JESSE LIBERTY'S
from scratch
PROGRAMMING SERIES

WebClasses

from scratch

Jesse Liberty

201 West 103rd Street,
Indianapolis, Indiana 46290

Trademarks

Warning and Disclaimer

Executive Editor
Tracy Dunkelberger

Acquisitions Editor
Holly Allender

Development Editor
Bryan Morgan

Managing Editor
Lisa Wilson

Copy Editor
Sara Black

Indexer
Schroeder Indexing Services

Proofreader
Louise Martin

Technical Editor
Donald Xie

Software Development Specialist
Andrea Duvall

Interior Design
Sandra Schroeder

Cover Design
Maureen McCarty and Anne Jones

Copy Writer
Eric Borgert

Layout Technician
William Hartman

Overview

Table of Contents

Foreword

Welcome to Jesse Liberty's Programming From Scratch series. I created this series because I believe that traditional primers do not meet the needs of every student. A typical introductory computer programming book teaches a series of skills in logical order and then, when you have mastered a topic, endeavors to show how the skills might be applied. This approach works very well for many people, but not for everyone.

I've taught programming to more than 10,000 students—in small groups, large groups, and through the Internet. Many students have told me that they wish they could just sit down at the computer with an expert and work on a program together. Rather than being taught each skill step by step in a vacuum, they would like to create a product and learn the necessary skills as they go.

From this idea was born the Programming From Scratch series. In each of these books, an industry expert will guide you through the design and implementation of a complex program, starting from scratch and teaching you the necessary skills as you go.

You might want to make a *From Scratch* book the first book you read on a subject, or you might prefer to read a more traditional primer first and then use one of these books as supplementary reading. Either approach can work; which is better depends on your personal learning style.

All the *From Scratch* series books share a common commitment to showing you the entire development process, from the initial concept through implementation. We do not assume that you know anything about programming: From Scratch means from the very beginning, with no prior assumptions.

Even though I haven't written every book in the series, as Series Editor I have a powerful sense of personal responsibility for each one. I provide supporting material and a discussion group on my Web site (www.libertyassociates.com—click on Books and Resources), and I encourage you to join my support discussion group (on my Web site) if you have questions or concerns.

Thank you for considering this book.

Jesse Liberty
From Scratch Series Editor

About the Author

Jesse Liberty is the author of the international best-seller *Teach Yourself WebClasses in 21 Days*, as well as *C++ from Scratch* and other books on C++ and object-oriented programming. He writes a regular monthly column for *C++ Report*, the premier magazine on the C++ language. He is president of Liberty Associates, Inc., which provides Web applications development as well as on-site training and mentoring in object-oriented software development.

Jesse was Distinguished Software Engineer at AT&T and Vice President of Electronic Delivery for Citibank. He lives with his wife, Stacey; his daughters, Robin and Rachel; his dog, Milo; and his cat, Fred, in the suburbs of Cambridge, Massachusetts. Jesse supports his books on his Web site at www.libertyassociates.com (click on Books and Resources).

Acknowledgments

My family makes this possible and worthwhile. Thank you again to Stacey, Robin, Rachel, Milo, and Fred.

My name is on the cover, but this book was created by a number of very dedicated people at Que, first among them Holly Allender and Tracy Dunkelberger. Among the many other hard-working people who helped put it together are Bryan Morgan, Lisa Wilson, Tonya Simpson, Sara Black, Louise Martin, Sandi Schroeder, Andrea Duvall, Sandra Schroeder, Maureen McCarty, Anne Jones, and Eric Borgert, all of whom worked tirelessly to make this book better than it was when I gave it to them. The glory is theirs; the mistakes are mine; so send me the email, not them.

Once again, I must thank Donald Xie, whom I've never met. He is a world-class technical editor. Donald: Finally a book on VB!

Additional thanks are due to the following wonderful folks who beta-tested *WebClasses from Scratch*:

> Dan Hurwitz is a database developer specializing in Paradox and Visual Basic. Dan has become a good friend, and I very much admire his openness and integrity.

> Cliff Gerald is the president of Gamma Software, where he provides a full range of database development services. Cliff is a wonderful person who has been more than kind to me. Cliff can be reached at `cgerald@gammasoftware.com`.

> Seth Weiss teaches mathematics and programs computers at Lincoln-Sudbury High School and is important to me beyond what I can write here.

Special thanks go to John Sequeira, who is the technical brains behind my understanding of WebClasses, ASP, and JavaScript. He has been putting data on the Web since 1994 and currently specializes in e-Commerce systems. John's contribution to this book cannot be overstated, and I'm very proud to consider him among my friends. He can be reached at `johnseq@pobox.com`.

Special thanks also go to Mike Kraley. Mike is a good friend and a brilliant programmer. I continue to learn from him every day.

Looking over this list, I realize again how lucky I am to work with good friends who know more about these things than I do. Their help has been critical to this book and to my life.

Tell Us What You Think!

As the reader of this book, *you* are our most important critic and commentator. We value your opinion and want to know what we're doing right, what we could do better, what areas you'd like to see us publish in, and any other words of wisdom you're willing to pass our way.

As an Executive Editor for Que Publishing at Macmillan Computer Publishing, I welcome your comments. You can fax, email, or write me directly to let me know what you did or didn't like about this book—as well as what we can do to make our books stronger.

Please note that I cannot help you with technical problems related to the topic of this book and that, due to the high volume of mail I receive, I might not be able to reply to every message.

When you write, please be sure to include this book's title and author as well as your name and phone or fax number. I will carefully review your comments and share them with the author and editors who worked on the book.

Fax: 317.581.4666

Email: programming@mcp.com

Mail: Tracy Dunkelberger
Executive Editor
Macmillan Computer Publishing
201 West 103rd Street
Indianapolis, IN 46290 USA

Introduction

This book is different from any book about Web development *ever* written. It is different in two ways. First, other books teach you a single language or development environment. Unfortunately, to build a world-class Web site, you need to know about a number of different technologies such as WebClasses, ASP, JavaScript, Visual Basic, and SQL Server. This book brings all these technologies together and teaches you *exactly* what you need to know.

Second, and perhaps just as important, other programming books start by teaching you simple skills that build in difficulty, adding skill upon skill as you go. When you've learned all the skills, the books then demonstrate what you can do, using a sample program.

This book does not start with programming technique; it starts with a project. We begin by analyzing and designing the project, and then we implement that design. Programming skills are taught in the context of implementation: First, you understand what you are trying to accomplish, and then you learn the skills needed to get the job done.

How Do WebClasses Fit In?

You certainly can build your Web pages using Microsoft Active Server Pages (ASP). Why bother with WebClasses? Here's the answer: As powerful as they are, ASP pages are oh-so-five-minutes-ago. The newest, hottest technology is WebClasses, and with good reason. WebClasses can do *everything* ASP can do, but it can do it better, cleaner, and with less work.

WebClasses serve the exact same role as ASP. However, rather than working in a text editor using a scripting language intermixed with HTML, you work in a full-fledged development environment, writng in a mature programming language with a clean distinction between the HTML and your code.

WebClasses are an integral part of Microsoft's Distributed interNet Applications (DNA) architecture. This book will teach you all about DNA and how WebClasses fit in with this approach to writing clean, scalable, robust, and reliable Web applications.

Who Should Read This Book?

This book is definitely for you if

a. You are a Visual Basic programmer who wants to make the transition to developing Web applications or

b. You are a database programmer who wants to put data on the Web or

c. You are a Web designer and coder who wants to begin writing the server-side and client-side code to support your increasingly complex and powerful Web sites or

d. You are a C or C++ programmer, or a programmer in another language, who wants to make the transition to Web development or

e. You are a Web developer who wants to apply object-oriented analysis and design and industry best-practices to your Web development.

Conventions Used in This Book

Some of the unique features in this series include

 Geek Speak—An icon in the margin indicates the use of a new term. New terms appear in the paragraph in *italics*.

 **How To Pronounce It**—You'll see an icon set in the margin next to a box that contains a technical term and how it should be pronounced. For example, "*cin* is pronounced see-in, and *cout* is pronounced see-out."

 Excursions—As short diversions from the main topic being discussed, excursions offer an opportunity to flesh out your understanding of a topic.

Concept Web—With a book of this type, a topic might be discussed in multiple places as a result of when and where we add functionality during application development. To help make this all clear, we've included a Concept Web that provides a graphical representation of how all the programming concepts relate to one another. You'll find it on the inside front cover of this book.

Notes—In addition to comments and asides about the topic at hand, certain concepts are explained more fully.

In addition, you'll find various typographic conventions throughout this book:

- Commands, variables, and other code appear in text in a special `computer font`.
- In this book, I build on existing listings as we examine code further. When I add new sections to existing code, you'll spot them in **`bold computer font`**.
- Commands and such that you type appear in **boldface type**.
- Placeholders in syntax descriptions appear in an *`italic computer font`* typeface. This indicates that you will replace the placeholder with the actual file name, parameter, or other element that it represents.

Breaking the Code

In some instances, when you look at a code listing, you'll notice that some lines of code have been broken in two and that the line numbers have letters. For example, see lines 10 and 10a:

```
10:     If Len(Session("SomeTextField")) = 0 Then
10a:        Session("SomeTextField") = "Any Value"
11:     End If
```

Here I have broken up a single line of code because it was too long to fit on a single line in this book. The rewrite is still legal code and can be typed in just as you find it (without the line numbers, of course).

The letter *a* is a signal to you that normally I would combine these two lines into one.

At other times, I use the VB line continuation character. In this case, the two lines are broken according to the rules of VB, and I use normal line numbering:

```
10:     If Len(Session("SomeTextField")) = 0 Then _
11:         Session("SomeTextField") = "Any Value"
```

Finally, the line may not lend itself to being broken. In this case, you'll see the line continuation character, indicating that what you are looking at is one very wide line that can't easily be divided:

```
19:  "<a href=""Javascript:OnChangeRequest('SearchByName')"""><em>A very long
➥prompt might have to go here</em></a>"
```

(Don't worry about the meaning of any of this code—it is all explained in the text of the book.)

Chapter 1

Getting Started

If you want to write a fairly serious Web application using Microsoft technologies, you need to master a vast array of skills, ranging from database design and programming to Active Server Pages and WebClasses, creation of COM controls, client-side scripting, and so forth.

You could simply pick up books on each of these subjects, but, judging from my bookshelf, you would be reading a minimum of 4,000 to 5,000 pages, much of which would be off-topic.

This book cuts through the clutter. My goal is to teach you what you need to know about each of the following tools:

- Database design
- SQL and Transact-SQL
- ADO and ODBC
- The ASP object model
- WebClasses
- Visual Basic
- COM and ActiveX
- JavaScript for client-side programming
- Distributed interNet Applications architecture
- Object-oriented analysis and design

Database Design. Databases can be complex beasts. You need to understand how to create a database, organize tables, create indexes, and support referential integrity (discussed in detail in Chapter 4, "Working With Enterprise-Scale Databases").

SQL and Transact-SQL. SQL is the universal language of choice for interacting with relational databases. Transact-SQL is Microsoft's variant on the language and the language of the SQL Server.

ADO and ODBC. You need these two Microsoft technologies to connect your application to a database.

The ASP Object Model. When managing a user's interaction with your application through a Web browser, you need the ASP object model to gain access to information you need.

WebClasses. This book is all about WebClasses. You need to create a WebClass before you can program an application that will be run over the Web.

Visual Basic (VB). For many Internet developers, Visual Basic is rapidly becoming the programming language of choice. As a C++ programmer, and author of a dozen books on C++ programming, I have a lot of explaining to do when I make that statement. This book attempts to prove that if you are building an application for the Internet, Visual Basic is the language to start with.

COM and ActiveX. Microsoft introduced Component Object Model (COM) and ActiveX to solve the problem of distributing small application components across the network. We explore how COM can help you build robust, maintainable, and scalable applications.

JavaScript. Because JavaScript is the development language of choice for client-side programming, we use it extensively for data manipulation and validation on the client (browser) machine.

Distributed interNet Applications (DNA) Architecture. Microsoft developed this architecture for building large-scale distributed applications. We look at DNA later in the chapter.

Object-Oriented Analysis and Design (OOAD). As a method for building maintainable and high-quality applications that ship, object-oriented analysis and design is nothing more (and nothing less!) than a structured approach for ensuring that you actually build what you set out to build.

How This Book Is Organized

My focus is on the drop-line approach to building a robust, maintainable, scalable, world-class Web application. By *drop-line*, I mean the shortest, most direct path with a minimum of distractions.

1

This approach does not lend itself to a comprehensive review of every nook and cranny of each of these languages and technologies—such a book would be at least ten times longer than this book.

On the other hand, after you have read this book, you'll be ready to create Web applications, and you'll be ready to read more. The appendix contains a suggested reading list for furthering your course of study.

WebClasses from Scratch provides all this information in the context of a nontrivial Web application. The approach is less of "here's what you need to know" and more of "let's sit down together and build something."

Unabashedly Microsoft Only

I don't apologize for the all-Microsoft strategy in this book. I could spend a lot of time explaining why I think this technology is superior to the alternatives, but the condensed version is that a significant amount of Web development is being done using these tools. They are robust, mature, and a pleasure to work with (except when they are unreliable, indecipherable, and sadistic).

In short, I have walked up to the roulette wheel of programming and put nearly all my chips down on the space that says Microsoft. The wheel is still in spin, but every year more and more of the slots have the Microsoft logo, and I'm fairly confident you can make a good living and have a lot of fun with this bet.

About the Project: EmployeeNet

I have chosen a project designed to be applicable to a wide variety of real-world commercial Web applications, both for those of you who are building intranet applications and for those building applications to be provided to a wider audience over the World Wide Web.

I imposed some design constraints. I wanted something large enough to take us into all the complexities of Web applications, without being overwhelming and distracting. I also wanted to draw from a domain familiar to every reader and yet not so hackneyed as to be boring and annoying.

What I've built is a fragment of an employee management system for middle-sized companies. It allows (theoretical) Human Resources personnel to enter data about their employees and to search for employees based on various characteristics.

This application is *not* complete, nor is it industrial-strength. I have intentionally stripped away everything but the essentials for the issues under consideration. Nonetheless, by working through this application, you will learn all you need to know to put your own data up on the Web in a robust and scalable design.

What Tools You Need

To build the application described in this book, you will need the following work environment:

1. A computer with Windows 9x or Windows NT and sufficient memory and hard disk space. I recommend no less than 32 MB of memory; 128 MB is far better. Even though disk space should not be a problem, unless it is already very tight, you may find that you'll need half a gigabyte by the time you're through.

2. Microsoft Internet Information Server (IIS) or Personal Web Server (PWS), both of which are available at no charge from Microsoft (http://www.microsoft.com) and are included in NT 4 Option Pack 4.

3. Visual Basic 6.0 (all versions).

4. An HTML editor. I use Microsoft's Visual Interdev briefly and then I go on to use DreamWeaver. Any editor will work fine, even Notepad. A number of free or low-cost editors are available on the Web.

5. SQL Server 7. The programs in this book are designed to work with SQL Server 7. You may be able to build all the projects with Access, but if you are serious about Web development, you'll need SQL Server sooner or later.

> **Note**
>
> DreamWeaver attempts to organize the tags in HTML files, and since it does not recognize WebClass tags, it occasionally changes their position. This is a significant problem which can be rectified by writing your own DreamWeaver data translators, or by using another text editor such as Visual Interdev or Notepad. For this reason, I do not recommend the use of DreamWeaver with WebClasses.

How Many Machines?

The code in this book was tested with three development environments:

1. All on one machine. I ran SQL Server desktop, the development environment, and Personal Web Server (PWS) all on my laptop running Windows NT4.

2. On two machines. I ran SQL Server on my server and the development environment and PWS on my workstation.

3. On three machines. I ran SQL Server on one machine, Internet Information Server (IIS) on a second machine, and the development environment on a third.

You may pick and choose among these development environments.

1

Setting Up Your Development Environment

Setting up Visual Basic, your HTML Editor, SQL Server, and IIS (or PWS) can be quick, easy, and trouble-free. It can also be a nightmare. Much depends on your existing configuration and how comfortable you are threading your way through the myriad options.

For what we're doing in this book, the default options are almost certainly correct. IIS is a bit more complicated, and PWS is quite straightforward. Setting up SQL Server 7 is nearly trivial compared with earlier versions.

That said, each of these is a commercial product and therefore is supported by the manufacturer (Microsoft). In this book, I assume that you bought a copy of these programs and will receive support from the vendor. I will not endeavor to walk you through the setup, nor can I support these products on my Web site.

I strongly advise you to begin by upgrading your NT installation to the latest service pack and read through all the read-me files and related documentation before beginning the installation.

What Do You Already Need to Know?

In this book, I assume that you have programmed *something* before. Even though I'll show you the syntax for if statements in both VB and JavaScript, you might be at something of a disadvantage if you don't know what an if statement is for or why you might use one. (If that is the case, run right out and buy my misnamed book, *The Complete Idiot's Guide to a Career in Computer Programming* in which all of this is explained. It will take you only a day or two to read, and then you'll be quite ready for this book.)

As I say in the Introduction, you may be a VB programmer, a database programmer, or an HTML programmer, so I assume that you know at least a little about what programming is all about.

I also assume that you've used Web sites and understand what databases are for. That's about it for my assumptions.

If you are completely new to VB, JavaScript, WebClasses, ASP, ADO, SQL Server, database programming, or object-oriented analysis and design, *don't panic!* I explain it all as I go, and there are additional shaded help sections that provide additional detail. If you are already proficient in any of these topics, you can skip the relevant shaded help sections and you won't be bored. (If you are already proficient in *all* these languages and technologies, thanks for the thirty-nine bucks, but why are you reading this book?)

Scale

When programmers talk about scale, they mean how many people will be using their product at once and how much data will they be handling. The programming techniques in this book are designed for fairly large projects, but I do not spend a lot of time on *enterprise-sized* applications (Web farms where there are thousands of simultaneous users).

I do this for two reasons. First, few programmers are actually doing that kind of work. Second, and more important, you need the skills I *do* cover before you can learn about scaling up to a large project. The appendix lists a number of books to read next. If enterprise-sized applications are one of your particular concerns, pay attention to the books on enterprise scale development.

In any case, I do build a solid foundation, so you won't be wasting your time reading this book.

Distributed interNet Applications—n-Tier Development

This book focuses on building Web applications using WebClasses and the SQL Server. Within that context, however, I follow Microsoft Distributed interNet Applications as an overarching architectural guideline.

DNA is a conceptual overview of how distributed applications, especially Web applications, ought to be built. It suggests that there should be a distribution of responsibilities into tiers, typically three or more. It is thus often called n-tier (n indicating some number greater than 2).

An n-tier design distinguishes between the user interface layer, the business layer, and the database layer, as illustrated in Figure 1.1.

The user interface (or presentation) layer is concerned with how the end user interacts with the program. This is where you determine what will be on the menus; what kinds of pages, screens, and dialog boxes the user will interact with; and what controls (screen widgets such as buttons and list boxes) you'll use.

The business layer handles the business logic and rules, especially the decisions about what data are valid and how those data will be used. It is here that you capture the procedures and rules of the business.

The database (or persistence) layer is where the data are stored. It is here that you design tables, indexes, and so forth.

Figure 1.1

n-Tier development.

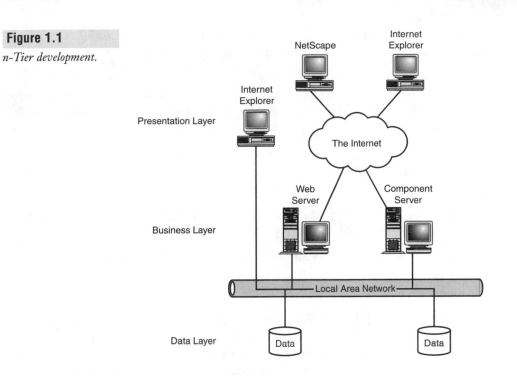

We talk more in detail about each of these layers later in the book. Our focus will be on Web browsers for the user interface (UI) layer and on the SQL Server for the database layer. We write our own COM objects for the business layer.

The goal of an n-tier architecture is to distribute responsibility to the location at which it can best be supported and to create an application in which components can be mixed and matched as needs change.

A Brief History

Early personal computer applications were one tier. The application was monolithic; you installed it and ran it on your computer, and everything was all-of-a-piece.

Two-tier applications were generally called client/server. In a client/server application, a program running on a desktop machine (the client) handled all the data processing and presentation, and the data were stored on a centrally administered server. Typically a client would connect to the server and stay connected until it was finished working with the data. These connections were created over a high-speed local area network (LAN). This worked well when not too many people were connecting at once.

The client/server architecture breaks down quickly when the connections are uncertain (over the Internet) and the number of simultaneous connections is difficult to estimate.

A partial solution is to move some of the processing to the server. Some client/server applications move some of the business logic to the database, encapsulating the rules of the business in stored procedures.

Even so, client/server applications tend to be brittle and inflexible. Because you must support a standalone client application, small changes in the specification of either the client or the server can mean significant upgrade and installation costs.

 Stored procedures—Short programs that run in the SQL Server. We talk about stored procedures in more detail later in the book.

This approach is sometimes whimsically known as two-and-a-half tier. In a true three-tier application, however, the business layer is separate both from the database and also from the user interface.

The big advantage of moving to a three-tier application is that it scales better. By separating business concerns from data concerns, and—even more important—by separating the UI layer from the business layer, we can have each layer located where it will be most efficient. We decouple the business layer from the UI layer and develop different interfaces depending on where the application will be run. For example, we might build a Web-based front end for searching and displaying data but choose to build a different UI for data entry, which will be accomplished only over a LAN, never over the Web.

In a three-tier application, the UI layer does not know the location or method of storage but rather treats the data layer as a magical repository of data.

Logical Versus Physical Layers

The distinction among these three layers is *logical*. It may well be true that all three layers run on the same physical machine. On the other hand, a given layer may be distributed among many machines, even across the globe. It is entirely possible, for example, for business objects to be distributed among many machines connected remotely by the Internet.

Components and Microsoft's COM

There are two contending technologies for component development (aren't there always?). One is CORBA—the Component Object Request Broker Architecture. The other is COM.

The argument for CORBA reminds me very much of the argument for the Mac. The proponents say it is better (better built, more object-oriented), but the market keeps going the other way. In any case, having decided on an all-Microsoft technology solution, this is a no-brainer: COM it is.

COM is a technology for breaking your program into smaller chunks (components) and distributing them across a network or around the world. COM and its distributed sister DCOM (Distributed COM) are the enabling technology.

COM programming can be a bit of a nightmare. The technology is fairly complex, and it is easy to get lost, unless, of course, you let VB solve the problem for you. We'll use COM throughout this project, but you'll barely notice it.

MTS and COM+

MTS is the Microsoft Transaction Server. This is a solution to the problem of handling updates to important data and ensuring that the data do not become corrupted. MTS is in the process of merging with COM in a new technology called COM+. MSMQ is Microsoft's message-handling technology, designed to ensure reliable, if delayed, delivery of messages between machines across a network.

MSMQ, MTS, and COM+ are beyond the scope of this book. They encompass a fairly complex topic, and we don't need it for this application. More important, the skills covered in this book lay the foundation for your work with transactions; this book is essentially the on-ramp to that highway.

Next Steps

The steps in this application, as in any other application, are these:

1. Figure out what you want to accomplish.
2. Create a specification detailing what is required.
3. Design a solution.
4. Implement that solution.

We work our way through each step in turn. Along the way, we consider issues relating to each of the technologies described in this chapter.

In Chapter 2, we turn our attention to the analysis of the problem we're trying to solve and the design of the program that will solve that problem. The remainder of the book focuses on implementing that design.

Chapter 2

Analysis and Design

This book is not about object-oriented analysis and design. I already wrote one of those (*Beginning Object-Oriented Analysis and Design*, Wrox Press, 1998, ISBN 1-861-00133-9), and it takes a few hundred pages to explain OOAD in any detail.

That said, we can't examine a program in depth without understanding how it will be used, so we must spend some time on analysis. In addition, before we examine the code, we need to understand the object model we plan to implement.

This chapter provides a whirlwind description of the analysis and design of EmployeeNet, an application for managing human resources in a middle-sized corporation. Hang on to your hat; we're going to do this very quickly.

Analysis and Design

With a large project such as EmployeeNet, I would expect to invest a significant amount of time on analysis (understanding the requirements) and design (modeling the solution) before beginning implementation (writing the code).

In 1992, I speculated that EmployeeNet would be a two-year project. I was wrong, of course; by the time we were done, it had slipped out to three years!

By 1995, we would have had less than a year to build a project like this because the world was speeding up, and Internet sites needed to hit the market in under a year.

The tools are getting better, we're all getting smarter about how to build Web applications, and the competition is getting increasingly fierce. Additionally, the time frame keeps shrinking. Today, I believe that we would need to get a first release out the door in four to six months, perhaps less. To do this, I would spend about a month on analysis, another month on design, two months on coding, and another month on testing. These estimates bring to mind a scenario where one phase ends before the other begins, even though it has no basis in reality. However, this tight scheduling does provide a good rough and ready approximation of how I would divide my time to get the job done.

Analysis

EmployeeNet will manage the human resources needs of middle-sized corporations. The project is sponsored by Acme Manufacturing, and we'll build it to meet their needs and then generalize for other companies as we go.

Acme employs 2,000 people in the manufacture of high-end consumer products. Their principal products are the Acme Widget and their world-famous Gizmo. They have manufacturing plants in East Podunk and New Boondock, and their main offices are in Gotham.

Conceptualization

EmployeeNet will allow the Human Resources department to track all benefits for employees and will allow employees to review and edit their own employment records.

Use Cases

There was a time when the typical requirements for a software project were expressed in terms of capabilities and performance. Even though this approach guaranteed that the resulting system met certain specified benchmarks, it did not ensure that anyone could or would want to use it. Typically the user didn't factor into consideration until after the product was out the door.

Object-oriented analysis begins with a thorough understanding of how the product will be *used*. A use case is a formal statement of the various ways in which users will interact with the system and what they will want to accomplish.

 Use case—A formal statement of one way in which the system will be used.

We begin the use-case analysis by identifying the principal actors—that is, the users of the system. These include

- Human Resources personnel (entering and updating records)
- Human Resources managers (reviewing the work done in their department and setting policies)
- Employees (reviewing their own records)
- Managers (reviewing the employee records of their direct reports)

Actor—A person or other software system that interacts with the system we're creating.

We will flesh out this list later. However, these are the principal actors, and we can begin to document how they will interact with the system—the use cases.

Adding an employee. In our first use case, the Human Resources representative adds a new employee. He must enter the employee's name, social security number, and contact information (home address and telephone, etc.) as well as the job title, salary, employment level, and so forth. In addition, he must enter the employee's choices about such benefits as health and life insurance, profit sharing, and 401(k) plans.

Searching for an employee. A Human Resources representative may need to locate the records for an employee based on his name, social security number, employee identification number, or other criterion. For example, he may want to locate all employees from a particular office or all employees with a given insurance option or investment decision. After finding these records, he may update them or create reports based on various additional grouping criteria.

Maintaining databases. The Human Resources department needs to maintain the various databases used by the system, including the list of offices in the company, the managers for each office, the insurance plans available for employees, and the investment options available. In addition, it must maintain the "business rules"—the rules about who is eligible for various benefits, how raises are assigned, and so forth.

Reviewing and editing. Human Resources personnel need to review and update records, and individual employees may wish to review their own records. They need to use the system to update their health insurance choices, change their investments, review their own past performance reports, and so forth.

Managing personnel. Managers need to be able to review the records of their direct reports, enter annual reviews, set objectives, and so forth.

Preparing reports. Both Human Resources personnel and team managers need to be able to run reports from the system. Some of these reports will be predefined standardized reports. In a robust system, it ought to be possible to generate custom reports spontaneously based on transient needs of managers and others.

Although this list of the use cases for the EmployeeNet system is by no means exhaustive, it will be more than enough to discuss the program as implemented for the purposes of this book.

In a full analysis of the system, we would flesh out all these use cases into scenarios, exploring the various requirements that arise. However, we won't take the time to do this here.

Domain Analysis

Before we go on to design, we need to achieve a better understanding of the problem domain—the real-world environment in which this program will be used. What problems are we trying to solve? How will this program integrate into how our customers do their work? With which other programs will EmployeeNet interact?

If I were writing this product as a commercial software package rather than as a demonstration for a book, I would certainly spend a fair amount of time with the potential end user of the product—the Human Resources manager. I would like to understand his job, what challenges he faces, and how this software will fit into his daily life.

For now, we can speculate that the principal relevant objects in his life include employees, managers, jobs, titles, salary ranges, job descriptions, annual reviews, addresses and personal contact information, insurance plans, and investment options. We want to understand in some detail how these objects interact, and we want to consider modeling these interactions in our design and ultimately in our application.

On to Design

Having raced through our analysis, let's briefly turn our attention to the design of our product. With a Web application, there are two types of design—object-oriented design and user interface design. They interact with one another but are quite distinct.

User interface design is the process of understanding how the user will interact with the application: what do the pages look like, what buttons does he click, what widgets are displayed on the page, and so forth.

Object-oriented design is the process of modeling the program in software, understanding the principal objects and detailing how they will interact. Object-oriented design is principally concerned with (surprise!) objects—things in the design that have both properties (attributes) and behavior (actions or methods).

Three-Tiered Development

As discussed in Chapter 1, we'll draw a bright and shining line between our user interface layer and our business layer. Our third layer will be the database layer, which will manage the data.

We can keep these layers somewhat distinct from one another, designing each relatively independently of one another. In Chapter 4, we discuss the database design in some detail, so I won't focus on that here. Instead, I'll briefly review the business and user interface layers, setting the stage for focusing on the implementation issues in the rest of this book.

The Business Layer

We encapsulate the business rules we'll be implementing in our program in the business layer. It is here that we consider questions such as:

- What health plan might this employee be eligible for?
- Can I have Dental Plan 1 with family coverage if I already have Health Plan 2 with individual coverage?
- Can I invest all my money in aggressive stocks if I have less than one year with the firm?
- When will I be eligible to convert my stock options?
- How long before I'm eligible for a raise?
- What is the most I can give this wonderful employee?
- What is the process for firing this slacker?

As you can imagine, in a large commercial project, this is where the action is. The business rules can be quite extensive, and determining an exhaustive list can consume much of the work of analysis. This is the area that novice programmers most often overlook, and getting this right may be the most difficult part of the analysis and design process.

For the purposes of this book, the Employee is the principal object we focus on. The Employee will be responsible for presenting all the information relating to an individual employee's records. It will form a bridge between the user interface layer and the back-end database.

The Presentation Layer

The presentation layer is the user interface—the look and feel of our project. This is the part of the program you will almost certainly want to hand over to a specialist. Expertise in graphical user interface design has very little overlap with expertise in programming. Although many programmers think they are quite good at user interface design (or that it is very easy), they are wrong. The difference between a first-class design and a mediocre design can be quite profound, and this difference can rest on very small changes.

I had a wonderful experience a few years ago. I created what I thought was a quite good home page for my business, shown in Figure 2.1.

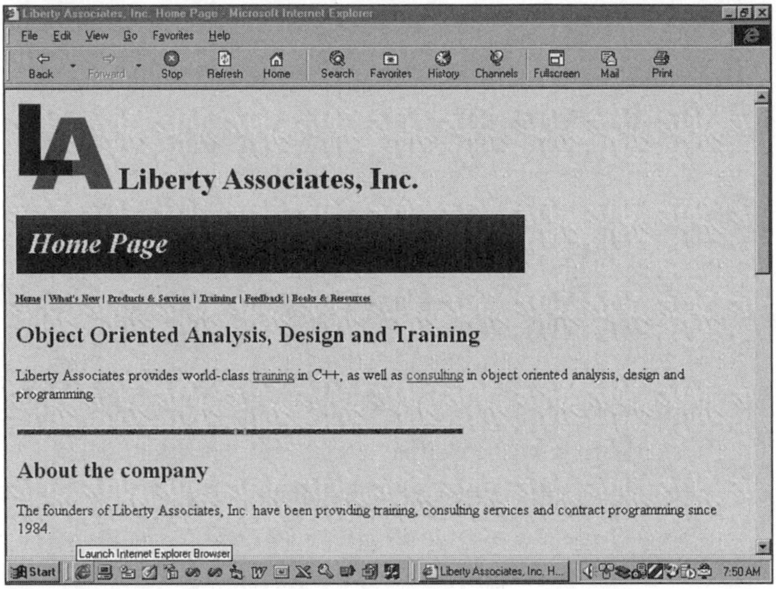

I received many compliments for this site and felt that I had done a professional job without bringing in a graphical design specialist. A couple of years later, business was booming, and I decided to contract with a few folks with whom I had worked before and who now had a consulting company called i-Collaborative (http://www.i-collaborative.com). I wanted to see what they might do with the site. The results, shown in Figure 2.2, have settled the question for me. Mine was, at best, competent. Theirs was in a whole different league.

For EmployeeNet, I turned to the services of a designer, Maethee Ratnarathorn, with whom I had worked before. Maethee is one of the most talented designers I have ever met and is responsible for design and interface for Atypica (http://www.atypica.com). Atypica was founded in January 1997 to design and develop Web applications to do business on the Web.

I sent the analysis and design documents to Maethee, along with some ideas about how we might organize the data. He sent back HTML pages that implemented the design and made it work, giving it polish and a professional look and feel. Figure 2.3 illustrates the opening screen for EmployeeNet as designed by Maethee.

Figure 2.2

My home page as created by i-Collaborative.

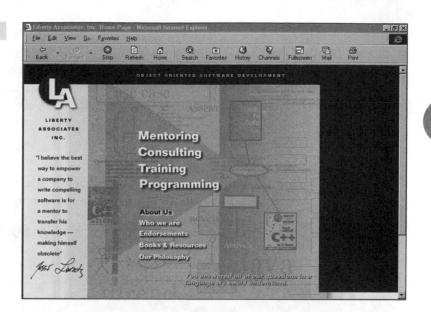

Figure 2.3

The EmployeeNet home page.

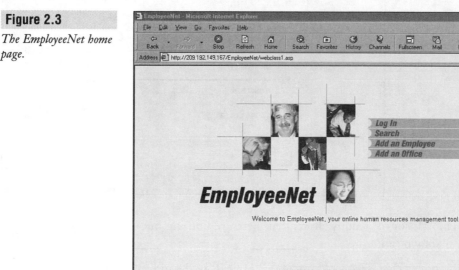

This page reflects the areas of the demo program we focus on in coming chapters—searching and adding employees and offices. Of course, in a final release of the application, these choices would not appear on the opening page. A real-world application would be somewhat more complex and would probably be divided into different areas or sections. Each section would then be under access control so that only staff with appropriate authorization would have right of entry to each section.

Searching

The Human Resources department will want to be able to search for employees based on each individual's name, home office, and a number of other criteria. One issue with building a Web application, which separates it from building a traditional two-tier application, is the question of bandwidth. If these pages are to be displayed across the Internet, then we must be concerned with the delay we might encounter if we send a lot of data to the client.

I asked Maethee to create his design based on an innovation I wanted to try—sending the contents of drop-down menus only on demand. Thus, when the user first navigates to the search page, there are no widgets visible at all, as shown in Figure 2.4.

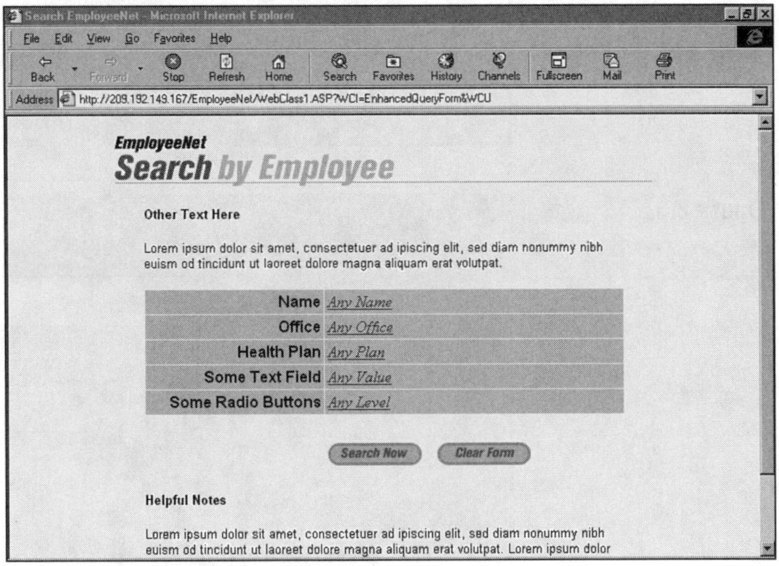

Figure 2.4

Search page.

The HTML source readily shows that these are nothing but links; no extra data were sent, as shown in Figure 2.5.

In subsequent chapters, we examine this HTML in detail because it relies on JavaScript to make it work. For now, the important thing to note is that there are no list boxes, buttons, or other widgets. Only when the user clicks on one of the fields (for example, on Any Name) do I open the widget and send the data, as shown in Figure 2.6.

We'll return to this user interface concept in later chapters when we need to implement the code. For now, the point is that the UI designer's job is to help you understand what works well from a human factor's perspective. Your job will be to design the code so that the UI can be implemented independently of the underlying business logic, which in turn should be somewhat independent of the data layer.

Figure 2.5

HTML source.

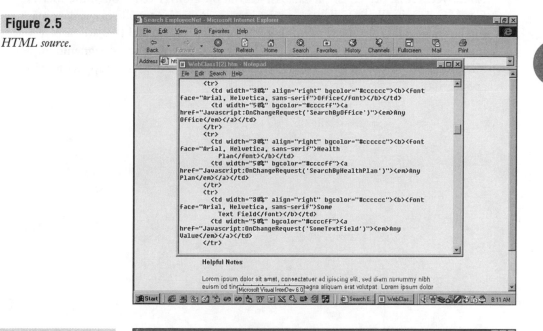

Figure 2.6

Open list box.

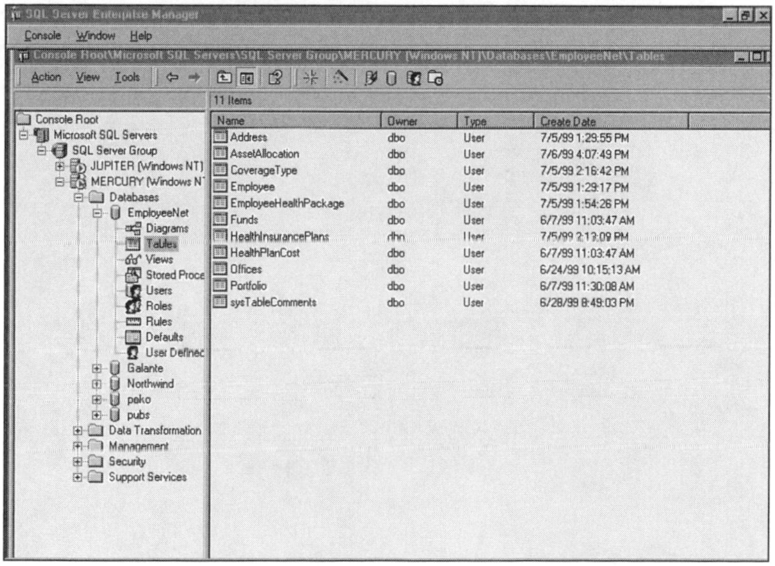

Next Steps

EmployeeNet is, principally, a database-driven program. Even though the user inter-face layer is critically important, and the business logic layer will encapsulate many of the business rules, our focus in this book is on the database and how we display and interact with that data on the Web. In Chapter 3, we explore the design and imple-mentation of the relational database, which will be the underlying support for this application.

Chapter 3

Proof of Concept

Enough theory! Let's look at the implementation technology and get something working before we go any farther in thinking through how to implement EmployeeNet.

Even though I believe in analysis and design, my number one rule of programming is this:

Get something working right away, and keep it working until it's done.

I implement this rule through incremental programming, in which I add features in small doses, ensuring that my working program *keeps* working as I go.

Which Technology: ASP or WebClasses?

Before we try to implement the design discussed in Chapter 2, we must make a technology decision: are we going to build this project using Active Server Pages or WebClasses?

Active Server Pages (ASP) is by far the more popular technology; WebClasses are still relatively new, there is far less written about them, and they appear to be targeted at Visual Basic programmers. I am not a Visual Basic programmer; I'm a C++ programmer. VB has been something of a toy I've played with in the past but not a language that I would have considered using to build a robust, extensible, maintainable, high-performance commercial application.

I certainly *can* implement this in C++: by using ASP for the front end and the ActiveX Template Library (ATL) for the back end. The problem is that I think WebClasses may be a far superior technology to ASP.

ATL or ActiveX Template Library—A set of objects and wizards designed to allow C++ programmers to create COM objects easily.

ASP or Active Server Pages—Microsoft technology for running Web applications on the server (rather than on the client) using HTML mixed with Script.

HTML or HyperText Markup Language—The language of Web pages.

Script—Simple programs written in a scripting language such as JavaScript or VBScript.

WebClasses—Microsoft technology for running Web applications on the server (rather than on the client) using Visual Basic.

SQL Server—Microsoft's enterprise-quality database technology.

ADO or ActiveX Data Objects—Microsoft technology that provides an object-oriented interface to databases and other data.

This book discusses each of these technologies in greater depth as we go, with the exception of ATL, which is beyond the scope of this book.

In addition, I can implement the business classes in VB far more quickly than I can in ATL, with fewer technological hurdles. For the *overwhelming* majority of business applications, the VB code will be plenty fast enough. Yes, there are a few sites in the world with such enormous traffic that I might want to implement some of the code in ATL, but these are rare and easily identified when the time comes. Most importantly, hardware is cheap and getting cheaper, and programmer time is expensive and looks to remain so for quite a while.

The real question is not ATL versus VB for the business objects, but ASP versus WebClasses to assemble the HTML for the user. To decide which to use, the best bet is to build a very tiny toy application in both.

ASP Versus WebClasses—A Prototype

Both Microsoft Access and SQL Server come with the Pubs database—a simple database that mimics a small publishing house. For this prototype, we display the list of publishers on a Web page. Figure 3.1 illustrates the table we want to display as seen from SQL Server.

Three Projects, One Chapter, No Waiting

In this chapter, I'll show you how to display this same data in three different ways.

First, we'll display this table using ASP only. It's quick, dirty, and effective.

Figure 3.1

Publishers table.

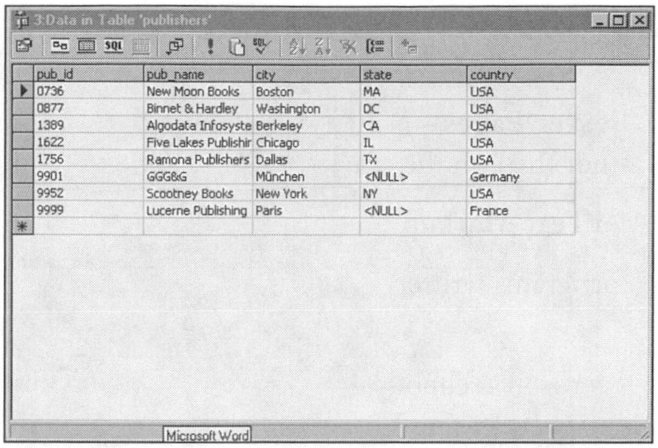

pub_id	pub_name	city	state	country
0736	New Moon Books	Boston	MA	USA
0877	Binnet & Hardley	Washington	DC	USA
1389	Algodata Infosyste	Berkeley	CA	USA
1622	Five Lakes Publishir	Chicago	IL	USA
1756	Ramona Publishers	Dallas	TX	USA
9901	GGG&G	München	<NULL>	Germany
9952	Scootney Books	New York	NY	USA
9999	Lucerne Publishing	Paris	<NULL>	France

Second, after we have that working, we'll peel off the responsibility for getting the data out of the database into a business object. We'll implement that business object in COM. The ASP page will then no longer talk to the database, it will talk to the business object, and the business object will, in turn, talk with the database.

Third, after our COM object is working, we'll throw away the ASP and build the same functionality using a WebClass.

ASP Only

We begin by displaying the data from the Publishers table in ASP. We can do this at break-neck speed, skipping over the details for now so that we can stay focused on the overall approach: comparing it with how we do it in VB using WebClasses.

To get started, let's fire up Visual InterDev (or your favorite editor) to create a new project. Note that we don't use Visual Basic at all for this first project.

geek speak **Visual InterDev (VI)**—Microsoft's integrated development environment for ASP. You can write ASP in any text editor, however, and you do *not* need VI for any of the exercises in this book.

Here are the steps for Visual InterDev.

Note As explained in Chapter 2, the exact details may be different on your computer or network, or if you are using different Internet enabling technology.

Create a new project called DataOnTheWebASP as shown in Figure 3.2.

Visual InterDev now begins a four-step process for creating the new project. It begins with Step 1 by asking you to choose your Web Server as shown in Figure 3.3.

Figure 3.2

Creating a project in Visual InterDev.

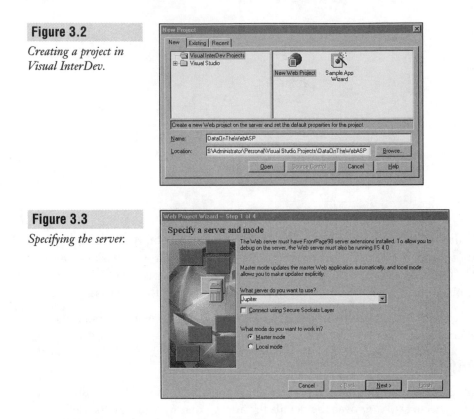

Figure 3.3

Specifying the server.

I will choose my server, which I've named Jupiter, on which I have IIS running. You might choose your local machine if you're using Personal Web Server. You are also asked to choose Master Mode versus Local Mode. Check the VI documentation for details, but this essentially asks if you'll be working on the master copy of the files or a local copy.

Step 2 involves deciding whether you are creating a new Web application or adding to an existing one, as shown in Figure 3.4.

In Step 3, shown in Figure 3.5, VI asks if you want a layout. Again, check the VI documentation for details. A layout allows VI to provide a consistent look and feel to your project. We'll choose none.

Step 4, shown in Figure 3.6, is similar. Here you are asked to choose a theme. We'll choose none.

Visual InterDev now creates your project, as shown in Figure 3.7. A number of files will be copied from the script library and used in the creation of ASP pages, but they are beyond the scope of this book. Because we use ASP sparingly, for reasons I'll explain shortly, these files really are not relevant to us.

Figure 3.4

Specifying the Web.

Figure 3.5

Choosing a layout.

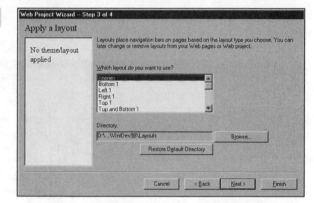

Figure 3.6

Choosing a theme.

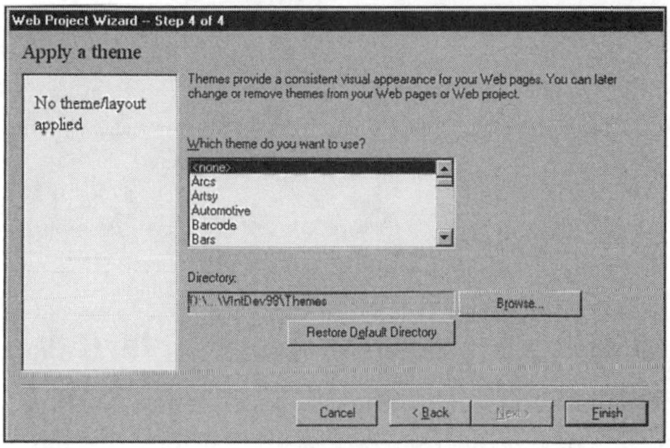

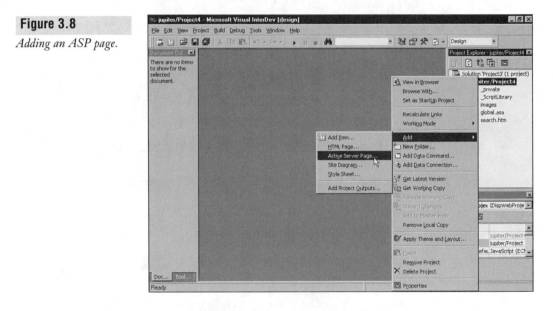

Figure 3.7

Creating the project.

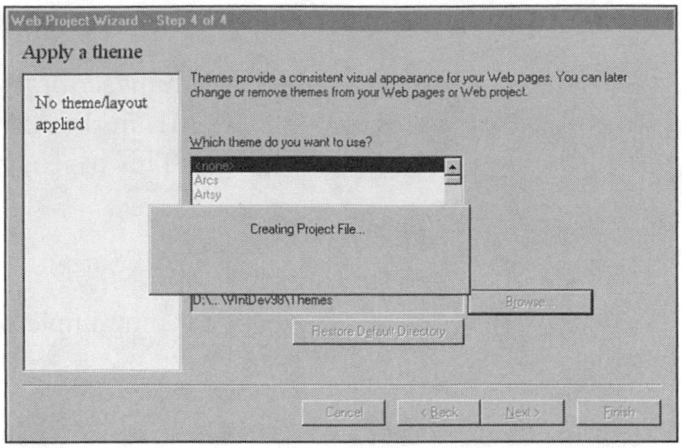

We are (finally!) ready to create our ASP page. Right-click on the project and choose Add Active Server Page, as shown in Figure 3.8.

Figure 3.8

Adding an ASP page.

Building the Project Without Visual InterDev

It's not a problem if you don't have VI. Simply open PWS or IIS and create a virtual directory for our new project. Now fire up your favorite HTML Editor (Notepad is fine) and follow along, creating the file you need. Visual InterDev is a luxury: we don't need it and really aren't using any of its power.

A Simple ASP Page

Essentially, ASP is HTML mixed with programming script. The *server* runs the script, mixing together the results with the HTML in the ASP page, and produces an HTML page (with no server script left in it). This page is then sent to the client for display in the browser.

ASP uses two scripting languages: JavaScript and VBScript.

Listing 3.1 provides the complete ASP listing for our simple page, entitled PubsASPOnly (that is Pubs ASP Only).

Listing 3.1—PubsASPOnly

```
0:   <%@ Language=VBScript %>
1:   <HTML>
2:   <HEAD>
3:   <META NAME="GENERATOR" Content="Microsoft Visual Studio 6.0">
4:   </HEAD>
5:   <BODY>
6:
7:
8:   <p><h1>Publishers</h1></p>
9:   <Table width = 75% border=1 cellspacing=1 cellpadding=1>
10:   <% dim rs
11:   set rs = server.CreateObject("adodb.recordset")
12:   dim sqlstmt
13:   sqlstmt = "select * from publishers"
14:   dim strConnect
15:   strConnect = "Driver={SQL Server};Server=myServer;Database=Pubs;UID=sa;PWD="
16:   call rs.Open(sqlstmt, strConnect )
17:
18:       while not rs.eof%>
19:       <tr>
20:           <td><%=rs("pub_id")%></td>
21:           <td><%=rs("pub_name")%></td>
22:           <td><%=rs("city")%></td>
23:       </tr>
24:       <%rs.movenext
25:       wend%>
26:   </table>
27:   <%rs.close()%>
28:   <P> </P>
29:
30:   </BODY>
31:   </HTML>
```

The first nine lines are straight HTML.

EXCURSION

HTML

If you are unfamiliar with HTML, let me briefly explain what is going on here. On line 0 we find a tiny bit of VBScript, which was generated by the tool. We can ignore it. This line simply tells the server which scripting language to use.

Notice the tag on line 1. A tag is an HTML instruction. All tags are surrounded by angle brackets. Typically tags come in pairs. For example, the tag on line 1 is an HTML tag. We would expect this to be matched by an HTML end tag. An end tag is just like its opening tag except that it begins with a forward slash (/). Thus, the end tag for <HTML> is </HTML>, which we find on line 31.

The HTML tag tells HTML that what follows is (surprise!) HTML. On line 2, we see the <HEAD> tag, which marks the beginning of the header. Any HTML page may have either one header or none. On line 3, we find more detritus from Visual InterDev. Again, ignore it. Line 4 marks the end of the header, and line 5 marks the beginning of the body. Easy, no?

Line 8 introduces two new tags. <p> marks a paragraph. At the end of the line we see the optional </p> end-of-paragraph tag. <h1> marks header 1.

HTML tells the browser *what* something is but not how to display it. This tag indicates that what follows is a level one header. It says nothing about how to display level one headers. This is entirely up to the browser. My browser makes level one headers centered, big and bold. But that is a browser decision.

Immediately after the <h1> tag is the word Publishers. This is not in a tag. Anything not in angle brackets is sent as-is to the browser and displayed on the screen.

The net effect of this line is that the word *Publishers* is displayed as a level one header.

Line 9 creates a table with a width equal to 75% of the width of the browser and a 1-pixel border. A 0 border would be invisible. I use invisible-border tables a lot to achieve alignment without showing the table itself.

Cell spacing is the amount of space between the individual cell boundaries within the table, whereas cell padding is the amount of space between the contents of a cell and its edges.

The <tr> on line 19 creates a row in the table (ended on line 23 by </tr>), and the <td> and </td> tags on lines 20–22 demark the individual cells within the row.

The table ends on line 26, the body of the page ends on line 30, and, as we discussed, the HTML itself ends on line 31.

There's more to HTML, but not a lot more. In the appendix, you'll find a recommended reading list for books that supply all the gritty details.

Line 11 begins the use of ASP server-side script. The ASP script is set off from the HTML by the special tag <%. Anything between the opening ASP tag <% and the closing tag %> is interpreted as ASP script. In this case, the closing tag comes at the end of line 18.

Line 10 uses the dim keyword to dimension a variable named rs. This essentially says, "I intend to use this name *rs* in a moment. I just want to let you know it is here on purpose." The point of dim is to say, "Let this name exist."

EXCURSION

Visual Basic

It is only necessary to "dim" variables if you have set Option Explicit. That said, you should *always* set Option Explicit in your VB projects. By doing this, VB will help you find other-wise difficult-to-find bugs. For example, suppose you create a variable called myInstitution, and later you assign Acme to myInstituton. It will be difficult to realize that you've misspelled myInstitution, and you'll get no error, unless you set Option Explicit.

On line 11 we use set to set the rs we just dimensioned to hold the results of calling CreateObject on the server object, passing in the string "adodb.recordset".

Quite a lot is going on here, but I don't want to explain it just yet. Let me make a few quick points to which I'll return later in the book. First, the ASP model makes available to you a number of powerful and complex objects. One of these is the server object, which represents IIS. A method that allows you to call on that object is CreateObject. You do this when you need to bring into existence objects from a library that the server knows about.

One such library is ADODB. ADODB is the library of objects that support ADO, the ActiveX Data Object model. ADO is built on top of OLE-DB (the COM model for accessing databases). OLE-DB, in turn, is built on top of ODBC (Microsoft's universal access engine for relational databases), and OLE-DB provides the ability to talk to nonrelational databases including mail files and text files. ADO brings an object-oriented interface to OLE-DB.

I won't go into details about any of this here, except to note that we'll use the ADODB library to interact with our SQL Server database. One object within the ADODB library is a recordset. A recordset acts as an iterator over a set of records.

Iterator—An object that keeps track of where you are in a collection. For example, if you have a calendar, which is a collection of dates, you might have an iterator named "today" which keeps track of where you are in the year.

Recordset—An object that acts as an iterator over a set of records in the database. It points to each record in turn, and you can tell it to move to the next record when you are done with the current record. This way you can *iterate* your way through (programmers say you "iterate over") the entire set.

Typically, a recordset is produced as the result of a query made against the database. We'll make such a query in the next few lines.

On line 12, we dimension `sqlstmt`, to which we assign a string on line 13. That string is the SQL statement we want to use to query the database. On line 16, we pass that statement in to the open method of our recordset object rs.

Remember to substitute your own computer's name as the server in line 15 (currently it is set to `myServer`).

The open method opens the database and issues the SQL command we've passed in.

On line 18, we iterate through the resulting recordset, printing out the publishers until we hit `rs.eof` (Resultset End Of File).

Note that lines 20–22 mix HTML and ASP freely. Let's examine line 20 in detail:

```
20:          <td><%=rs("pub_id")%></td>
```

The first four characters `<td>` are HTML; they indicate a column in a row of a table. This is followed by a burst of ASP script: `<%=rs("pub_ID")%>`. The effect of this ASP is to print (to the HTML page) the contents of the pub_id field. We'll examine this syntax in detail later in the book; the point to note here is that this is ASP script running right inside of HTML. Line 20 ends with HTML `</td>`, closing the column.

The result of running this code is shown in Figure 3.9.

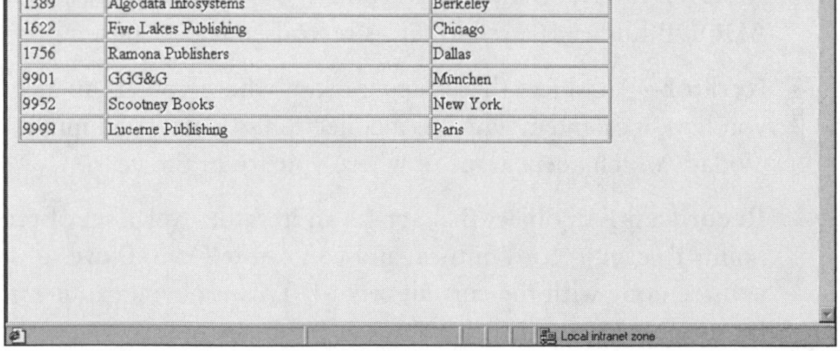

Figure 3.9

Publishers in your browser.

0736	New Moon Books	Boston
0877	Binnet & Hardley	Washington
1389	Algodata Infosystems	Berkeley
1622	Five Lakes Publishing	Chicago
1756	Ramona Publishers	Dallas
9901	GGG&G	München
9952	Scootney Books	New York
9999	Lucerne Publishing	Paris

In the End, It Is Just HTML

So, what was sent to the browser? After all, the browser doesn't know how to interpret ASP server-side script. This is the power of ASP: what is sent is *just HTML*. Select View Source in your browser to see for yourself, as shown in Figure 3.10.

Figure 3.10

Viewing the source.

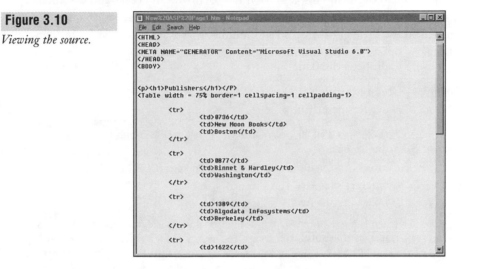

By the time this page is generated, all the code has been executed, and all the fields have been substituted. What is sent to the user is just HTML.

This is great for two reasons. First, *any* HTML browser can display the results. Second, and perhaps more important, the business logic and database structures are hidden from your readers; they see only the results, not the possibly confidential and certainly ugly details of how you generate these results.

Adding a COM Object

Now that we have this working with pure ASP, we can make our code somewhat easier to maintain and a good deal cleaner by adding a tier. Let's separate at least some of the presentation layer from the business layer by breaking out the job of understanding the Publishers table into a separate object, pubBizObject (clever name, no?).

Note that we are only going to separate presentation from business logic. We won't yet separate business concerns (such as business rules) from data concerns (such as table layout and database schema). This will come later, if needed.

About COM

COM, the Component Object Model, is a very big topic in and of itself. The details of COM are well beyond the scope of this book, but that is not a problem. We can think of COM objects as small-component dynamic link libraries (DLLs), which provide services to our program, and we'll find that we can create and use them without delving into their details. This is one of the great pleasures of Visual Basic: we can treat these little gum-drop sized modules as reusable code without diving into the intricacies of COM. *Don't panic!*

EXCURSION
ADO

To connect to the database from VB, you must have a system DSN set up for the Pubs database. Here's how to do it...

1. Open your control panel and click on ODBC Data Sources (ODBC32).
2. Choose the System DSN tab and click Add...
3. Choose SQL Server from the list of drivers and click Finish.
4. Enter a name; I suggest **Pubs**. Enter a description if you'd like (for example, "Access the Pubs Database") and choose a server. You should see the server on which you are running SQL Server or (local) if you're running SQL Server locally. If not, contact your system administrator. (Don't you hate when they say that and you *are* the system administrator?!) Click Next.
5. Click the With SQL Server authentication using a login ID and password entered by the user radio button. Delete Administrator from the loginID and enter **SA**. Leave the password blank. Click Next.
6. Click in Change the Default Database and scroll down and select Pubs. Click Next.
7. Accept all the defaults on the Create A New Data Source to SQL Server dialog box by just clicking on Finish.
8. Click on Test Data Source. If the test does not complete successfully, you'll need help from your SQL Server administrator, system administrator, or Microsoft. In all likelihood, however, you'll see the magic words TEST COMPLETED SUCCESSFULLY!
9. Congratulations, you now have a system DSN to Pubs. Click OK. This will return you to the ODBC Data Source Administrator dialog box. Click OK.

We'll encapsulate our knowledge of how to get the Publishers table inside a COM object written in VB. This isn't as hard as it sounds. Start by opening Visual Basic and enter File/New Project. Choose an ActiveX DLL project, as shown in Figure 3.11.

Name the new project PubsGetDataProject and create a new class module (right-click on the project and choose Add/Class Module).

Figure 3.11

Creating an ActiveX DLL in VB.

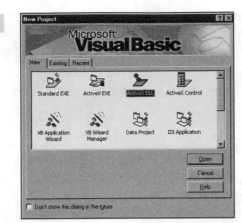

Click on Projects/References…, scroll down to Microsoft ActiveX Data Objects 2.1 Library, and click in the check box to include it in your project. (If you have a later ActiveX Data Objects library, use that instead.)

Name the new class PubsGetData and enter the code from Listing 3.2.

Listing 3.2

```
1: Function GetTheData() As Recordset
2:     Dim rs As ADODB.Recordset
3:     Set rs = New Recordset
4:     Call rs.Open("select * from publishers", "dsn=pubs",  UID=sa; PWD=;")
5:     Set GetTheData = rs
6: End Function
```

Your screen should look like Figure 3.12, with the project listed in the project window on the right and the code shown in the GetTheData method on the left.

Run, build, and save this project to your disk. Hey! Presto! You built a COM object. Wasn't that easy? Take the rest of the day off.

Visual Basic registered the DLL you created on your local machine. If you need to run it on another machine, copy the resulting DLL to your server machine and register it using regsvr32. (The easiest way is to locate regsvr32.exe in your Windows/Systems directory and drag a shortcut to the desktop. Then drop the DLL on the shortcut to register it.)

Whoa! You just registered a COM object on a foreign machine: instant distributed COM application. Take another day off!

Figure 3.12

The project and the code.

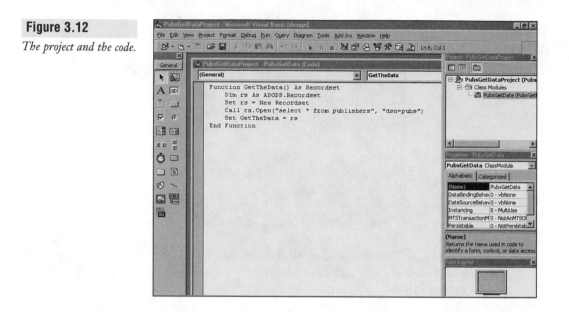

Using the New Module with ASP

 Note

For these exercises, be sure to log in using the administrator account. Failing that, you'll need to pass an account and password in with the DSN. See your network administrator.

We are now ready to modify the ASP document so that we can take advantage of the reusable, highly encapsulated, wicked-cool COM object we just built. Modify your ASP file as shown in Listing 3.3.

Listing 3.3

```
0:   <%@ Language=VBScript %>
1:   <HTML>
2:   <HEAD>
3:   <META NAME="GENERATOR" Content="Microsoft Visual Studio 6.0">
4:   </HEAD>
5:   <BODY>
6:   <%' get the data
7:   'display the data%>
8:
9:   <%dim pubBizObj
10:  set pubBizObj = server.CreateObject
10a:     ("pubsgetdataproject.pubsgetdata")
11:  set rs = pubBizObj.GetTheData%>
```

```
12:
13:    <P><h1>Publishers</h1></P>
14:    <TABLE WIDTH=75% BORDER=1 CELLSPACING=1
14a:       CELLPADDING=1>
15:       <%while not rs.EOF%>
16:       <TR>
17:           <TD><%=rs("pub_id")%></TD>
18:           <TD><%=rs("pub_name")%></TD>
19:           <TD><%=rs("city")%></TD>
20:       </TR>
21:       <%rs.movenext
22:       wend%>
23:    </TABLE>
24:
25:    </BODY>
26:    </HTML>
```

This code may not appear to be much simpler than the ASP-only version shown in Listing 3.1 (it is only four lines shorter), but the potential is here for great things. We've allocated much of the work of interacting with the database into the COM object you created in VB, and the ASP page can now use this object as a magic black-box for accessing the database.

When working in a team, one person might write the COM control and hand it off to the UI programmer, who will write the ASP that uses it. In any case, the output results are identical to those you got the last time you ran the program, as illustrated in Figure 3.13.

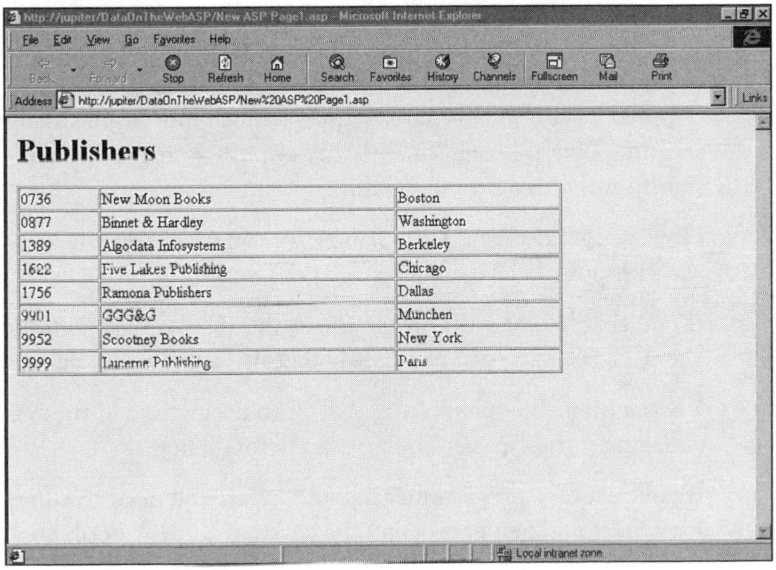

Figure 3.13

The output using a COM object.

More important, the HTML that results is also identical, as you can prove by choosing View Source in your browser, and as illustrated in Figure 3.14.

Figure 3.14

The source.

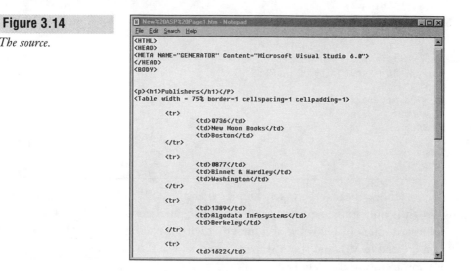

Converting It to a WebClass

Although this is great, ASP suffers two tremendous drawbacks:

1. It is very difficult to debug.
2. The code is mixed in with the HTML.

In addition, the code itself is either JavaScript or VBScript, and neither language is a full-bodied, rich, and aromatic programming language. VBScript is, in fact, a crippled version of VB. JavaScript is a much more robust language, but it is still a scripting language, and mixing the script in with the HTML makes for code that is significantly harder to maintain.

However, if we create WebClasses, we can write code in Visual Basic and then interact with pure HTML files.

If you are already a VB programmer, this discovery is fantastic: skill reuse results. In about 12 seconds, you will decide that this is the one true path of righteousness.

VB is a blast. It couldn't be more fun to program, and there is great satisfaction in churning out three-tier applications before lunch.

If you're a C++ programmer like me, relax. You need to run out and buy *Visual Basic from Scratch*. Then photocopy the cover of Knuth's book on algorithms, and paste it over the cover of the VB book, so no one will know what you're really reading. This way the construction workers won't laugh at you as you walk by, and you can still get your work done in half the time.

Rewriting It in WebClasses

To write this same application using a WebClass, we take three steps:

1. Create a template HTML file.
2. Create the WebClass file.
3. Stitch them together.

We explore each of these steps in detail in coming chapters. For now, let's quickly look at how this works, in keeping with our whirlwind tour.

I began by creating a new project in Visual Basic. This time, however, I chose an IIS application, as shown in Figure 3.15.

Figure 3.15

Creating an IIS application (WebClass).

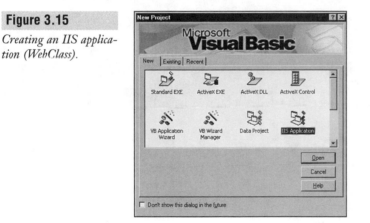

I renamed the project PubsWCProj and then changed the name WebClass1 to PubsWC. (Note that, to rename the WebClass, you must first double-click on WebClass1 to open the WebClass designer and then click on the Name property.) I also changed the NameInURL property to something short because it will become the URL to access the page.

I saved the project, clicked on Project/Resources..., scrolled down to Microsoft ActiveX Data Objects 2.1 Library, and clicked in the check box to include it in the project. (If you have a later ActiveX Data Objects library, use that instead.) While I'm at it, I'll add PubsGetDataProject as well.

Next, I started up DreamWeaver (my HTML editor) and created a new HTML file. I put in some simple text and saved it with the name PublisherTemplate.html, as shown in Figure 3.16.

Figure 3.16

DreamWeaver.

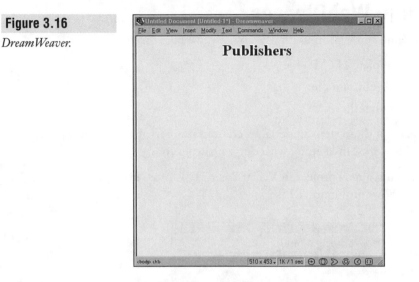

Because I like to save these templates in the same directory tree in which I keep the Visual Basic WebClass project, I created a subdirectory called templates and saved the .html file there.

Returning to the WebClass project, I right-clicked on HTML Template WebItems and chose Add HTML Template…, as shown in Figure 3.17.

Next, I navigated to the template I just created to add it. VB added it to the list of HTML Template WebItems, named it Template1, and immediately highlighted it for renaming, as shown in Figure 3.18.

Note that VB actually makes a copy of the original HTML file when it adds it to the HTML Template WebItems list. Consequently, I renamed the copy to Publishers, right-clicked on it, and chose Edit HTML Template, which will open the copy in my editor. (I already set my editor to DreamWeaver.)

Once again, we cover the details of working with WebClasses later in this book, but for now we just want to port over the code created in ASP. Template files are essentially straight HTML, with one special tag—the template tag. The default template tag is <WC@???></WC@???>, where you substitute any text you like for the question marks.

Figure 3.17

Adding the HTML template.

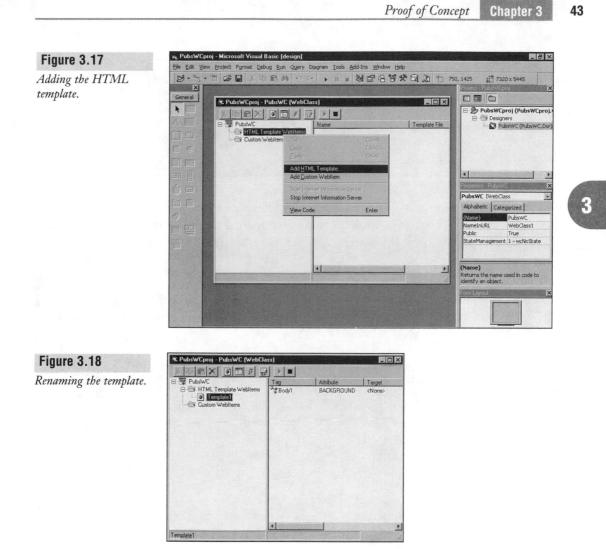

Figure 3.18

Renaming the template.

For example, I created the tag `<WC@Publishers>`. When my code sees this tag, it will process the tag and substitute whatever I tell it to substitute: typically more HTML. This allows me to manipulate this page dynamically at runtime, sending to the browser all the HTML from the file plus whatever I create at runtime to substitute for the template tags.

In our example, we want to create a table and fill it with the data from the database. Figure 3.19 illustrates the HTML we generate for this page in the template file.

Figure 3.19

Examining the tags.

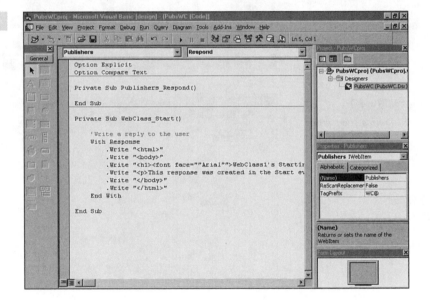

If we return to the WebClass and double-click on our Web template, we'll be brought to WebClass_Start. This is the first method that will run when this project is started. Right now it has dummy data put in by Visual Basic, as shown in Figure 3.20.

Figure 3.20

WebClass_Start.

Before we go any farther, let's run this program as-is by pressing F5. The debugger pops up and asks for our start component, as shown in Figure 3.21.

Let's just accept the defaults as offered. Next, VB asks where to create a virtual root for the new WebClass application, as shown in Figure 3.22.

Again, we just press OK. Our default browser is launched, and we see the text shown in Figure 3.23.

Where did this text come from? It is simply the result of the code added by VB. It attaches this code so that *something* will work when you start up the project.

Figure 3.21

Project properties.

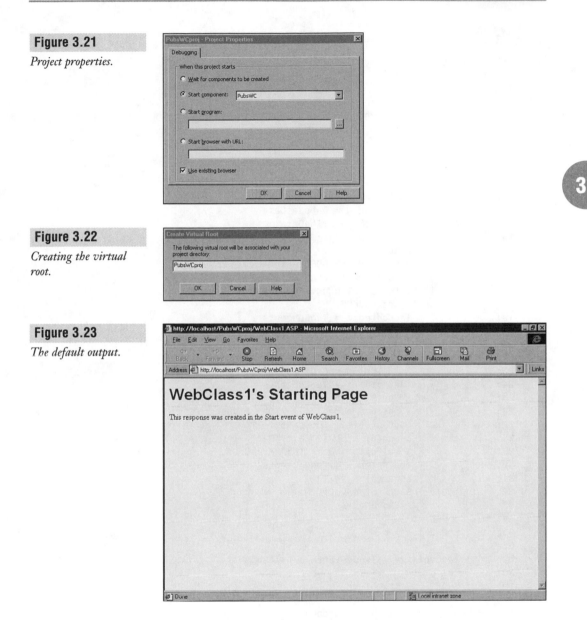

Figure 3.22

Creating the virtual root.

Figure 3.23

The default output.

Return to VB and delete all the code currently in WebClass_Start() and replace it with this line:

```
Set NextItem = Publishers
```

This sets the next Web item to be processed to the Web item we've just created: Publishers. The result is that Publishers_Respond is called. Listing 3.4 shows all the code for this module.

Listing 3.4

```
0:   Option Explicit
1:   Option Compare Text
2:
3:   Private Sub Publishers_ProcessTag_
4:   (ByVal TagName As String, TagContents As String,_
5:    SendTags As Boolean)
6:
7:       Select Case TagName
8:
9:       Case "WC@Publishers"
10:          Dim rs As Recordset
11:          Dim bizObj As New PubsGetData
12:          Set rs = bizObj.GetTheData
13:
14:          TagContents = _
15:          "<TABLE WIDTH=75% BORDER=1 " _
16:          & "CELLSPACING=1 CELLPADDING=1>"
17:          TagContents = TagContents & vbCrLf & vbCrLf
18:          While Not rs.EOF
19:              TagContents = TagContents _
20:              & Chr(9) & "<TR>" & vbCrLf
21:              TagContents = TagContents _
22:              & Chr(9) & Chr(9) & "<TD>" & rs("pub_id") _
23:              & "</TD>" & vbCrLf
24:              TagContents = TagContents _
25:              & Chr(9) & Chr(9) & "<TD>" _
26:              & rs("pub_name") & "</TD>" & vbCrLf
27:              TagContents = TagContents _
28:              & Chr(9) & Chr(9) & "<TD>" _
29:              & rs("city") & "</TD>" & vbCrLf
30:              TagContents = TagContents _
31:              & Chr(9) & "</TR>" _
32:              & vbCrLf & vbCrLf
33:              rs.MoveNext
34:          Wend
35:       End Select
36:
37:       TagContents = TagContents & "</table>"
38:
39:   End Sub
40:
41:   Private Sub Publishers_Respond()
42:       Publishers.WriteTemplate
43:   End Sub
44:
45:   Private Sub WebClass_Start()
46:       Set NextItem = Publishers
47:   End Sub
```

Whenever NextItem is set, the Respond method is called. In this case, it is Publishers_Respond. This code appears on line 41, and we invoke the WriteTemplate method on line 42. This tells VB to write the template file to the browser and call ProcessTag.

In ProcessTag, we respond to the tags in the template with code. Whatever we put into TagContents is injected into the HTML stream in place of the tag. In other words, our template is streamed to the client line by line, and each time a tag is found ProcessTag is called, giving us an opportunity to read the tag and respond appropriately.

Let's examine ProcessTag in some detail. On line 10, we declare a recordset object; on line 11, we create a new business object from the PubsGetData object we created in the previous exercise. On line 12, we call its GetTheData method and assign the resulting recordset to the rs variable we created on line 10.

We then start spitting out HTML. Note on line 14 that we assign to TagContents the string "<TABLE WIDTH=75% BORDER=1 CELLSPACING=1 CELLPADDING=1>". We then add in HTML for the rows, interspersing the strings returned from the recordset. When we're done, TagContents is one long string of HTML. We can set a break point on line 17, as shown in Figure 3.24, and use the *Immediate* window to examine the contents of TagContents.

You can see what is in TagContents by opening the Immediate window (Ctrl G), as shown in Figure 3.25.

Note, however, that this is produced within a loop. The next time through we *add* to the TagContents string, building up the table as we go. By the time the loop is finished and we hit the final line (where we add the closing tag for the table), we have built up a complete HTML string for output to the browser.

Figure 3.24

A break point.

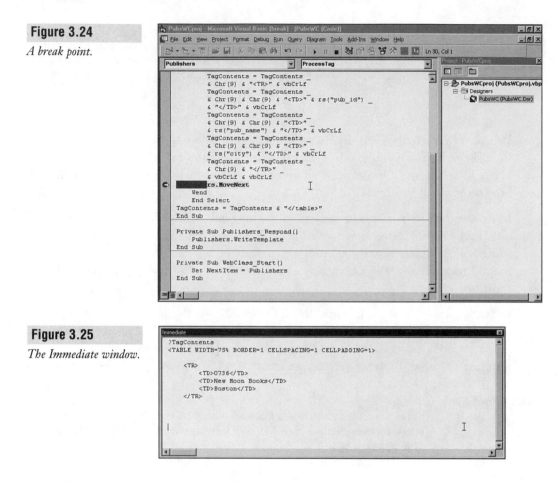

Figure 3.25

The Immediate window.

The output of all this is nearly identical to the previous ASP page, as shown in Figure 3.26.

Again, the browser receives nothing but plain HTML as shown by View Source and shown in Figure 3.27.

Comparing the Three Approaches

In our initial approach, all the code was mixed together with the ASP in a single file. In our second approach, we broke out a business object and implemented it as a Visual Basic COM DLL. This made our ASP somewhat cleaner.

Figure 3.26

Publishers.

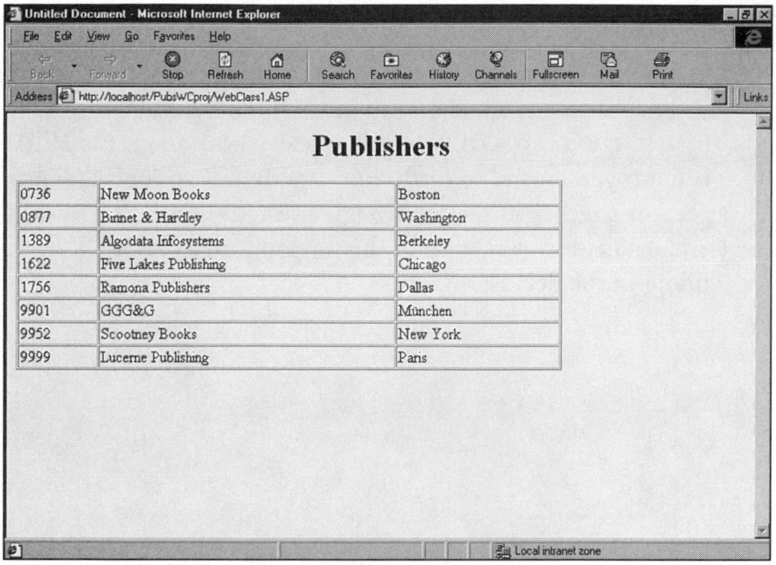

Figure 3.27

The source.

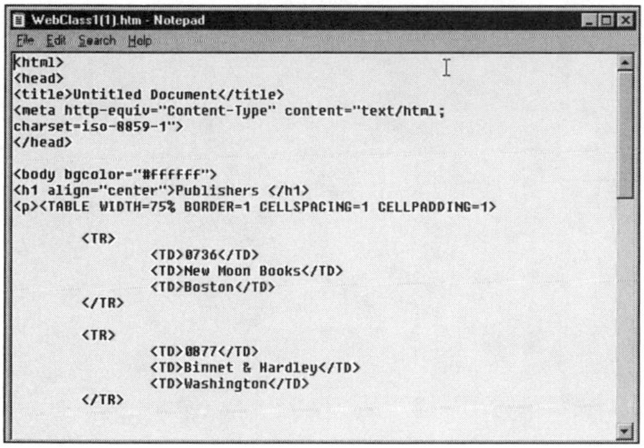

In the third approach, we set aside ASP and created a WebClass in VB. This allowed us to use the full power of Visual Basic, as well as its robust debugging abilities. The presentation layer is encapsulated in the template HTML file, and the logic of replacing tags with dynamically determined data is encapsulated in the WebClass. The business object is still used, but this time it is called within the WebClass code. All in all, this makes for a far more scalable and robust architecture, and it is the approach I use for the rest of the book.

Next Steps

In coming chapters, we explore many of the issues raised by this code in far greater detail. You need to understand more about the database and the interface to the database (ODBC and ADO) as well as learn more about the HTML, how the WebClass is put together, and so forth. For now, however, you've seen that it is not difficult to present pages that iterate through a resultset produced by a SQL call against a back-end database. We're well on the way now. In a sense, all the rest of the work is just filling in the details.

Chapter 4

Working with Enterprise-Scale Databases

In keeping with our all-Microsoft approach to this project, we use SQL Server 7 as our back-end database.

how tōo prō nouns′ it	*SQL Server* is pronounced as if it were written Sequel Server.

SQL Server is a high-end enterprise-level database, which is the latest version of a product originally created in 1987 by Sybase for the UNIX market. It was codeveloped by Sybase, Ashton-Tate, and Microsoft over a few years and has been through numerous releases since that time.

Note	The code for this book has been tested with SQL Server 7 and works well with that database. Nothing I do is all that unusual, however, so I would be very surprised if you couldn't get it to work with Oracle, Informix, Access, or virtually any SQL-compliant database.

We draw on only a fraction of the power of SQL Server to create our tables, establish relationships, and enforce the database rules of EmployeeNet.

Getting Started with SQL Server

Even though setting up SQL Server has become much easier with the release of version 7, it still makes sense to take a few moments with a good book on the subject to *get it right*. SQL Server comes complete with a number of very powerful tools, which we will draw upon as we work our way through the EmployeeNet project.

The details of setting up SQL Server are beyond the scope of this book, but I will walk you through the creation of the EmployeeNet database step by step. In truth, if you accept all the defaults when you set up SQL Server, you will probably be just fine.

Creating the EmployeeNet Database

Let's start by firing up Enterprise Manager, as shown in Figure 4.1.

Figure 4.1

Enterprise Manager.

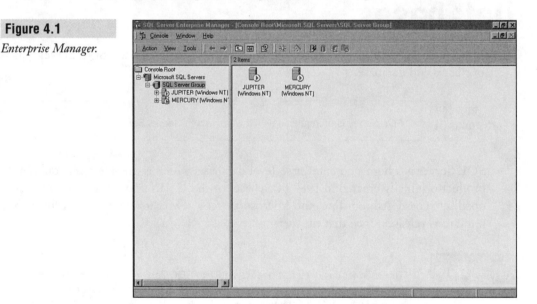

As you can see, my machine has links to two different database servers. Jupiter is a server machine running Windows NT. On the other hand, Mercury is a desktop instance of SQL Server running on the machine on which I'm capturing these images. Each of these databases runs independently on my small local area network.

We'll put our new database on Mercury. To do this, I'll expand Mercury (by clicking on the + mark), and then I'll right-click on the Databases entry to choose New Database..., as shown in Figure 4.2.

Figure 4.2

Creating a new database.

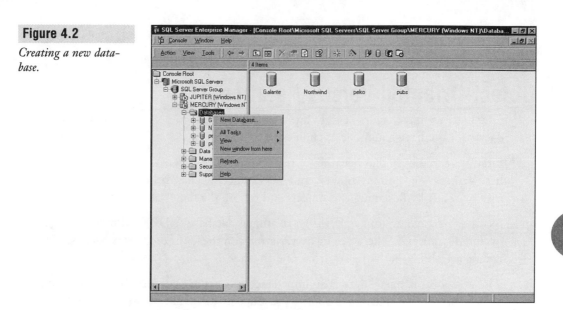

This brings up the Database Properties dialog box shown in Figure 4.3. I'll fill in the name for the new database, **EmployeeNet**, and accept the default location for the database. In this version of SQL Server, the database and its log files will grow as needed. Managing the log file is a task we can ignore during development, and, with luck, our Data Base Administrator (DBA) will handle it for us.

Figure 4.3

Database properties.

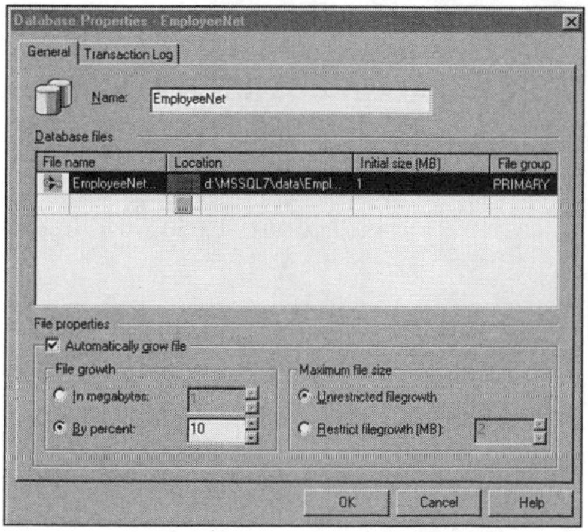

After the database is created, it is added to the list of databases. Clicking on it displays details about the database, and expanding the plus mark next to EmployeeNet displays a list of related database objects such as tables, diagrams, views, and stored procedures. All these will be empty (except for the tables created to manage the database system information).

Object-Oriented Versus Relational

One issue we must confront right away is how we want to deal with the back-end database. We have a number of choices.

First, we can decide that because we're building an object-oriented project, the database will serve as nothing more than a persistence mechanism for our objects. In this case, we start by designing our objects and ignore the database altogether.

As an alternative, we can start with a relational database (RDB) and build an object-oriented front end. There are many variations on these different approaches, but the results are somewhat different from one another.

The key point is this: There is an impedance mismatch between object-oriented programs and relational databases, so we must decide in advance who is setting the course. Let's begin by looking at using relational databases as a persistence mechanism for our object-oriented design.

 Programmers talk about an impedance mismatch between object-oriented programs and relational databases. In electrical engineering, an impedance mismatch refers to a condition that makes it difficult to wire two segments together. Here, by analogy, we refer to a difficulty in mapping the object-oriented perspective to that of a relational database.

Database as Persistence Mechanism (Object Store)

In this model, we design the objects and their relationships (association, aggregation, inheritance, and so on) without regard to the database. The database becomes nothing more than an implementation choice for storing the objects when they can no longer live in memory.

When we finally do turn our attention to the database, each table represents a single object, each column in the table represents an attribute of the object, and each row represents one instance. This is a fairly clean, but imperfect, mapping to the object-oriented perspective, but it doesn't utilize the relational aspects of our relational database. Thus it underutilizes the database technology.

If we were to take this approach, we would be far better off using an object database. That said, object-database technology is still relatively immature; consequently, the tools are not as robust. In addition, few programmers have an expertise in object-oriented database OODB technology, and our customer (or employer) may not want to take that risk.

The details of using a relational database as a persistence mechanism for an object-oriented design are, in some ways, beyond the scope of this book. The vast majority of applications putting data on the Web begin with a back-end database. We create an object-oriented n-tier design to support that existing (or planned) database.

The Data Layer

If, therefore, we decide to use the relational database for its own power, we start with the database and its data structures. Designing the database is a significant undertaking, and it is the thrust of this chapter.

Nevertheless, the problem remains: there is a mismatch between objects and the relational database. We need a plan before we begin to handle this, and n-tier architecture provides some help. First, we need to create an interface layer between the business objects on the one hand and the database tables on the other. This layer will be the data layer. The responsibility of the data layer will be to translate cleanly between the (object-oriented) business layer and the (relational) database itself.

In EmployeeNet, the objects we consider are relatively simple and have a fairly straightforward mapping to the tables we build. The data layer will be manifest principally in stored procedures (more about these shortly) rather than in objects. The Windows DNA architecture allows for this or for the creation of data objects in their own right, depending on the complexity of the interface you require.

Designing the Database

With this plan in mind, we are ready to design our database. The principal entities we'll be concerned with are

- Tables
- Indices (indexes)
- Relations (foreign key constraints and join tables)
- Constraints and rules

Let's consider these entities one at a time.

Creating the Tables

When building a relational database, we typically start by designing the tables. It is fair to say that RDBs are, in large measure, defined by their table structure.

It is traditional to think of tables as columns and rows. Each row represents a "record," and each column represents a "field" of that record.

Even though I've drawn a sharp distinction between objects and relational databases, the distinction begins to blur the moment we look at tables. For example, our tables ought to have some relationship to the entities in our design and thus indirectly in the problem domain.

In the EmployeeNet application, the central object is the employee, and it is more than reasonable to start with an Employee table.

We might be tempted to pour everything we know about an employee into an Employee table. This might include the employee's name, address, phone, fax, start date, job description, salary, Social Security number, health benefits, and investment plan.

The problem is that some of this information may be repeated in other tables, and this makes for a system that is harder to maintain and more error-prone. To eliminate these problems, database programmers *normalize* their databases, putting them into *normal form*. In other words, they squeeze out the duplicate information. There are a number of normal forms, but we'll only be concerned with the third normal form.

This book does not provide a precise definition of these terms, but a working understanding of the third normal form will help you understand how to design your database to be efficient.

First Normal Form

To understand the third normal form, let's start with the first normal form, referred to as 1NF. When a database is in 1NF, each attribute (column) in a given table represents a single piece of data. It is said to be atomic rather than an aggregate or a set.

Figure 4.4 shows a table that violates the first normal form. Employee 003 works in two cities: NYC and LA. Her office ID is a set of two, which is not legal. To fix this, we must rewrite that entry, moving the table into 1NF, as shown in Figure 4.5.

Figure 4.4

Unnormalized table.

EmpID	OfficeID	EmpName	OfficeCity	Salary
001	A01	Liberty	Acton	10,000
002	A02	Smith	NYC	20,000
003	A02/A03	Jones	NYC/LA	30,000
004	A01	Brown	Acton	20,000

Figure 4.5

Table in first normal form.

EmpID	OfficeID	EmpName	OfficeCity	Salary
001	A01	Liberty	Acton	10,000
002	A02	Smith	NYC	20,000
003	A02	Jones	NYC	30,000
003	A03	Jones	LA	30,000
004	A01	Brown	Acton	20,000

Second Normal Form

Second normal form (2NF) builds on 1NF and requires that each row in the database be uniquely identifiable. A table has a *primary key*, which is the field (or set of fields) that uniquely identifies each record. In Figure 4.5, if we said that the EmpID was the primary key, we would violate 2NF because EmpID 003 appears twice. We cannot point to any single column that currently guarantees that each record is unique. One way to solve that problem is to declare that the primary key is the combination of the first and second columns. Thus, each row is identified by the combination of the EmpID *and* the OfficeID.

Third Normal Form

The purpose of the third normal form (3NF) is to build on the 2NF, while eliminating duplicate information. Duplication of data is necessary in all databases, but what ought to be duplicated is the identification of data, not the data itself. For example, in Figure 4.5 the Employee name Jones is duplicated for records 003-A02 and 003-A03. Similarly, the officeCity NYC is duplicated for records 002-A02 and 003-A02. In this case, the duplication is trivial, a few wasted bytes. But duplicate data adds up (perhaps the duplicated data is a long comment). More important, it is hard to maintain (if we change the designation A02 from NYC to "New York City" we must update every record that contains A02.

The solution is to "factor out" the common data into separate tables, as shown in Figure 4.6.

We have divided our table into three smaller tables and eliminated all duplication. The first row in the assignments table tells us that Employee 001 is in office A01. By looking up Employee 001 in the Employees table, we can determine his name and salary. By looking up office A01 in the offices table, we can find out what we need to know about the location of this office.

We have decoupled information about offices from information about employees, which makes maintaining and modifying either one independently of the other far easier. If the NYC office moves across the water to NJ, we can change only the one record in the offices table, and the information is changed for every NYC employee.

Figure 4.6

Factoring out common data.

Assignments

EmpID	OfficeID
001	A01
002	A02
003	A02
003	A03
004	A01

Offices

OfficeID	OfficeCity
A01	Acton
A02	NYC
A03	LA

Employees

EmpID	EmpName	Salary
001	Liberty	10,000
002	Smith	20,000
003	Jones	30,000
004	Brown	20,000

Building the EmployeeNet Tables

With that background, we're ready to start building the EmployeeNet tables. To do this, we need to expand our newly created EmployeeNet database and right-click on the Tables entry. This will bring up a context menu from which we choose New Table..., as shown in Figure 4.7.

We are prompted to enter a table name (as shown in Figure 4.8).

From here we can enter all the columns (fields) for this table. The very first field should be the primary key field: EmployeeID. Because we know that we want each employee to have a unique ID, EmployeeID satisfies the requirement that every record be unique. We will use this EmployeeID in the other tables we'll build to refer to all employees.

Figure 4.7

New table.

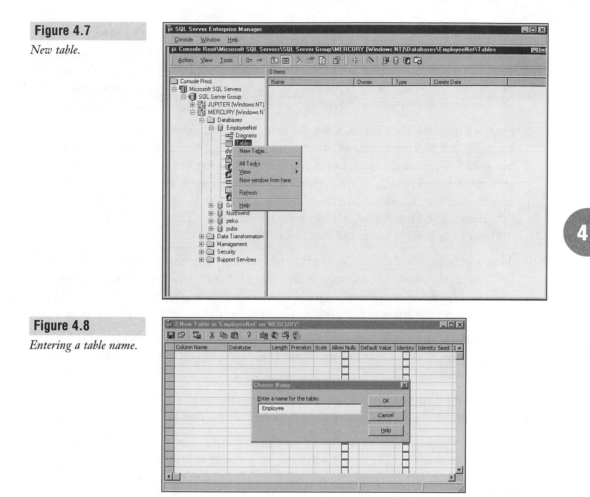

Figure 4.8

Entering a table name.

SQL Server will create a unique ID for us, if we

- Set the Datatype to int.
- Do *not* allow null values.
- Set the identify property.

SQL Server creates a unique number for each record. The *identity seed value* is the first value assigned to the first record. The *identity increment* is the value by which each subsequent identity number will be incremented. Thus, if you set these to 1 and 1, the first record will be 1 and the next three will be 2, 3, and 4. If you set the identity seed to 100 and the increment to 5, then the first four values will be 100, 105, 110, and 115. The default values are 1 and 1.

By designating this column as the primary key, we create a *primary key constraint*, which dictates that this value must always be unique for each record.

Adding Fields

It is now time to fill in the data fields for the employee object. We know that we want to capture the employee's name, but we must separate out first, middle, and last names into individual fields. This gives us greater flexibility when building our Web site (for example, we can say "Hello John" rather than "Hello John Q. Public").

First, we must decide what to name the field. You would think this would be an easy question, but like everything in programming it takes a bit of thought. We might call this field FN (for first name), but that might be a bit hard to maintain. When you see a table with FN, MI, LN, T, A1, A2, C, S, Z, you *might* figure out what kind of information is in the table. But the table is much easier to understand when we use field names like First Name, Middle Initial, Last Name, Title, Address Line 1, Address Line 2, City, State, and Zip Code.

That said, spaces in field names are frowned upon. If you choose First Name as the field name, the computer will turn it into [First Name], which is difficult to work with. It is better to turn it into a single word, either First_name or FirstName. I personally prefer the latter because I hate reaching for the underscore character.

FirstName is an example of *camel notation*. In this convention, you use a capital letter for each new word, so that the words are easier to read (FirstName is easier to read than Firstname).

Camel notation—All the names are formed together without spaces, but each new word begins with a capital letter. Examples include myBigDogMilo or MyCatFred.

The second decision we must make is to determine the data type. The data type tells SQL Server what kind of data it will be storing and thus how much space to allocate. For fields such as FirstName, which will store characters, we might choose char or varchar. Char allocates a fixed number of bytes (1–8000), but the data must fit in however many bytes we allocate. The alternative is varchar, which allocates a variable number of bytes but brings some overhead. In short, if we expect the data to vary in length, we should use varchar. We'll use varchar to handle names from Amy to Zachariah. We could, I think, use a char(15) and be pretty sure we have enough room, but varchar works well.

Decision number three is whether or not to allow this field to be *null*. If we check Allow Nulls (or more accurately, if you just leave it checked, as that is the default), then we are not required to provide a value for this field. If we do uncheck this field, then every record must have some value for FirstName. Because all the employees will have a first name, let's uncheck this, and force the value.

We could enter a default value (for example, we might enter "Unknown"). This way, if we don't know a new employee's first name, we'll at least have *something* in this field.

Let's go ahead and fill in MiddleName, LastName, Title (for example, Mrs.), and Suffix (for example, Jr.). FirstName and LastName will be required fields; MiddleName, Title, and Suffix will be optional (and thus will allow nulls), as shown in Figure 4.9.

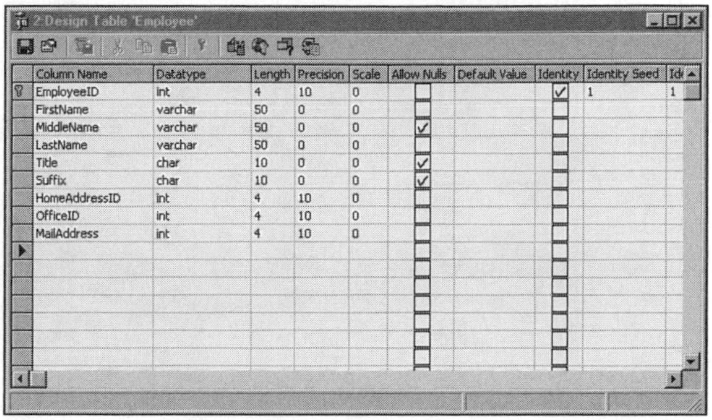

Figure 4.9

Designing the Employee table.

When we tell the database that a field will not have nulls, it will object when we try to add a record that, in fact, does have a null value for that field. Why bother? Why let the database pester us in this way? After all, if we just tell it to allow nulls on every field, we won't have this annoyance.

The answer is this: We want the design to model the *semantics* of our understanding of the business domain. If every employee will always have a last name, but may or may not have a middle name, then we want the database tables to reflect this information. This makes for software that is much more reliable and easier to maintain.

First, the model maps to reality, so we are not surprised by what we see. Second, when we make the inevitable human error of leaving out a first name, the database has an opportunity to remind us *before* the data we are working with becomes corrupted.

I make a point of checking Allow Nulls as infrequently as the problem domain allows. That is to say, I use it only when it makes sense for the field to be null, not as a convenience to make data entry simpler. We'll return to this thought when we talk about referential integrity. First, however, we need to add more tables.

Normalizing Out the Address

Note that the HomeAddressID field in this table definition is just an integer. What's going on here?

Every employee will be associated with (at least) two addresses: his home address and his office address. Each of these addresses will have very similar data: address line 1, address line 2, city, state, zip code. Rather than duplicate these fields and keep them aligned with each other, I chose to create a separate address table. Every address will have an ID, and the employee record stores that ID for home and office address.

The final field in the Employee table is MailAddress. The employee might get his employment-related work at home or at the office; we keep track of his individual choice here, as shown in Figure 4.10.

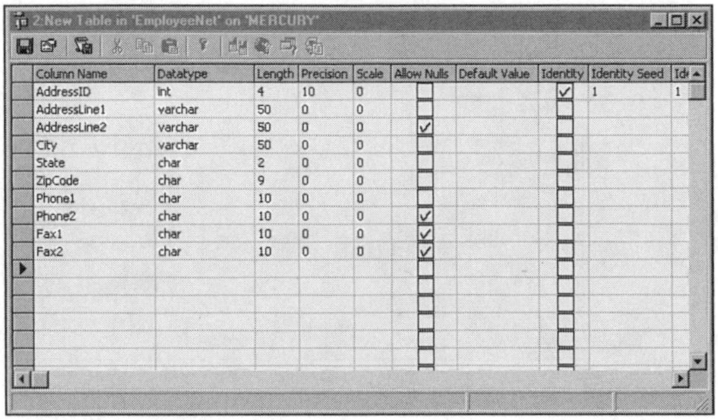

Figure 4.10

Creating the Address table.

There are no great surprises in this table: AddressID is followed by the fields you'd expect, adding only two entries for phones and two for fax.

Again, the use of nulls reflects our conservative guesses about which fields *might* legitimately be empty, including the second line of the address, the second phone, and any fax at all.

If you reflect on this design for a moment, however, you'll find that it is somewhat limited. Why designate two home telephones and not one or three? Many employees will have only one home phone, but some will have many more than that (for a while, I had seven, but I'm a geek and don't count).

A better and more flexible way to design this would be to call out the phones and fax into a separate table. Each record in the telephone table would have only two fields: the telephone number and the AddressID that it belongs to. By this method, any given employee might have any number of phone numbers associated with his address (either home or office).

For those of you who program in C or C++, this is the equivalent of going from an array (fixed size) to a linked list (dynamically allocated). In a commercial application, I would certainly make this change, but for the purposes of this book, we'll keep things as they are with just two phone numbers. It will make our analysis of the tables somewhat simpler.

Declarative Referential Integrity

It is our intent to relate each employee record to address records. Specifically, the HomeAddressID, OfficeID, and MailAddress are all aimed squarely at the Address table. Each of these fields in the Employee table will hold the identity value of exactly one record in the Address table.

We can enforce this by simply remembering to enter these values each time we add an employee, or we can ask the database to enforce it. We do this by creating an explicit relationship between these fields.

The simplest way to create such a relationship is to use the SQL Server Database Design Diagram tool. Right-click on Diagrams and choose New Database Diagram....

This will bring up the Create Database Diagram wizard. The first question involves which tables to include in the diagram; we'll add Address and Employee. After adding these, the diagram shows two tables, complete with their fields, as shown in Figure 4.11.

Figure 4.11

Diagram of the database.

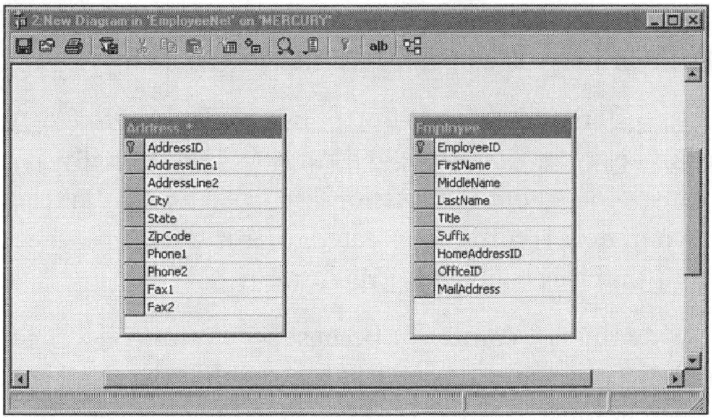

No explicit relationship is shown between the tables, despite the fact that the Employee table refers to the Address table. Or does it? After all, the database has no way of knowing that HomeAddressID refers to the primary key of the Address table, and thus it has no way of enforcing this relationship (unless we tell it).

We do so by clicking in the HomeAddressID field of the Employee table and dragging it to the AddressID field of the Address table. (You can drag either one to the other; SQL Server will figure out what relationship you want by which one is a primary key.)

This brings up the Create Relationship dialog box shown in Figure 4.12.

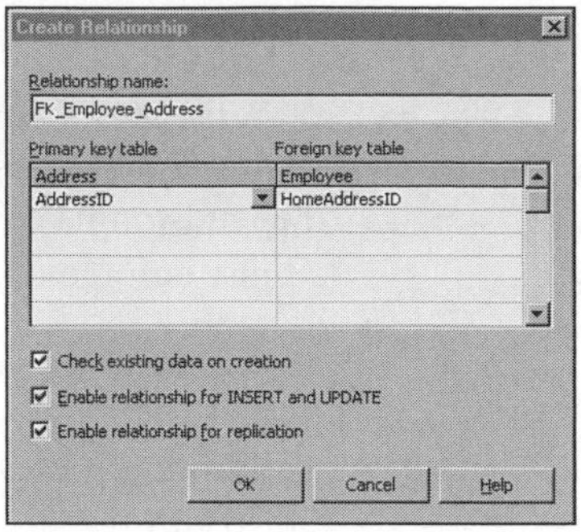

Figure 4.12

Creating a primary key relationship.

This dialog box creates a *primary key* relationship between the Address and Employee tables. In this relationship, the table whose primary key is used is called the primary key table.

When a table (such as Employee) holds a value that is a primary key in another table (such as Address), that value is referred to as a *foreign key*. The table with a field that is a foreign key in another table (in our case, Employee) is called the foreign key table. Upon close examination of this dialog box, we see that SQL Server has correctly identified Employee.HomeAddressID as the foreign key; the value will be found in the primary key of Address.AddressID.

SQL Server offers to name this relationship FK_Employee_Address–Foreign Key relationship between Employee and Address. Additionally, it defaults to enforcing certain constraints about the relationship, specifically that the relationship should be checked when new records are created, that it should be checked both for insert and update, and that it is enabled for replication.

Let's set aside the last constraint because we're not concerned about replication. The first two, however, are interesting. They say that the database is empowered to *enforce* this relationship. That is, if you add an employee, there had better be a valid address entry for that employee *before* you try to add her.

This is the essence of Declarative Referential Integrity (DRI). We have declared that one field in the Employee table refers to a specific field in the Address table, and we are asking the database to protect the integrity of this relationship.

This is a *good* thing. It means that the database will flag any employee who has no home address, and that is what we want. Let's ask the database to help us find these corrupted records.

Why Use DRI?

Declarative Referential Integrity makes working with your database much harder. You must be careful about the order in which you *add* data (ensuring that the reference data is in place before you add data that depends on it) as well as the order in which you *delete* data. Why not skip all this and just enforce data integrity through careful programming?

Do not give in to this temptation! What you hear is the Devil of Development denoting degenerate design; the Pariah of Programming postulating pusillanimous punditry; the Satan of Software suggesting sophistry to the susceptible.

The true path—the one, correct, golden, bright and shining road to software nirvana—is to enlist the database in helping you find bugs *before* you ship the product. The more constraints you can encapsulate in the software, the fewer must be embodied in "wet ware"—that unreliable medium housed between your ears. Let the database find your mistakes; it is less expensive and less embarrassing than allowing your customer to do so.

The Complete Database Design

For the purposes of this book, we'll keep the database design relatively simple. Consequently, we use only 10 tables:

Address

Asset Allocation

Coverage Type

Employee

EmployeeHealthPackage

Funds

HealthInsurancePlans

HealthPlanCost

Offices

Portfolio

The Tables in Detail

Let's examine these tables in detail and consider their interrelationships. As discussed, the Employee table is the central repository of information about each employee. Its data structure is shown in Figure 4.13.

Figure 4.13

Employee table.

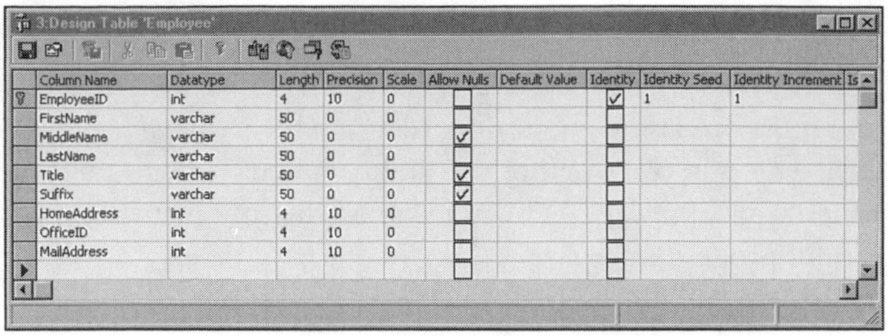

There are no surprises in this table. We looked at the Address table previously (see Figure 4.10), so I won't reproduce it here.

We are concerned with two sets of information: the employee's insurance and his investments. To track his insurance, we must know what health plan he has chosen and what dental plan. For each plan, we need to know the coverage type he's chosen (for example, family or individual).

Many-to-Many Relationships

At first glance, this would appear to be a one-to-many relationship. Each employee has a single health plan and a single dental plan. The problem is that the difference between a health plan and a dental plan is trivial. Almost all the information required about one is required about the other (health plan provider, coverage type, deductibles, and the like). Why not combine these two tables (health plan and dental plan) into a single table?

In that case, each employee has more than one plan—one for dental and one for health. Each plan, of course, is attached to more than one employee. This is a many-to-many relationship.

This is still not quite right, however. We don't want to allow the employee to participate in three such relationships, but rather exactly two. The answer is to create a new table to represent this relationship between an employee and one health plan (and coverage type) and one dental plan (and coverage type). This is the EmployeeHealthPackage table, as shown in Figure 4.14.

Note in this figure that each plan and each coverage type is represented by an integer. These are each, in turn, the ID of records in other tables. Similarly, the employee himself is represented by an integer—the EmployeeID of the employee in this particular relationship with the health plans.

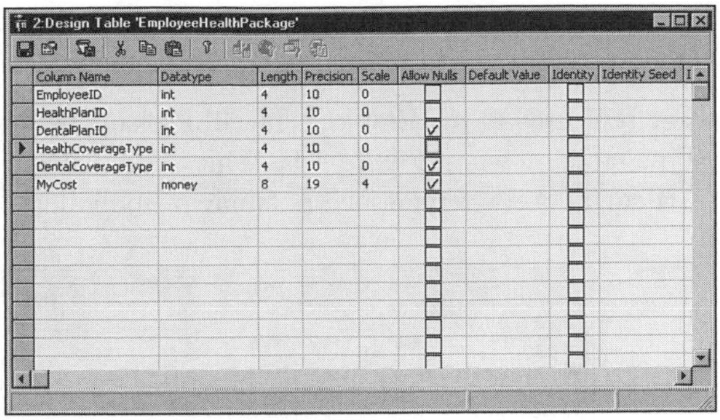

Figure 4.14

EmployeeHealthPackage table.

The design of the EmployeeHealthPackage table also indicates that participation in a health plan is mandatory but that participation in a dental plan is optional (note the use of null fields). This table captures the business rule in a very straightforward manner.

So, EmployeeID (Jesse Liberty) might subscribe to HealthPlan (Blue Cross) with CoverageType (family) and to DentalPlan (Delta Dental) with CoverageType (individual). The final field is the aggregated cost of these choices.

One-Way Relationship

Note that the relationship between a particular employee and his health plan is not reciprocal: the EmployeeHealthPackage table tracks EmployeeID numbers, but the Employee table does not track the health package. This is good design; the Employee table need not know anything about this relationship because all the information about an employee's health decisions is captured in this single table.

To fully understand this table, we need to examine two others—the health insurance plans and the coverage types. Figure 4.15 shows the plans.

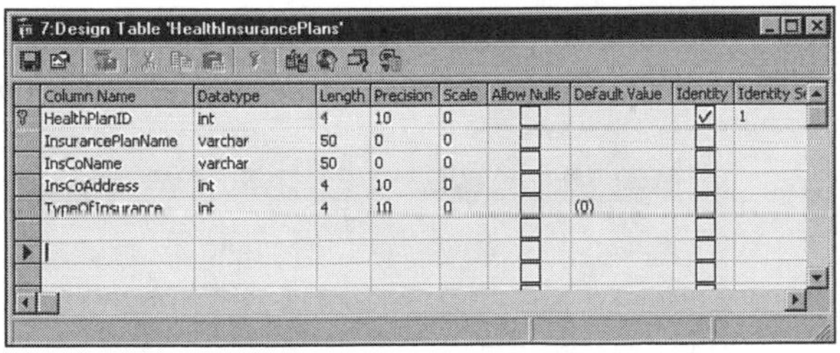

Figure 4.15

HealthInsurancePlans table.

Note here that the InsuranceCoAdd is, again, captured in the Address table. The final column, TypeOfInsurance, is a simple integer in which 0 represents health insurance and 1 represents dental insurance. In a more robust and complicated application, these in turn might be offsets into an insurance type table.

The coverage type used in the EmployeeHealthPackage table is looked up in the CoverageType table shown in Figure 4.16. This ties a CoverageTypeID to a description of a particular coverage type such as family or individual.

Figure 4.16

CoverageType table.

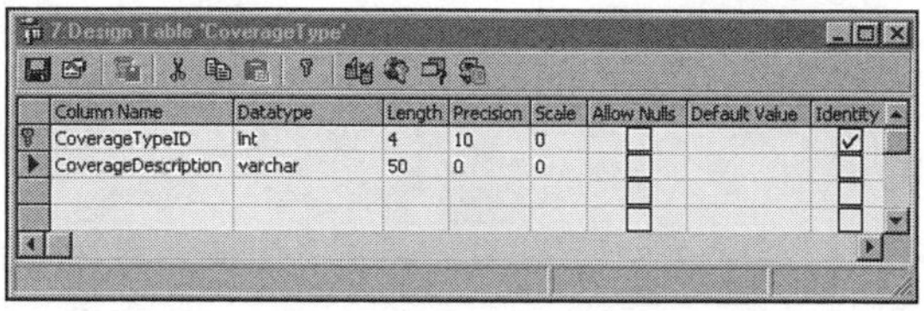

Column Name	Datatype	Length	Precision	Scale	Allow Nulls	Default Value	Identity
CoverageTypeID	int	4	10	0			✓
CoverageDescription	varchar	50	0	0			

The cost field in the EmployeeHealthPackage is computed from the HealthPlanCost table shown in Figure 4.17. Each HealthPlanID coupled with a CoverageType makes for a unique record, each of which is assigned a cost.

Figure 4.17

HealthPlanCost table.

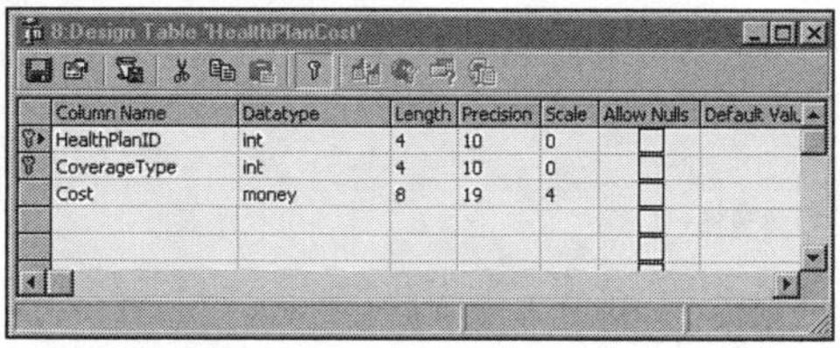

Column Name	Datatype	Length	Precision	Scale	Allow Nulls	Default Value
HealthPlanID	int	4	10	0		
CoverageType	int	4	10	0		
Cost	money	8	19	4		

That closes the circle. A given employee has both a health plan and a dental plan, with a specific coverage type in each. This is captured in EmployeeHealthPackage. The various plan types are captured in HealthInsurancePlans, the cost is in HealthPlanCost, and the coverage types themselves are captured in CoverageType.

Asset Allocation

We also want to track the employee's investments. To do this, we create the concept of a *portfolio*, which will represent a collection of funds, as shown in Figure 4.18.

Figure 4.18

Portfolio table.

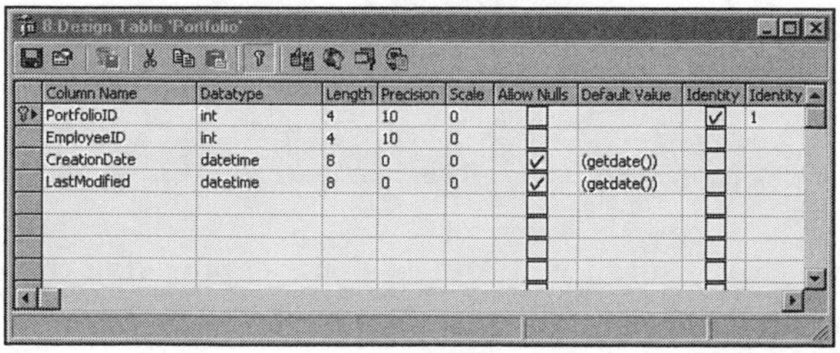

Column Name	Datatype	Length	Precision	Scale	Allow Nulls	Default Value	Identity	Identity
PortfolioID	int	4	10	0			✓	1
EmployeeID	int	4	10	0				
CreationDate	datetime	8	0	0	✓	(getdate())		
LastModified	datetime	8	0	0	✓	(getdate())		

Each record in the Portfolio table represents the entire portfolio for a given employee. We expect that there will be one record in this table for each employee.

A given employee can divide his assets into as many as four funds, telling us what percent to allocate to each (for example, 100% to one or 50% each to two or 50, 30, 15, and 5% to four).

We use a second table, *AssetAllocation*, to track these decisions. The AssetAllocation table is shown in Figure 4.19.

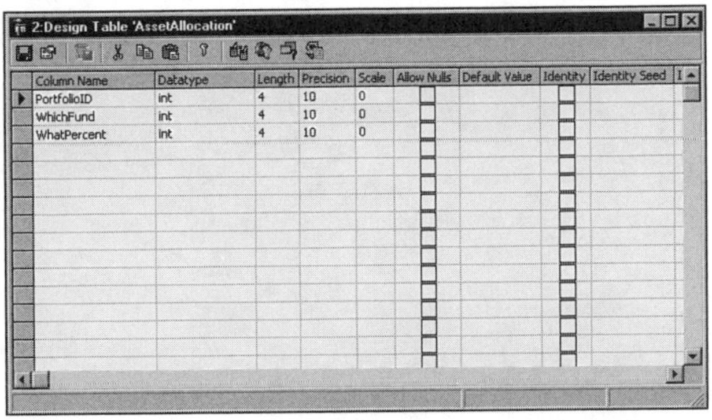

2:Design Table 'AssetAllocation'

Column Name	Datatype	Length	Precision	Scale	Allow Nulls	Default Value	Identity	Identity Seed
PortfolioID	int	4	10	0				
WhichFund	int	4	10	0				
WhatPercent	int	4	10	0				

Figure 4.19

AssetAllocation table.

As you can see, there is a record in the AssetAllocation table for each allocated fund. These are tied back to the employee by way of the Portfolio table, based on the PortfolioID.

Thus, a given employee has a portfolio represented by a record with that employee's ID in the Portfolio table. For each employee's portfolio, there are up to four allocations of funds. Each of these allocations is represented by a record with the appropriate portfolio ID in the AssetAllocation table.

The only missing piece of the puzzle is the description of the various funds. We keep these in the funds table, with one record for each fund, as shown in Figure 4.20.

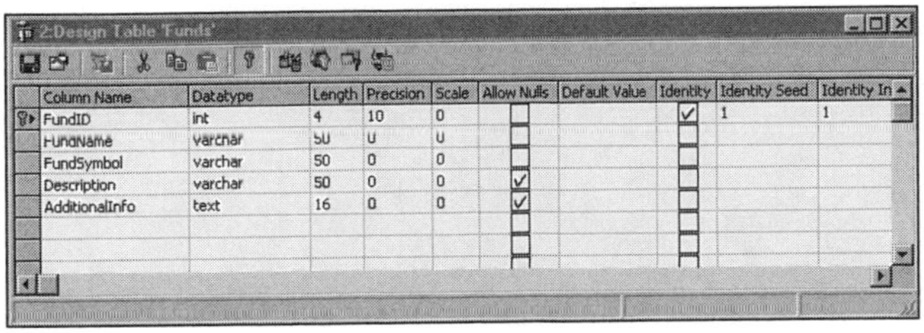

2:Design Table 'Funds'

Column Name	Datatype	Length	Precision	Scale	Allow Nulls	Default Value	Identity	Identity Seed	Identity In
FundID	int	4	10	0			✓	1	1
FundName	varchar	50	0	0					
FundSymbol	varchar	50	0	0					
Description	varchar	50	0	0	✓				
AdditionalInfo	text	16	0	0	✓				

Figure 4.20

Funds table.

With this, we can keep track of the employee's health investments and insurance choices.

Next Steps

We have enough of a design to be able to turn our attention to the task at hand: How do we display this data on the Web? After we have that working, we go on to build data-entry pages. Then, we return to the database design to add the appropriate constraints and rules to guarantee that the data being added are what we need.

Chapter 5

EmployeeNet Release 1.0

Now that we have a design for EmployeeNet, we must decide how to implement it. The first option is to follow the design step by step, adding each page and all its related functionality. The second option is to start with a far simpler first iteration, get it working, and then add to it. I will pursue this second option because it is far closer to how I actually like to work.

Page—In Web development, each HTML file is referred to as a page.

The expression "above the fold," which was originally used to refer to articles that began above the fold of newspapers like the *New York Times*, now refers to articles or images that appear on the top of an HTML page, so that you don't have to scroll to find them.

Get Something Working, Keep It Working

There is great advantage to getting something working quickly and then adding to it. If the additions are guided by a sound design, there is positive feedback between that design and what you learn while you implement it. To get us started, I'll scale back the design and implement the simplest, most bare-bones version of EmployeeNet. We'll begin with just four pages:

1. A very simple start page with just one link to the search page.

2. A very simple search page with just one simple control: a drop-down of the offices already existing in the system. Choose an office and we'll report on all the employees in that office.

3. A list of all the matching employees. Every employee will be presented as a link. Click on the link to see details about that employee.

4. A simple details page that provides a little data about the employee.

Although these pages will be Spartan and will implement virtually none of Maethee's UI design, they will allow us to explore the underlying technology in great detail.

We'll build this simple project together, step by step. It won't take very long.

Step 1—Data in the Database

In order to have something to search for, we must have some data in our database. We begin by bringing up SQL Server Enterprise Manager and navigating to the EmployeeNet database. Once there, we can click on the EmployeeNet table to see a list of our tables, as shown in Figure 5.1.

Figure 5.1

The EmployeeNet tables.

Name	Owner	Type	Create Date
Address	dbo	User	7/5/99 1:29:55 PM
AssetAllocation	dbo	User	7/6/99 4:07:49 PM
CoverageType	dbo	User	7/5/99 2:16:42 PM
Employee	dbo	User	7/5/99 1:29:17 PM
EmployeeHealthPackage	dbo	User	7/5/99 1:54:26 PM
Funds	dbo	User	6/7/99 11:03:47 AM
HealthInsurancePlans	dbo	User	7/5/99 2:13:09 PM
HealthPlanCost	dbo	User	6/7/99 11:03:47 AM
Offices	dbo	User	6/24/99 10:15:13 AM
Portfolio	dbo	User	6/7/99 11:30:08 AM
sysTableComments	dbo	User	6/28/99 8:49:03 PM

> **Note** You will note sysTableComments in some of the figures showing the database. This is a special table added by the SQueaL tool, which is described in Chapter 11.

Because of referential integrity constraints, we must be a bit careful about the order in which we add our data. Right-click on HealthInsurancePlans and choose Open Table/Return All Rows, as shown in Figure 5.2.

Figure 5.2

Viewing all rows.

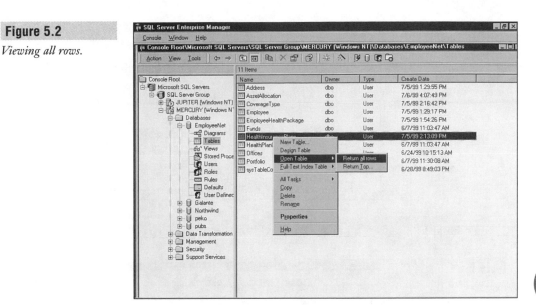

This will open the table for your editing. Let's add seven plans—five for health insurance and two for dental, as shown in Figure 5.3.

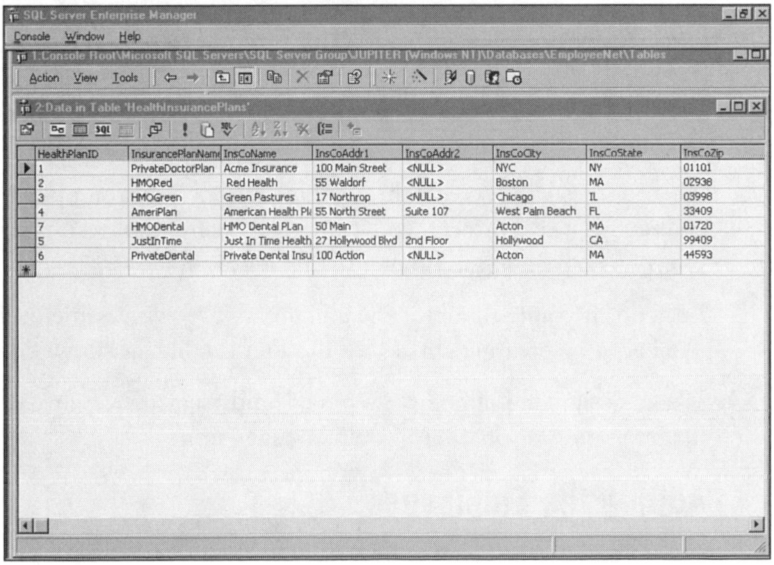

Figure 5.3

Open for editing.

Next, we need to provide data in the CoverageType table to designate the four types of coverage we'll consider: individual, two person, family, and extended family, as shown in Figure 5.4.

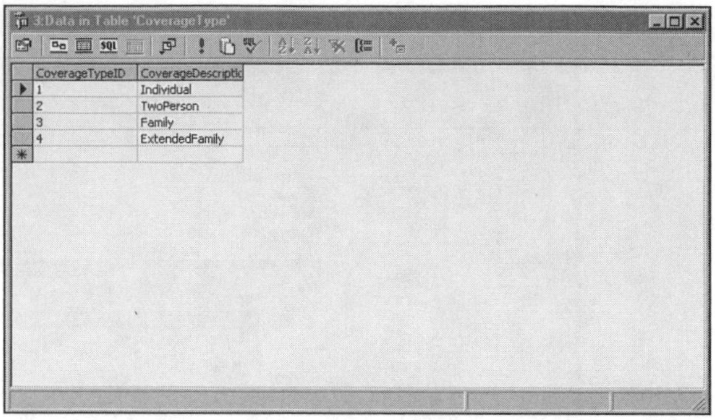

CoverageTypeID	CoverageDescriptic
1	Individual
2	TwoPerson
3	Family
4	ExtendedFamily

Figure 5.4

Filling the CoverageType table.

For HealthPlanCost, fill in the data, as shown in Figure 5.5.

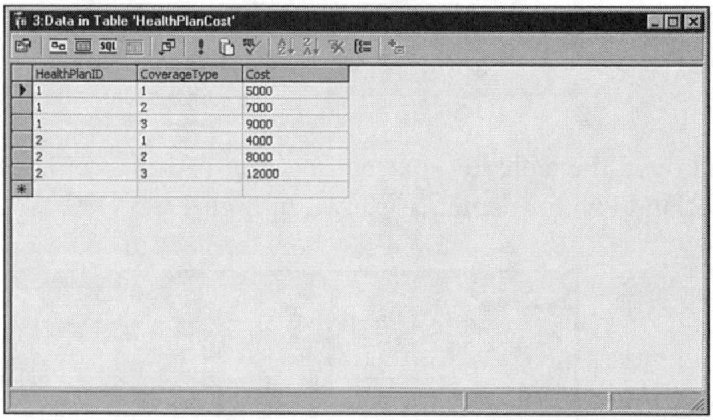

HealthPlanID	CoverageType	Cost
1	1	5000
1	2	7000
1	3	9000
2	1	4000
2	2	8000
2	3	12000

Figure 5.5

Filling the HealthPlanCost table.

These tables will serve us throughout this book as we implement all the code. Of course, for a real project, you would eventually want to plug in the accurate data—often by connecting to other, existing legacy systems.

Let's do the same thing for the lookup tables for investments and asset allocation. We begin by creating entries for the Funds table, as shown in Figure 5.6.

We've designated only three types of funds: aggressive, mixed, and cautious. Again, in a real application, there would be many more.

Adding the Employees

We're ready now to add employees and assign health coverage and a portfolio of funds to each one. We do have a problem however. Our design has an interesting flaw.

Figure 5.6

Creating entries for the Funds table.

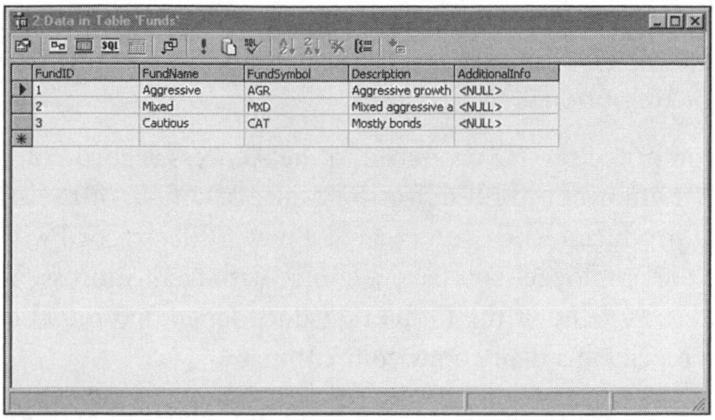

Every employee must be assigned to an office. To do this, we must first create an Office record. The problem is that every office must have a manager, and the manager must be an employee. We are stuck. We can't create an office until we have a manager, and we can't create a manager until we have an office to assign to that manager.

Let's finesse this problem by temporarily relaxing the requirement that an office must have a manager so that we can create our first office. We'll then create an Employee record for the manager of that office and then go back to the Office record and assign that employee as the manager.

In a robust program, we would have to allow for this design issue. One way to solve it is to initially assign the manager of a new office to a different office, create the new office, and then reassign the manager. Of course, steady-state operations are easier to design for than startup (first office, first employee) conditions.

Creating the Employee Record

Before you can add an office or an employee, you must first add records to the Address database. This is because each employee (and office) has an address.

At this point, you have a choice: you can do as I did, filling in a few records of dummy data for the address and the employee, or you can "cheat" and just restore the Employee database provided on the CD.

Note

Later, when we are farther into the project, we'll create the data-generator program that I used to produce the data on the CD. This procedure is described in Chapter 11.

After you add the employee's address, you are ready to add your first Employee record. Recall that the first and last names are required fields; the middle name, title, and suffix are optional.

I hope you noted the ID produced in the Address record you just added because that's what you want to fill in for the AddressID field of the employee. Similarly, the OfficeID produced when you created a new Office record will go in the OfficeID field for the employee. You have a choice with MailAddress: You can use either the HomeAddress value or the OfficeID value, depending on where your employee wants to receive his mail about your company.

The system will provide an EmployeeID in the identity column of the Employee record you just created. With that ID, you can not only add a Portfolio record but also allocate assets for that employee by creating records in the AssetAllocation table using the PortfolioID just generated.

You need to create at least a couple of Employee records to work with for this exercise. Again, adding the test data from the CD might be a better bet.

Creating the Pages

We are now ready to turn our attention to creating the project. The very first step is to fire up Visual Basic 6.0 and then start a new IIS application as we did in Chapter 3. This time we'll name the project EmployeeNetR1 (EmployeeNet Revision 1). Click on the plus sign next to Designers to open the Designers dialog box to open the Properties window so that you can change the name of your WebClass from WebClass1 to EmployeeNetWCR1. Also change the NameInURL value to EmployeeNetR1. You are now ready to save this project. Click Save and create a new directory, EmployeeNetR1. Save the .DSR (designer) file to that directory, as shown in Figure 5.7.

Save the project to the same directory, and by all means add your project to Source Safe or whatever you use for source code control.

 Source control—The ability to keep copies of your software as it evolves. Sophisticated source code control (SCC) software allows you to create "branches" to support bug fixes to one version while working on the next as well as to "roll back" changes as problems arise. The principal job of SCC software, however, is to ensure that two developers are never working on the same code—each developer "checks out" the code, works on it, and then checks it back into the system.

Figure 5.7

Saving the designer file.

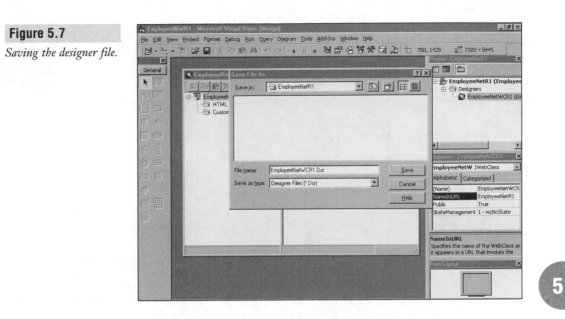

> **Note**
>
> You won't see source code control shown in my demonstration program because the computer on which I capture the images is not the computer on which I actually develop code.

We are now ready to create the template pages for our program. Begin by firing up your favorite HTML editor. I use Macromedia DreamWeaver. Let's start by creating the opening page, which will have nothing more than a link to the search page, as shown in Figure 5.8.

Creating the Search Page

Next we need to create the search page so that we can establish the link.

We add a form to this page, and within that form we add both a menu (drop-down list box) and a button, as shown in Figure 5.9. Save this page as SearchPageTemplate.htm.

EXCURSION

HTML

A form is the mechanism by which data are gathered on the Web. An HTML form presents text and elements, such as text fields, lists, check boxes, and radio buttons. After the user completes the form, it is then "submitted" to the server where it is processed.

Figure 5.8

The search page template.

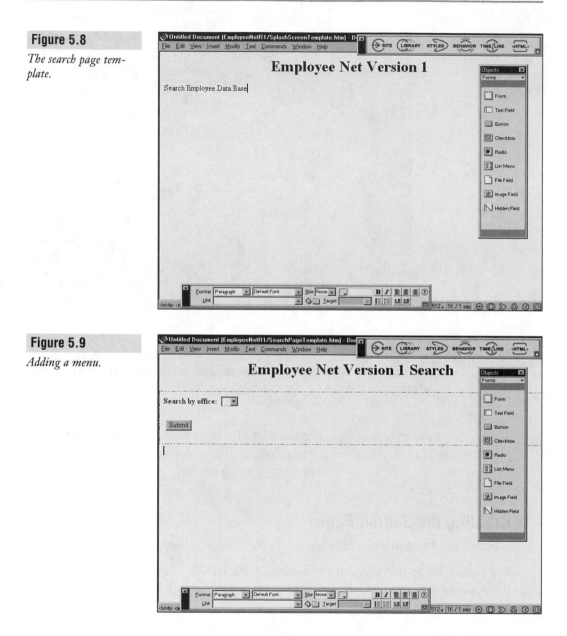

Figure 5.8

The search page template.

Figure 5.9

Adding a menu.

Now let's go back to the first page and create a link from the text "Search Employee Data Base" to the search page and then save this first page as SplashPage-Template.htm.

We need to get these pages working before we go any farther. Exit your HTML editor and return to Visual Basic. Double-click on the EmployeeNetWCR1 designer and then right-click on HTML Template WebItems, choosing Add HTML Template. If you haven't done so already, now is a good time to save the project. You must save the project before adding these.

> **Note**
>
> Before you go any farther, consider setting the VB environment to save your files every time you run the program. That way, should the program crash your system, you won't lose your work. To do this, open the Tools menu, choose Options, click on the Environment tab, and choose When A Program Starts: Save Changes.

Choose the first of the two HTML files you just created. It will be added and you'll be prompted to provide a name; name it SplashScreen. Do the same for the second page, but name it SearchPage.

Copies of the original pages are made in the new directory. Click on SplashScreen and you'll see that the designer has identified two objects on the page: the body of the page and a hyperlink, as shown in Figure 5.10.

Figure 5.10

SplashScreen's objects.

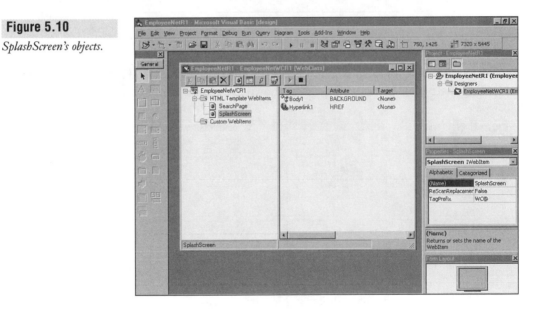

Note that the hyperlink has no target listed under Target. Right-click on that tag and choose Connect To WebItem, as shown in Figure 5.11.

This brings up the Connect To WebItem dialog box, as shown in Figure 5.12. Choose SearchPage.

Figure 5.11

Connecting to a web item.

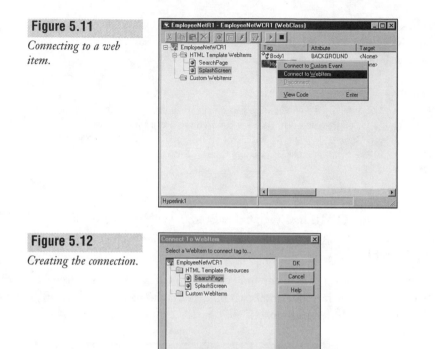

Figure 5.12

Creating the connection.

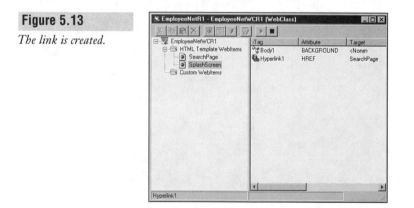

Presto! You've linked the text in SplashScreen to SearchPage. This is reflected in the Target attribute of SplashScreen, as shown in Figure 5.13.

Figure 5.13

The link is created.

Let's try it out! Click Play. The debugging window pops up, as shown in Figure 5.14. Accept the default to start with the designer component.

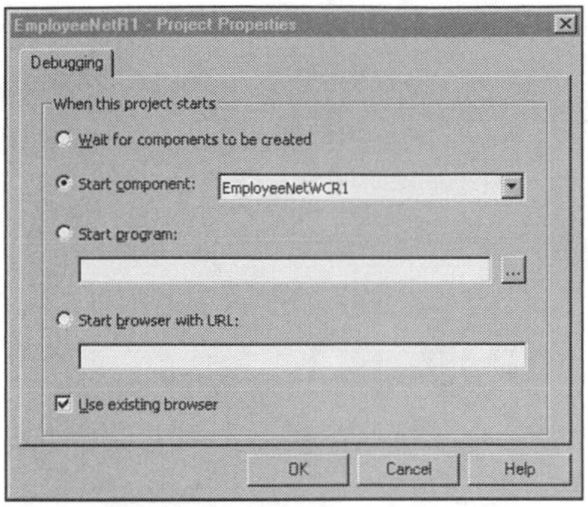

Figure 5.14

Project properties.

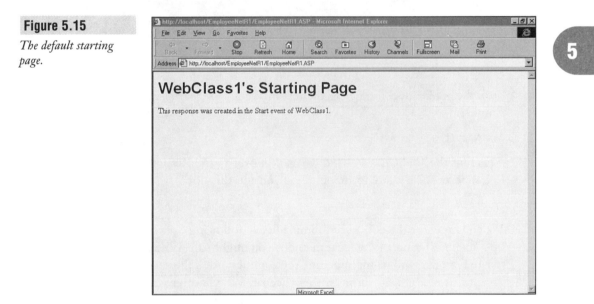

The results are not quite what we expected, as shown in Figure 5.15.

Figure 5.15

The default starting page.

5

This isn't the page we created, and where did this text come from? To answer this question, we must delve just a bit deeper into how WebClasses work.

How WebClasses Work

When your WebClass application begins, control is passed to the WebClass Start method, as shown in Figure 5.16.

Visual Basic added this code so that *something* would show in your browser. The usual way to display a page, however, is to call WriteTemplate on the appropriate item, which is SplashScreen in this case). Here's how you do it.

Figure 5.16

WebClass_Start.

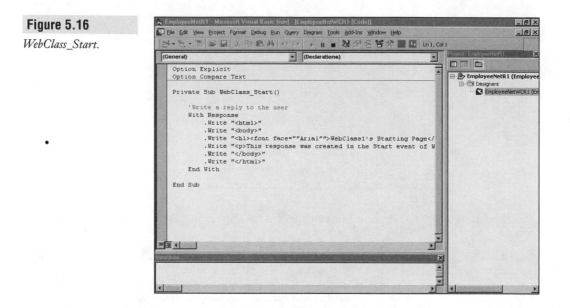

Stop the application and delete the text in WebClass_Start(), replacing it with this simple line:

```
Set NextItem = SplashScreen
```

This tells the WebClass to hand navigation over to the Respond method of SplashScreen. Navigate to that method and add this line:

```
SplashScreen.WriteTemplate
```

When you enter the dot (period) immediately following SplashScreen, VB will pop up a menu offering all the legal methods you might call. When you press W, WriteTemplate will be highlighted. You can then press the spacebar or Enter to accept this method. If you press the spacebar, VB will offer you help on the optional parameters to WriteTemplate, but we'll not use a parameter.

WriteTemplate will cause the Process Tags method to be invoked, but we don't need to take any action in ProcessTag for now. The net effect will be to write the template out to the browser, which is just what we want.

ProcessTag allows us to replace tags in the file with the result of work we do in the ProcessTags method, as we saw in Chapter 3. Later in the book, we'll come back and look at ProcessTag in greater detail.

When we click on the link, we transfer control to the search page, and so we must update its Respond() method as well with the line:

```
SearchPage.WriteTempate
```

Click on Play, and you should see the SplashScreen displayed, as illustrated in Figure 5.17.

Figure 5.17

Displaying a SplashScreen.

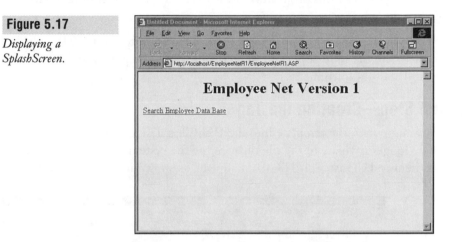

Clicking on the link brings you to the search page, as shown in Figure 5.18.

Figure 5.18

The search page.

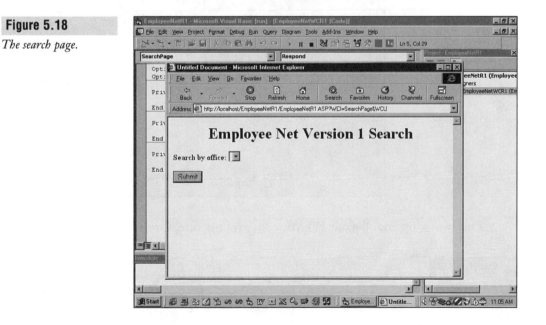

The good news is that the page draws and the widgets are in place. The bad news is that there are no contents for the drop-down menu. Filling that menu will be our first significant programming task.

Filling in the Drop-Down Menu

The simplest way to fill in this drop-down list is to create the widget programatically: filling in the values as we go.

Doing so is a two-step process. The first step is to put a tag into the HTML, which we will replace with the fully populated widget. The second step is to replace the tag with a data-filled drop-down menu.

The First Step—Creating the Tag

Recall that we imported the template into the WebClass designer. When we want to edit it, we no longer navigate to the file through the file system but rather right-click on the web item and choose Edit HTML Template, as shown in Figure 5.19.

Figure 5.19

Editing the template.

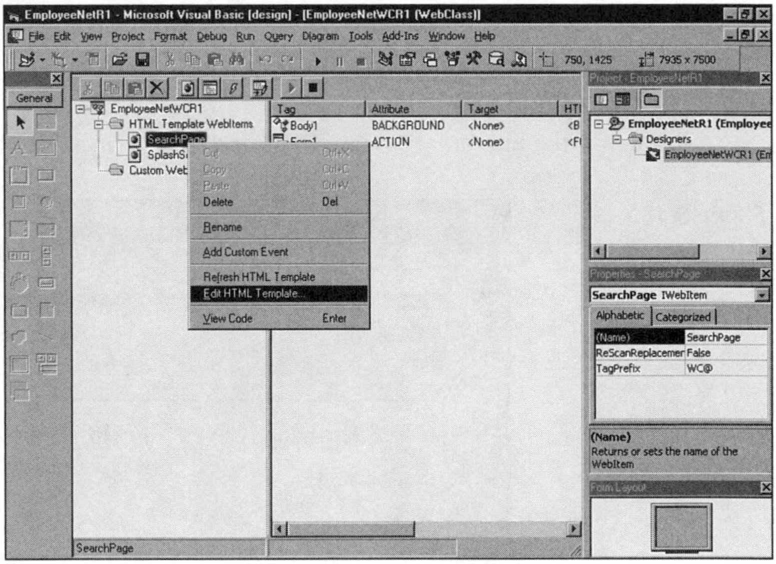

This brings up your default HTML editor (in my case, DreamWeaver).

> **Note**
>
> To set the default HTML editor to your favorite HTML editor, click on the Tools menu and choose Options.... Click on the Advanced tab (don't be frightened), and enter the full path in the External HTML Editor box.

Delete the drop-down menu that you just added moments ago, and substitute the following tag:

```
<WC@OFFICEMENU></WC@OFFICEMENU>
```

Your entire page looks much like the page shown in Figure 5.20.

Figure 5.20

Adding tags to the HTML.

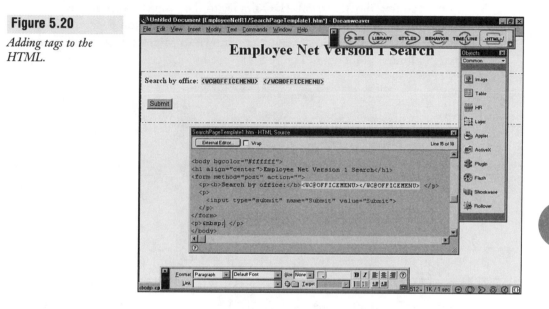

> **Note**
>
> DreamWeaver and many other editors prefer to have these tags entered in HTML mode rather than in the WYSIWYG editor.

With this tag in place, we can save the file and return to Visual Basic. VB will inform you that the WebItem has changed. Click Yes.

The Second Step—Implementing the Process Tag

We want to process that tag as follows:

1. Create a drop-down list box (menu).
2. Get the list of offices from the database.
3. Create an entry in the list for each office.
4. Display the page.

This begs the question of how we get the data from the database.

To get the data from the database, we must create an ADO recordset. In the next version of our program, we'll separate this responsibility out to an object in the business tier. For now, to keep this simple, we do the search right in line with creating the drop-down list box.

We begin by adding the Microsoft ADO library to the project. Stop the program if it is running and click on Project from the VB menu. Then click on References.... This will bring up the references menu. Scroll down to Microsoft ActiveX Data Objects 2.1 Library, as shown in Figure 5.21.

Figure 5.21

Adding the references.

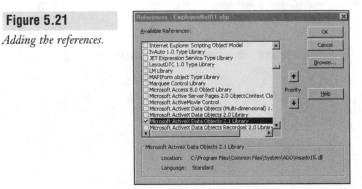

This tells Microsoft to include the ActiveX Data Object library, which allows us to create recordsets and other objects from ADO.

EXCURSION

YAA—Yet Another Acronym: ADO

The Microsoft ActiveX Data Object library supplies a number of COM (ActiveX) controls that provide access to the database. Although the details of ADO are beyond the scope of this book, the short story is that ADO provides an object-oriented interface to Microsoft's OLE-DB.

OLE-DB is a set of interfaces that data sources can implement through special drivers. This provides your program with uniform access to a wide variety of data sources including mail systems, files, spreadsheets, graphics, object databases, and relational databases.

OLE-DB is designed to replace open database connectivity (ODBC), which was Microsoft's first attempt to provide universal data access. ODBC is complex to use and provides access only to relational databases. OLE-DB is more flexible, is easier to use, and can be extended to other data providers.

ADO is the successor to data access objects (DAO) and relational data objects (RDO). Each of these technologies continues to be supported by Microsoft, but the train is leaving the station soon; it is time to get on board.

The big news with ADO is that it provides a robust object model. This is one of a series of object models with which we'll be concerned. Others include the ASP object model and the document object model, each of which is discussed later in the book.

Having included the ADO library, we are now ready to create a recordset. Navigate to the SearchPage object and add a ProcessTag method, as shown in Figure 5.22.

Figure 5.22

ProcessTag method.

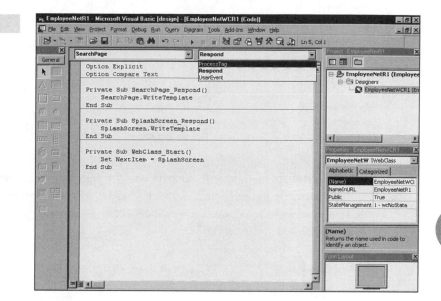

This will create a skeleton for the ProcessTag function. Before we fill in this function let's look at the HTML that will invoke it.

When the WebClass WriteTemplate method is called, the template HTML is pumped out to the client browser.

Listing 5.1—HTML for search

```
0:   <html>
1:   <head>
2:   <title>Untitled Document</title>
3:   <meta http-equiv="Content-Type"
3a:     content="text/html; charset=iso-8859-1">
4:   </head>
5:
6:   <body bgcolor="#ffffff">
7:   <h1 align="center">Employee Net Version 1 Search</h1>
8:   <form method="post" action="WebClass1.ASP?
8a:   WCI=ResultsIndex&amp;WCU">
9:     <p><b>Search by office: </b><WC@OFFICEMENU></WC@OFFICEMENU></p>
10:    <p>
11:      <input type="Submit" name="Submit" value="Submit">
12:    </p>
13:    <p> </p>
14:  </form>
```

continues

Listing 5.1—continued

```
15:   <p> </p>
16:   </body>
17:   </html>
```

EXCURSION

HTML

You've seen all this HTML before, except the code on line 11. This creates a button (`input type="Submit"`), which is used to "submit" the form. The name of this button is currently set to Submit, and its value (which is the text shown on the button) is also "Submit."

The WriteTemplate method will work its way through this code line by line, passing the HTML directly to the client's browser where it will be interpreted. When WriteTemplate sees the tag on line 9 (`WC@OFFICEMENU`), it recognizes this as a special tag to be processed at the server.

EXCURSION

How Tag Processing Works

When you generate your WebClass application, VB creates a very small ASP page for you. In that page, VB initializes the WebClassManager object, provided by the WebClassRuntime library, which comes with VB6. The WebClassManager object is then stored in the ASP application variable ~WC~WebClassManager.

WebClasses have a tag prefix property, which is set to WC@ by default. When you call WriteTemplate, the HTML file is passed to the WebClassManager, which in turn sends it to the browser. When the WebClassManager sees the `WC@` prefix in your HTML file, it sends the tag to the ProcessTag method for processing and then sends the TagContents string on to the browser. Note that this method is called once for each tag found in the HTML file.

This tag is passed as the TagName parameter to ProcessTag. The second parameter to ProcessTag is TagContents. Your job is to fill TagContents with the HTML you want substituted into the HTML in place of the WC tag you just received.

It is as if the WriteTemplate method and the ProcessTag method were in the following dialog:

> WriteTemplate: "I have this OfficeMenu tag. Do you have anything you want to give me as a substitute?"

> ProcessTag: "Yes, substitute the following HTML...."

The HTML returned by ProcessTag in the TagContents parameter is then sent along to the client browser. The client is oblivious to this processing; it just gets back HTML.

Let's look at what is substituted. The code for ProcessTag is shown in Listing 5.2.

Listing 5.2—Search_ProcessTag

```
0:   Private Sub Search_ProcessTag(ByVal TagName As String, _
1:       TagContents As String, SendTags As Boolean)
2:
3:       Select Case TagName
4:
5:           Case "WC@OfficeMenu"
6:               Dim sqlCmd  As String
7:               sqlCmd = "Select officeID, OfficeName from offices"
8:               Dim searchByOfficeRS As New Recordset
9:               searchByOfficeRS.CursorType = adOpenStatic
10:               searchByOfficeRS.CursorLocation = adUseClient
11:               searchByOfficeRS.LockType = adLockBatchOptimistic
12:               Call searchByOfficeRS.Open(sqlCmd, _
13:                   "DSN=EmployeeNet; UID=sa; PWD=;")
14:               searchByOfficeRS.ActiveConnection = Nothing
15:               TagContents = "<select name=OfficeMenu>"
16:
17:               With searchByOfficeRS
18:
19:                   While Not .EOF
20:                       TagContents = TagContents & _
21:                           "<option value = " & .Fields("OfficeID") _
22:                           & ">"
23:                       TagContents = TagContents & CStr("" & _
24:                           .Fields("OfficeName")) & "</option>" & _
25:                           vbCrLf
26:                       .MoveNext
27:                   Wend
28:
29:               End With
30:
31:               TagContents = TagContents & "</select>"
32:       End Select
33:
34:   End Sub
```

On line 5 of TagContents, we match the TagName passed in (WC@OfficeMenu) and so enter the body of the Case statement. We are in VB and so can use the full complement of Visual Basic tools, including in this case the ADO library we added to this project.

On line 6, we dim a string sqlCmd. On line 7, we fill sqlCmd with the SQL statement we'll want to issue to the database. This command

```
7:                sqlCmd = "Select officeID, OfficeName from offices"
```

will search the database and return the fields officeID and OfficeName for every record in the Offices database. This is just what we want.

EXCURSION

Visual Basic

In Visual Basic, you can choose among a number of values by using the Select Case statement. In this case, we examine only one of the cases. A case is a single potentially matching value.

In this example, we select a case for a value in TagName. If TagName matches one of our Case statements, the code following that Case statement will run until the Next Case statement. The Select itself ends with an End Select statement on line 32.

This code uses the With statement on line 17. When we write With followed by a recordset, we can leave off the recordset name when accessing its methods or member data. For example, on line 19, we would normally write

```
While not searchByOfficeRS.EOF
```

But because of the With statement, we can just write

```
While not .EOF
```

This is much easier. This While statement says that all the code from lines 20 to 26 will be repeated as long as the condition remains true. That is, as long as it is true that the recordset is *not* EOF (end of file)—as long as there are records to work with.

While loops end with the keyword Wend (line 27), and the With statement ends with the statement End With (line 29).

This entire set of code is housed within a subroutine, which begins on line 0 and ends on line 34. The subroutine is marked Private, which means that it can only be used by other subroutines and functions in this code module. A subroutine differs from a function in that the latter can return a value to the calling routine, whereas a subroutine simply does work and then ends.

Note

There are two ways to work with VB. You can just use variables as you need them, creating them by using them, or you can turn on Option Explicit, which demands that you declare your variables before they are used. This extra step, while occasionally annoying, can save you hours of debugging. The compiler will complain if you use a variable that you haven't declared, which helps you catch typos.

Suppose that you have a variable OfficeName that you want to assign a value "Home Office." Now suppose Option Explicit is not set and you write the following line of code:

```
OficeName = "Home Office"
```

You may not notice right away that you have misspelled OfficeName (you only wrote one *f*). The compiler will not complain; it will assume that you are creating a new variable, OficeName, and will assign "Home Office" to that variable. Of course, your real variable, OfficeName, will not have the value you expect. You could waste a lot of time finding it. If you had set Option Explicit, VB would complain that OficeName did not yet exist when you tried to assign to it. The bug would have been found instantly.

We'll display each OfficeName and stash away each officeID so that we can find the right office when we need it.

To do this, we need a recordset. We declare one on line 8, allocating space for it with the keyword new.

The next three lines, 9–11, set the CursorType, CursorLocation, and LockType, respectively. The goal here is to create a disconnected recordset. A disconnected recordset contains all our results but does not maintain a connection to the server.

Note The details of the CursorType, CursorLocation, and LockType settings are not difficult, but they are beyond the scope of this book. You can learn more about each by consulting the Microsoft Developer Network (http://msdn.microsoft.com) or by consulting a book on ADO (see the appendix for a recommended reading list).

Finally, on line 12, we open the recordset, passing in the SQL command we want to issue along with the DSN, which will connect a user ID and a password to the database. The result of this is that searchByOfficeRS is filled with the records that match our search criteria (all the offices in the offices table). We then disconnect from the database by setting ActiveConnection to nothing, as shown on line 14.

Note The details of creating and managing DSN settings are not difficult, but they are beyond the scope of this book. You can learn more about each by consulting the Microsoft Developer Network (http://msdn.microsoft.com).

We are now ready to fill the drop-down list, the code for which begins on line 15.

Here's the trick: we'll build up the string TagContents to have whatever we want to send to the browser. In short, TagContents starts out empty, and we fill it with HTML.

On line 15, we create the list by using the HTML `select` tag, naming the resulting widget OfficeMenu. We iterate through the recordset we just created, beginning on line 19 and ending on line 27. We'll add one line to the list for each record until we hit the end of the file (EOF).

 **Note**   The statement on line 17 allows us to refer to the member variables of the searchByOfficeRS recordset object using the dot notation (.Fields) rather than the entire name (searchByOfficeRS.Fields). It is nothing more than a useful shorthand.

For each record in the recordset, we grab the OfficeID and assign it to the value of the next Option tag and then grab the OfficeName and assign it to the text to be displayed. The result is a traditional HTML statement, which creates the drop-down menu and fills it with values. We concatenate a carriage-return-line-feed on the end of each line, shown on line 25, to make the resulting HTML easier to read in the browser.

Finally, when the end of the recordset is hit, we end the While loop and close the Select statement on line 31.

Clicking on Play will run this code, and the drop-down menu will be populated with the dummy data you put in the database, as shown in Figure 5.23.

Figure 5.23

The drop-down menu.

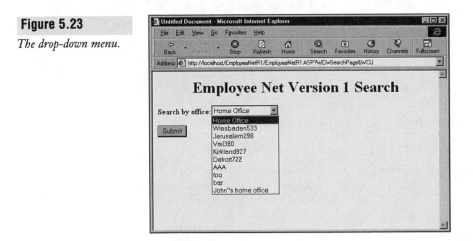

Click on View Source to look at the source code sent to create this page, as shown in Figure 5.24.

Figure 5.24

Examining the source code.

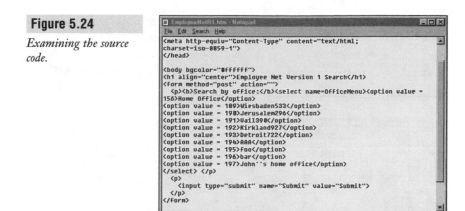

Note that each option has a value, which is the officeID from the database, and a city name, which is the officeName from the database. Open up the SQL Enterprise Manager and view the contents of Offices; they should match, as shown in Figure 5.25.

Figure 5.25

Examining the results.

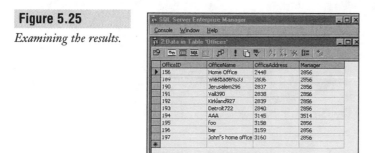

That's it. The rest of the book is just the details. You can stop here and go get an ice cream if you'd like. Get one for me too; I'll keep working....

On with the Details

Having filled the list box, we'll allow the user to choose an office and click Submit. When he does, we'll figure out which office was selected and display every employee from that office in a list.

Submitting the Form

When a form is submitted, it must be submitted *to* some page. In our case, we want to submit to the results index page. Of course, to do this, we must create the index page (oh, yeah, that!).

We begin by creating a template file and then adding it to the project. Once again we open DreamWeaver. Let's put a simple title at the top of the page, and then create a one-column table to hold our results. We only need one row in the table because we'll add each new row programmatically. Figure 5.26 shows the HTML file we'll save to create our template.

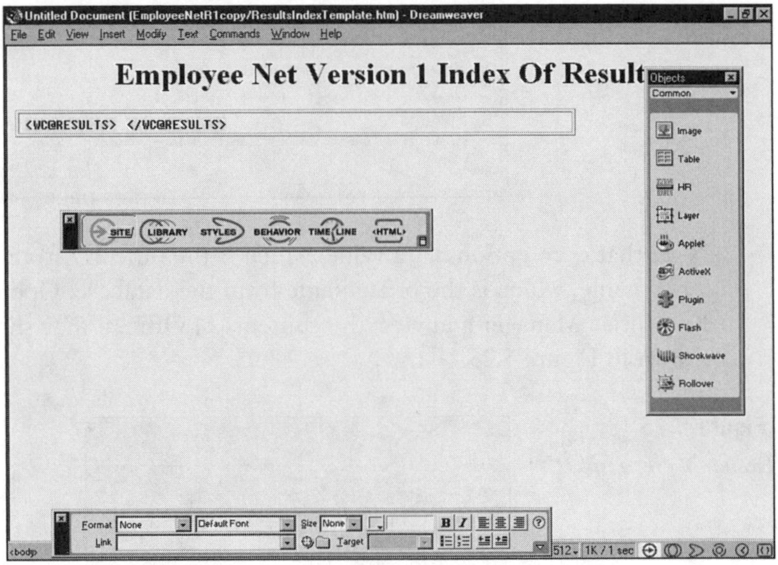

Figure 5.26

The template file.

Notice that, once again, we've created a tag that we'll use to substitute the results of the search.

Import this into your WebClass Designer (right-click on HTML Template WebItems and choose Add HTML Template) and name it ResultsIndex.

Now click on SearchPage and notice that the Form1 tag has no associated target. Right-click on it and choose Connect to WebItem, which will bring up the Connect To WebItem dialog box. This time choose ResultsIndex (the item you just added). This sets up the connection you require: When the form on Search is submitted, it will be submitted to ResultsIndex, invoking the ResultsIndex_Respond method.

Preparing ResultsIndex to Respond

In ResultsIndex_Respond, add the line:

```
ResultsIndex.WriteTemplate
```

This causes the ProcessTag method to be invoked, writing out the contents of the HTML document to the client, integrating in the processing of each tag in turn.

We are ready to program the ProcessTag method in ResultsIndex, but what do we want it to do?

Here are the steps we want to take:

1. Find every record for every employee in the office the user has chosen.
2. List the first and last name of the employee as a link.
3. Set up the link so that clicking on it will invoke the details page for that employee.

This is easier than it sounds. VB supports the URLFor method, which takes two parameters—a WebItemObject (for example, an HTML Template WebItem) and an event name. We'll use this as the URL for the details page (passing in the employee's record ID as the event name), and we'll use the employee's first and last names as the display text in the link.

The code for the ResultIndex_ProcessTag method is shown in Listing 5.3.

Listing 5.3—ResultIndex_ProcessTag

```
0: Private Sub ResultsIndex_ProcessTag(ByVal TagName As String, _
1:     TagContents As String, SendTags As Boolean)
2:
3:     Select Case TagName
4:
5:     Case "WC@Results"
6:         Dim sqlCmd      As String
7:         sqlCmd = "Select employeeID, FirstName, "
8:         sqlCmd = sqlCmd & "LastName from Employee "
9:         sqlCmd = sqlCmd & "where officeID = "
10:         sqlCmd = sqlCmd & Request.Form("OfficeMenu")
11:         Dim rs          As New Recordset
12:         rs.CursorType = adOpenStatic
13:         rs.CursorLocation = adUseClient
14:         rs.LockType = adLockBatchOptimistic
15:         Call rs.Open(sqlCmd, "DSN=EmployeeNet; UID=sa; PWD=;")
16:         rs.ActiveConnection = Nothing
17:
18:         With rs
19:
20:             While Not .EOF
21:                 TagContents = TagContents & "<tr><td><a href="""
22:                 TagContents = TagContents & URLFor(Details, _
23:                     CStr(rs("employeeID"))) & """>"
24:                 TagContents = TagContents & rs("FirstName")
25:                 TagContents = TagContents & " " _
26:                     & rs("LastName") & "</a></td></tr>"
27:                 .MoveNext
28:             Wend
```

continues

Listing 5.3—continued

```
29:
30:          End With
31:     End Select
32:
33: End Sub
```

 Note The lines are kept artificially short to fit in this book. In a normal program, each line might be a bit wider and less choppy.

EXCURSION

Visual Basic

This code takes advantage of a VB feature—robust strings. A string is a series of characters. VB strings are very powerful and easy to work with. For example, in this code on line 6, we declare a string `sqlCmd`. We then begin building this string by concatenating one string after another, using the & operator. After line 7, sqlCmd has in it `"Select employeeID, FirstName, "` (note the space). After line 8, this string variable now holds `"Select employeeID, FirstName, LastName from Employee "`.

As you can see, each line concatenates another phrase on to the end. By the end of line 9, the command has `"Select employeeID, FirstName, LastName from Employee where officeID = "`. We now need to add in the office ID that is in the form. No problem! We concatenate in the string returned by calling `Request.Form("OfficeMenu")`. This builds up the string exactly as we want.

On line 5, we catch the single tag we put into the HTML, `"WC@Results"`. The very first thing to do is to search the database for the employeeID and first and last names of every employee whose officeID matches that passed into this method as a result of choosing a particular office in the drop-down of the form.

Accessing the User's Choice

How do we figure out which city was chosen? Recall that the user dropped down our list of cities and then pressed Submit (turn back to Figure 5.23 to refresh your memory).

How is this choice transmitted to the current page? As the target of the previous page's form, this page has access to the ASP Request object. The Request object is one of the five objects in the ASP object model available to you in your WebClasses.

The Request object provides access to five collections: the QueryString, the Form, the ServerVariables, the Cookies, and the ClientCertificate. The QueryString is the complete query, which would be populated with the contents of the form's controls had you used the Get submission method rather than the Post.

Get is somewhat simpler to work with and so was a favorite of Web developers for a while. These days, it is scorned because all the search criteria are submitted in the URL of the target frame (making them visible to the end user) and because they are limited in length (about 1K characters). There is little advantage to using Get when submitting forms to WebClasses.

If you submit using Post, however, the same information is available in the Response object's Form collection. This is far cleaner and is how we'll work with forms in this book.

The other three collections are not important to us now. We won't need to work with Cookies directly because we'll use session variables (discussed later in the book) and the ServerVariables and ClientCertificate collections are, again, beyond the scope of this book and not relevant to our work.

Using the Form Collection

The Form collection, however, is quite relevant to us. If you look back to Listing 5.1, you'll see that the HTML for the search page had this line:

```
8:   <form method="post" action="WebClass1.ASP?
8a:    WCI=ResultsIndex&amp;WCU">
```

This declared a form and designated that its submission method should be "post". That's just what we want. It also shows that the action of posting will be to an ASP page WebClass1—this is the ASP page that wraps our WebClass, and it is through this ASP page that we receive the Request object and with it the Form collection. The WCI tag indicates the WebClass item that will be invoked (ResultsIndex).

Returning to Listing 5.3, lines 7–10 formulate the SQL statement. When these lines are concatenated, the SQL statement is:

```
Select employeeID, FirstName, LastName from Employee where officeID =
```

And then the value from the list box is inserted. We get that value by accessing the value of the "OfficeMenu" item in the Form collection of the Request object, using the syntax `Request.Form("OfficeMenu")`.

The name of the item ("OfficeMenu") is the name of the control (the drop-down list). The value returned is the value of the particular item currently selected. Because that value is an office ID, our SQL statement will work as we intend.

Lines 11–16 open a recordset using that SQL statement exactly as you saw previously.

Lines 18–30 will use that resulting recordset to form the new TagContents, which will be sent to the browser. We loop through each record (one for each employee in the targeted office) and build up the HTML to print out their first and last names, building the HREF target for the link using the URLFor() method described earlier. Let's examine it step by step.

Building the Table of Links

Line 21 adds the text

```
<tr><td><a href=
```

to the TagContents. This creates a new row in the table and begins a new column. It also sets down an anchor tag for a link. The anchor tag expects two parts: a URL to link to and text to display. On lines 22 and 23, we create that URL by using the URLFor method. The first parameter to that method is the page we want to link to (Details). The second parameter is the value to pass in as an associated "event." We'll see how this is used shortly.

We continue to build up the HTML, closing the `href` tag and adding the text to display: the user's first and last names. We then close the anchor tag and close the column and row.

On line 27, we move to the next record, and then on line 28 we return to the top of the While loop on line 20 until the record set is at EOF.

After we add all the rows we want, we fall out of the While loop, end the With (recordset) statement on line 30, and then on line 31 close out the Select Case statement. On line 33, the function ends.

Details, Details...

This will work well, but we need a details page if we're going to tell our URLFor to connect to it. Once again, fire up your HTML editor, and let's create a very simple page. We can add to this later.

As shown in Figure 5.27, this page can be an extremely rudimentary stand-in for our details page; we need just enough to link to in the URLFor statement.

Figure 5.27

The details page template.

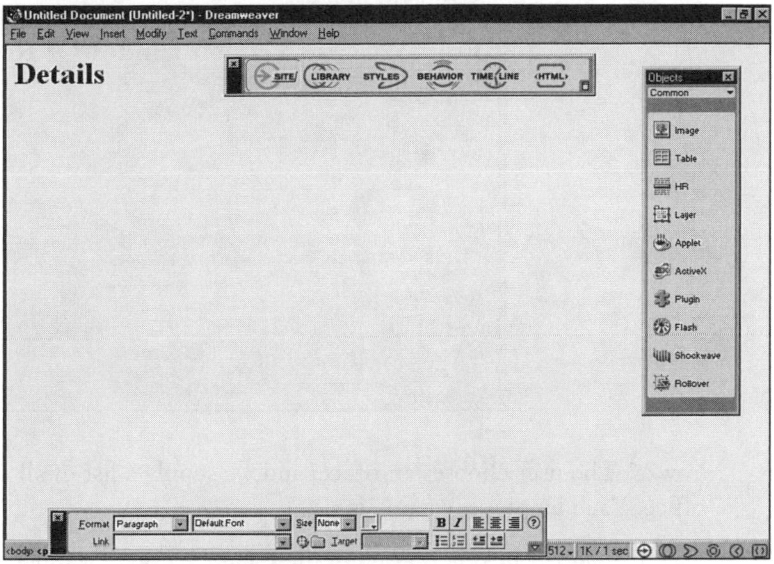

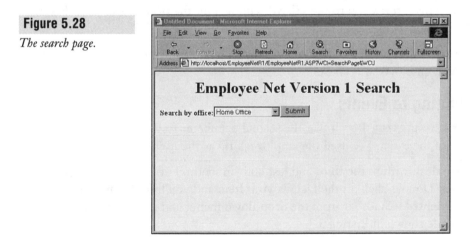

Add this page in the usual way (right-click on HTML Template Web Items and choose Add HTML Template) and be sure to name it Details.

Okay, we're ready to rock and roll. Click Play and watch the magic, as illustrated in Figures 5.28 and 5.29.

Figure 5.28

The search page.

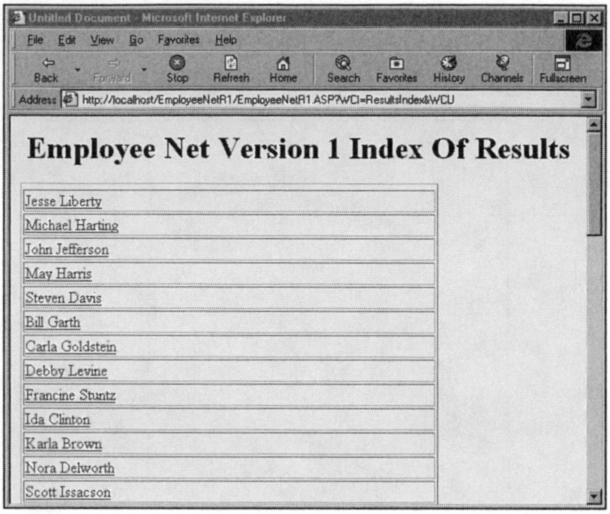

Figure 5.29

The results.

Yowza! The user chooses an office, and we supply a list of all the employees in that office. Each employee's name is a link.

Unfortunately, clicking on one of these names won't do much yet because we haven't set the Details Respond method—but one thing at a time.

Let's now implement these links so that they bring up a demonstrable level of detail.

The Devil Is in the Details

Stop the application and right-click on the Details Web Item. Choose Edit HTML Template. This returns you to the HTML editor. Edit the page as shown in Figure 5.30. Note the new tag WC@Details.

Now we are ready to respond to the user's click on any employee. But how do we know which employee was chosen?

Responding to Events

URLFor fires an event. Recall that the second parameter to the URLFor method is the name of the event. We used the employee's ID as the event name.

Events are dealt with in the third and last built-in method of every WebClass: UserEvent. Double-click on the Details Web Item and you'll find that UserEvent is not implemented. Choose it from the drop-down menu, and a stub will be created. Add the code shown in Listing 5.4.

Figure 5.30

Editing the template.

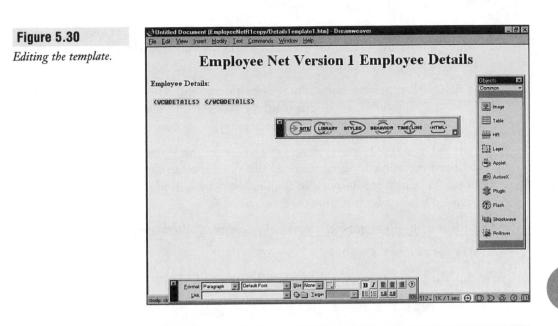

Listing 5.4—Handling the event

```
0: Private Sub Details_UserEvent(ByVal EventName As String)
1:     Dim sqlCmd As String
2:     sqlCmd = "Select * from Employee "
3:     sqlCmd = sqlCmd & "where employeeID = "
4:     sqlCmd = sqlCmd & EventName
5:
6:     Set detailRS = New Recordset
7:     detailRS.CursorType = adOpenStatic
8:     detailRS.CursorLocation = adUseClient
9:     detailRS.LockType = adLockBatchOptimistic
10:
11:     Call detailRS.Open(sqlCmd, "DSN=EmployeeNet; UID=sa; PWD=;")
12:     detailRS.ActiveConnection = Nothing
13:     Set NextItem = Details
14: End Sub
```

> **Note**
>
> Earlier in this file, detailRS was defined as a class-level variable.

There is nothing terribly surprising here. The important thing to note is that the name of the event is passed in as a parameter EventName. Thus, the employeeID is passed in as the parameter EventName, and we can use that value to access the appropriate record.

On line 1, we declare SqlCmd, and on lines 2–4, we create a SQL statement requesting every field from the Employee record where the employeeID matches the ID passed in as the Event name parameter.

With that SQL statement, we can now open a recordset. The recordset variable was declared at the module level so that it will be available to the other methods in this module. After the recordset is filled, we are ready to process this page.

To start the processing, however, we need to invoke the WriteTemplate method. Visual Basic recommends against calling this directly from any method except Respond. We can force Respond to run, however, by setting the next item to this very page, Details, which is what we do on line 13.

This invokes the Respond method, which consists of exactly one line of code:

```
Details_Respond.WriteTemplate
```

Writing the template invokes the ProcessTag method, shown in Listing 5.5.

Listing 5.5—Writing out the details

```
0: Private Sub Details_ProcessTag(ByVal TagName As String,
0a:            TagContents As String, SendTags As Boolean)
1:  Select Case TagName
2:  Case "WC@Details"
3:   TagContents = "<h1>" & detailRS("FirstName")
4:   TagContents = TagContents & " " & detailRS("LastName")
5:   TagContents = TagContents & "</h1><br>"
6:   TagContents = TagContents & "Details here about "
7:   TagContents = TagContents & "this employee..."
8:  End Select
9:
10: End Sub
```

On line 2, we begin processing the WC@Details tag. We print out the first and last name within h1 tags (for heading level 1), and then we stub out where we would supply further details about this employee. We'll return to this topic in greater detail in the next iteration of this program.

Figure 5.31 shows what happens when you click on one of the employees in the table of employees at a particular office.

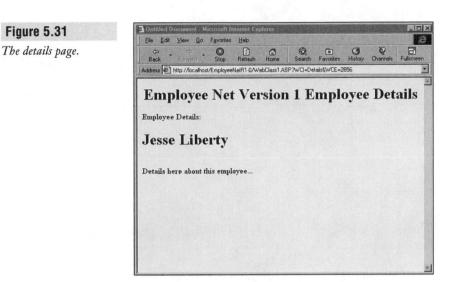

Figure 5.31

The details page.

5

Next Steps

We've built our first version of EmployeeNet. It allows us to browse through all the offices in the database, choose one to find all the employees in that office, and choose an employee to see details about that employee. That is quite remarkable for what represents about two hours' work.

In subsequent chapters, we'll add a number of advanced features, including more complex searching, data input with client-side validation, and a fancier user interface. The reality, however, is that you've already seen the hard part, and it isn't all that hard.

Chapter 6

Using WebClasses and the ASP Object Model to Create a Form

Now that we've built the fundamental site, we can begin adding features and fleshing out the design. In the coming chapters, we review the code that contributes to the entire demonstration program.

At this point, however, it will be more profitable to analyze the final product in great detail than to build this site up piece by piece. Along the way we'll discuss the subtleties of using WebClasses, the ASP object model, SQL programming, JavaScript, and more.

How the Opening Page Works

The opening page for EmployeeNet is shown in Figure 6.1.

This page was supplied to me by my UI designer: Maethee Ratnarathorn of Atypica (http://www.atypica.com). The code for this page is fairly complex because we are using rollovers, which make each choice light up when you roll the cursor over it. More important, most of this code was generated by DreamWeaver and so is not terribly human-readable.

 Rollover—The effect of "lighting up" or otherwise changing an element on a Web page when the cursor moves over it.

The details of how this works are beyond the scope of this book and not terribly interesting. The goal of this screen is simply to provide an entry point for the demonstration.

Clicking on Search brings us to the first page of significant interest (see Figure 6.1).

Figure 6.1

The splash screen.

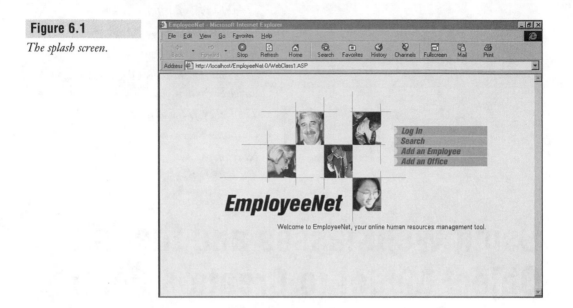

How the Search Page Works

The search page does a number of very complex things, some of which require the use of JavaScript, hidden fields, and other advanced topics. This chapter explains the problem I was trying to solve and how I went about creating this page.

What Problem Was I Trying to Solve?

The specifications for EmployeeNet called for a complex search form with a number of drop-down list boxes. One of these lists every employee in the company. Another lists all the offices.

The problem, from a Web design perspective, is that we must push all this information through a very tiny wire. If the application will be used via dial-up modems, the best we can hope for with today's technology is 5K bytes per second (56KB is 56 kilobits). With overhead, each byte is about 10+ bits on average). The best bet is to figure that you get about 2–3K with an average connection.

A middle-sized company might have 1000–2000 employees. Each name could be about 30 bytes on average. Using rough numbers, we need to send as many as 60,000 bytes for the names list. That is 60K. At 2–3K bytes per second (average) we're looking at a 30-second delay.

If we were to put the names drop-down, the city drop-down, the HMO office drop-down, and a few other drop-downs along with perhaps a few multiselect lists for stocks and so forth, we could be looking at a full minute to draw a page. Clearly such performance is not acceptable.

There are a few ways to solve this problem. We could decide that the application will never be used over a dial-up modem. T1 line speed would cut this down to far more acceptable performance, but we're not certain we can guarantee such performance.

The Solution

Certainly we can minimize the amount of data we send, and there are a number of optimizing strategies (precaching and so forth) that we might try. Part of the solution we've arrived at, however, is to send the contents of the drop-down list only when it is requested. Perhaps we'll find that 90% of the users never even look at the drop-down of names. Why bother sending all that information if it is not needed?

 **Note**

In these examples, many of the text fields are filled with G*reeking*. This is a common technique in design, in which pseudo-Latin is substituted for actual text.

Figure 6.2 shows the search screen as it will appear when you first click on Search. Remember that this is a demonstration program for the book and that an actual employee search might have many more fields.

6

Figure 6.2

The search screen.

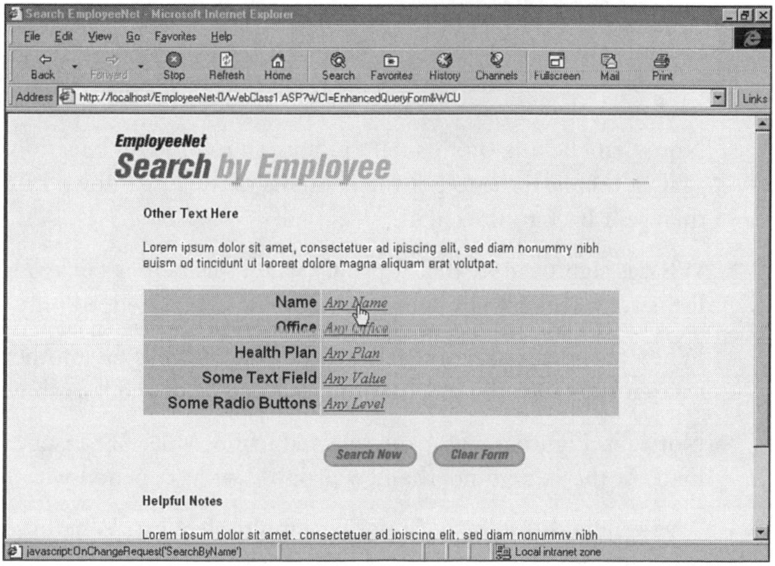

Notice that each of the five fields is represented by a phrase, written in text rather than in a control (widget). The phrase is underlined and, in fact, is an actual link. As verification, sneak a look at the status line. Because this picture was taken with the cursor hovering over the Name field, the status line reveals that there is in fact a link to a JavaScript method called OnChangeRequest with the parameter "SearchByName." We'll return to this shortly.

Clicking on Any Name opens the drop-down list of names, as shown in Figure 6.3.

Figure 6.3

Viewing the list of names.

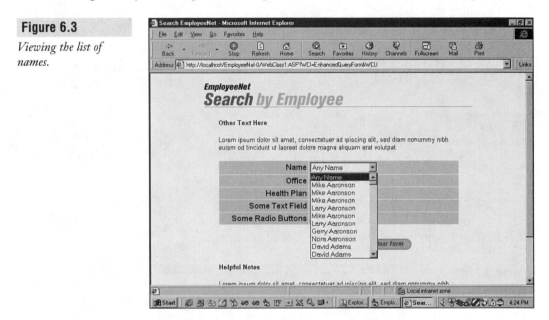

Note that clicking on this field requires a round-trip back to the server and a query against the database to get the contents of the drop-down list. This information is then sent back to the client.

What is significant is that it is only when this field is clicked and made "live" that the list is sent. If there is a delay, therefore, it is experienced only on demand.

When the user makes her selection and then clicks on another field, the selection is written back into the link and the new field is opened, as shown in Figure 6.4.

Notice in Figure 6.4 that the selected name, Mike Aaronson, is the linked Name field. At the same time, the new drop-down has opened with health plan choices.

The middle drop-down, Office, is a multiselect list. When it opens, rather than dropping down, a five-line list box opens, and the user can multiselect using the standard Windows conventions of Shift-click or Control-click when viewing this page through Internet Explorer, as shown in Figure 6.5.

Figure 6.4

Just-In-Time controls.

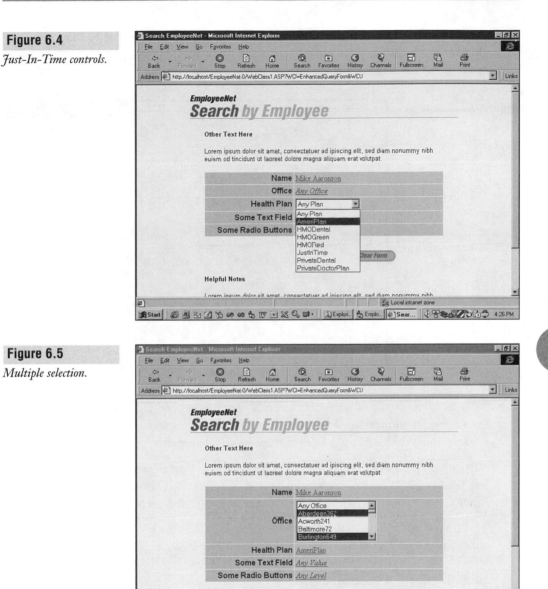

Figure 6.5

Multiple selection.

Text and Radio Buttons

At this stage in the development of EmployeeNet, I couldn't think of a good use for either text boxes or radio buttons, even though they would certainly be necessary in a fleshed-out system. However, I did want to illustrate their use in the book. I've added two stub fields (stand-ins for future fields) named SomeTextField and

SomeRadioButtons. Clicking on these opens the appropriate field. For example, clicking on SomeTextField's value (currently "Any Value") opens a text field that can be filled in, as shown in Figure 6.6.

Note in Figure 6.6 that when the text box opens I prepend a dollar sign ($) before the entry and add the word "thousand" afterwards. This text is created along with the control. We'll see how all this is done in just a moment.

Notice also, and this is very important, that all the selected values from the multiselect list Office are shown comma-delimited. The user has chosen more than one office to search, and it is imperative that we give him the correct feedback.

The final field is SomeRadioButtons (see Figure 6.7). The trick here is to make room for them. The answer is just to expand the row in the table.

Customizing a Clear Event

On a typical form, when the user clicks Submit, the form is submitted. When she clicks Clear, all the data she has entered is deleted, and she's presented with a blank form. Our equivalent of a blank form is that all fields return to "Any Name," "Any Office," "Any Value," and so forth. Even though most Clear buttons require no additional programming, we must be a bit more clever in this case.

Figure 6.7

Radio buttons.

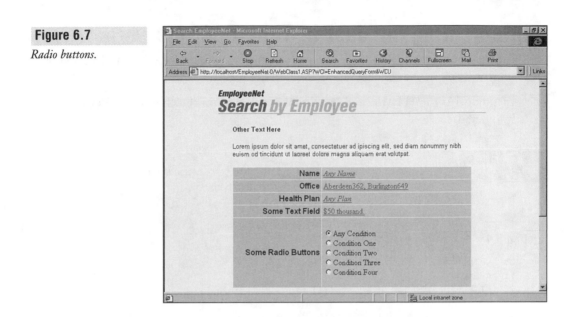

Finalizing the Design for Just-In-Time Controls

These Just-In-Time (JIT) controls (a term I coined, not a standard term of the industry) meet my goal of not sending any more data to the client than is actually required. The problem with them is that each time the customer clicks on a field a round-trip back to the server is necessary to handle the request and send the new data.

In a commercial application, I would probably change this design to use JIT controls for data-intensive drop-downs and use standard always-in-place controls for those controls that are not data-intensive like text fill-in and radio buttons. For now, we'll implement them all as JIT controls to see how it's done.

When this form is submitted, all the user's selections will factor into the search. When the user asks to modify that search, however, we must be able to restore this page exactly as it was when originally submitted. Thus, we must keep track of the form's state.

Although this point is trivial in a client/server application, it is not quite the same with a Web application. HTTP (Hypertext Transfer Protocol) is by its nature stateless. We solve this problem by using the state variable, as you'll see in just a moment.

6

Implementing the Just-In-Time Controls

Implementing the JIT controls takes a little bit of work on the client and a good bit of processing in the ProcessTag method on the server.

Listing 6.1 is the HTML, and JavaScript is required on the client-side. Let's examine it in detail.

 Note

This listing is longer than it would normally be because I've been forced to keep each line of code narrow for display in this book.

Listing 6.1

```
0:   <HTML>
1:   <HEAD>
2:   <TITLE>Search EmployeeNet</TITLE>
3:
4:   <script language="JavaScript">
5:
6:   // EnhancedQuery.htm
7:   // Lines shortened for presentation purposes
8:   // If we want to keep track of what was selected so that we
9:   // can show it in the browser when the field is not
10:  // displaying the widget we have two ways of doing so:
11:  // 1. we can keep the ID and each time we write the display,
12:  // we can search the database records for the matching fields
13:  // for their text or...
14:  // 2. we can use GetSelected to find out what is selected and
15:  // then stash the text in a hidden field
16:
17:  function GetSelected(element)
18:  {
19:      value = "";
20:      for ( var i = 0; i< element.options.length; i++ )
21:      {
22:          if ( element.options[i].selected )
23:          {
24:              if ( value )
25:                  value += ", ";
26:              value += element.options[i].text;
27:          }
28:      }
29:      if ( ! value )
30:      {
31:          element.options[0].selected = true;
32:          value = element.options[0].text;
33:      }
34:      return value;
```

```
35:  }
36:
37:  function OnChangeRequest(whichRequest)
38:  {
39:      document.forms[0].ChangeRequest.value = whichRequest;
40:      if ( document.forms[0].SearchByName )
41:          document.forms[0].SearchByNameDisplay.value =
42:              GetSelected(document.forms[0].SearchByName);
43:      if ( document.forms[0].SearchByOffice )
44:          document.forms[0].SearchByOfficeDisplay.value =
45:              GetSelected(document.forms[0].SearchByOffice);
46:      document.forms[0].submit();
47:  }
48:
49:  </script>
50:  </HEAD>
51:  <body bgcolor="#ffffff">
52:  <center>
53:    <table width="560" border="0" cellspacing="0"
54:       cellpadding="0">
55:       <tr>
56:        <td width="413">
57:        <A href="WebClass1.ASP?WCI=Login&amp;WCU">
58:        <IMG alt=EmployeeNet border=0 height=23
59:         src="images/p2_logo.gif" width=413></a></td>
60:        <td align="right"> </td>
61:       </tr>
62:       <tr>
63:        <td colspan="2"><IMG border=0 height=37
64:        src="images/p2_searchemp.gif" width=560></td>
65:       </tr>
66:    </table>
67:    <br>
68:    <table width="500" border="0" cellspacing="0"
69:    cellpadding="0">
70:       <tr>
71:        <td>
72:          <p><font face="Arial, Helvetica, sans-serif">
73:          <b><font size="2">Other Text
74:            Here </font></b></font></p>
75:          <p><font face="Arial, Helvetica, sans-serif" size="2">
76:              Lorem ipsum dolor sit amet, consectetuer ad
77:              ipiscing elit, sed diam nonummy nibh euism
78:              od tincidunt ut laoreet dolore magna aliquam
79:              erat volutpat.</font></p>
80:        </td>
81:       </tr>
82:    </table>
83:
84:       <form method="post" onSubmit="OnChangeRequest('Search')"
85:       action="WebClass1.ASP?WCI=EnhancedQueryForm&amp;WCU">
```

continues

Listing 6.1—continued

```
86:        <table width="500" border="0" cellspacing="1"
87:           cellpadding="3">
88:          <tr>
89:            <td width="30%" align="right" bgcolor="#cccccc"><b>
90:            <font face="Arial, Helvetica, sans-serif">Name</font>
91:            </b></td>
92:            <td width="50%" bgcolor="#ccccff"><WC@SEARCHBYNAME>
93:            </WC@SEARCHBYNAME></td>
94:          </tr>
95:          <tr>
96:            <td width="30%" align="right" bgcolor="#cccccc"><b>
97:            <font face="Arial, Helvetica, sans-serif">Office
98:            </font></b></td>
99:            <td width="50%" bgcolor="#ccccff"><WC@SEARCHBYOFFICE>
100:             </WC@SEARCHBYOFFICE></td>
101:          </tr>
102:          <tr>
103:            <td width="30%" align="right" bgcolor="#cccccc"><b>
104:            <font face="Arial, Helvetica, sans-serif">Health
105:              Plan</font></b></td>
106:            <td width="50%" bgcolor="#ccccff">
107:            <WC@SEARCHBYHEALTHPLAN></WC@SEARCHBYHEALTHPLAN></td>
108:          </tr>
109:          <tr>
110:            <td width="30%" align="right" bgcolor="#cccccc"><b>
111:            <font face="Arial, Helvetica, sans-serif">Some
112:              Text Field</font></b></td>
113:            <td width="50%" bgcolor="#ccccff"><WC@SomeTextField>
114:            </WC@SomeTextField></td>
115:          </tr>
116:          <tr>
117:            <td width="30%" align="right" bgcolor="#cccccc"><b>
118:            <font face="Arial, Helvetica, sans-serif">Some
119:              Radio Buttons</font></b></td>
120:            <td width="50%" bgcolor="#ccccff">
121:            <WC@SomeRadioButtons></WC@SomeRadioButtons></td>
122:          </tr>
123:          <tr>
124:            <td width="30%" align="right"> </td>
125:            <td width="50%"> </td>
126:          </tr>
127:          <tr>
128:            <td width="30%"> </td>
129:            <td width="50%">
130:              <input type="image" src="images/search_now.gif"
131:              width="97" height="23" border="0" alt="Search Now">
132:                
133:            <a href="<WC@CLEAREVENT></WC@CLEAREVENT>"> <img
134:            src="images/clearform.gif" width="97"  height="23"
135:            border="0" alt="Clear Form" ></a>
```

```
136:            </td>
137:          </tr>
138:        </table>
139:       <input type="hidden" name="ChangeRequest" value="Search">
140:      </form>
141:
142:      <table width="500" border="0" cellspacing="0"
143:        cellpadding="0">
144:        <tr>
145:          <td>
146:            <p><font face="Arial, Helvetica, sans-serif"><b>
147:            <font size="2">Helpful
148:              Notes</font></b></font></p>
149:            <p><font face="Arial, Helvetica, sans-serif"
150:              size="2">Lorem ipsum dolor
151:              sit amet, consectetuer ad ipiscing elit, sed diam
152:              nonummy nibh euism od tincidunt ut laoreet dolore
153:              magna aliquam erat volutpat. Lorem ipsum dolor sit
154:              amet, consectetuer ad ipiscing elit, sed diam
155:              nonummy nibh euism od tincidunt ut laoreet dolore
156:              magna aliquam erat volutpat.</font>
157:            </p>
158:          </td>
159:        </tr>
160:      </table>
161:      <p> </p>
162:    </center>
163:   </body>
164:  </HTML>
```

This code can be divided cleanly into two parts: JavaScript (from lines 4 to 49) and HTML (the rest of the file). The JavaScript consists of two functions: GetSelected() and OnChangeRequest(). The purpose of GetSelected() is to return those items selected in a multiselect list box. We'll return to this one shortly.

EXCURSION

HTML

There are a few new HTML tags in this bit of code. On line 51, we see a more extensive body tag than we've seen before. In this case, we're setting the background color to white.

On line 57, we see an anchor tag. This tag is used to create a link. It begins with the anchor tag <A followed by the href, which tells the browser where to go when the user clicks on the link. In this case, we're linking to a WebClass item, so this is an unusual anchor tag. What makes it even more unusual is that this anchor tag includes an IMG tag. What is going on here is that we're putting a link behind an image rather than behind words. The image is the EmployeeNet logo (the stylized words EmployeeNet) shown as the first line in Figure 6.7. We'll see more conventional anchor tags shortly.

6

> **Note** What if you don't know JavaScript? If you are a C++ or Java programmer, you'll have little trouble following this code and the discussion. If you have little experience with C++, Java, or JavaScript, however, you may want a bit more of an introduction to JavaScript.
>
> Check out the JavaScript Excursions for tips on using JavaScript. The truth is, however, that you really need to know very little about the language to use it. Most of the time you can find a bit of JavaScript that someone else has written and adapt it to your needs. If you decide you really need to understand JavaScript in detail, take a look at the suggested reading list in the appendix.

The function OnChangeRequest serves two purposes. The first, and most important, is to determine which field has been requested (which field the user is trying to modify). The second, subsidiary purpose of this method is to help with implementing controls that display a text string different from the value they manage.

For example, if we want to display an employee's first and last names, but track which employeeID to search for, how do we accomplish this? We'll solve this dilemma in two ways; this function will help with one of the two ways.

EXCURSION

JavaScript

Let's walk through GetSelected one line at a time. It begins on line 17 with the function statement, followed by `GetSelected`. This means that you can "call" GetSelected from elsewhere in your JavaScript code, and this function will run and do its work. A parameter named `element` is passed in. In many languages, you would have to say what kind of "thing" element is, but not in JavaScript.

On line 19, we create a variable, `value`, by using it. We fill it with the empty string.

On line 20, we begin a For loop. A For loop begins with parentheses, within which are three sets of statements. The first statement sets up the loop conditions. In this case, the variable i is created and initialized to hold the value 0.

The second statement is a test. As long as i is less than element.options.length (this value is explained later), then the loop will continue.

The third statement is an action that is taken *after* each iteration of the loop. In this case, i is incremented.

The body of the loop begins on line 21 and ends on line 28. This body repeats once for each time the loop executes.

On line 22 is an If statement. This is another powerful flow-of-control device. It says that if the condition between the parentheses is true, then whatever is in the body of the If statement will execute. Note that the body of this If statement contains *another* If statement.

We read this entire If statement, from line 22 to 27, as follows: "If it is true that element.options[i].selected evaluates to true, then, if value evaluates to true, add a comma

> to whatever is in value. Then add whatever is in element.options[i].text to whatever is in value."
>
> Note that value will evaluate true any time it is not empty, and thus we must add the comma after every element, but not before the first element.

The HTML beginning on line 50 is fairly straightforward. Nevertheless, there are a few things to note.

On line 84, we declare the form itself, with a method of Post (indicating that we'll get the form's values from the request.Forms collection rather than from the request.Query collection).

More important, we've attached an action to the onSubmit event. onSubmit is called when the Submit button is pressed. If we don't catch this event, the default action is to submit the form. We instruct the form that the JavaScript function OnChangeRequest is to be called instead, passing in the value "Search". The action attached to this form is set on line 85 to the Web item EnhancedQueryForm, which is this very page. Thus, this page submits its results to itself!

Before we examine how this all works, let's continue looking at the HTML. The next lines do nothing more than fill in the table with WC tags that we'll use for substitution in the ProcessTag method of our Web class. On line 139, however, we find a hidden field: ChangeRequest, which is given the default initial value of "Search". This hidden field will be used to capture the user's specific request: Which field did he want to edit?

The point of the function OnChangeRequest, shown on line 37, is to determine which field is to be edited and to store that information in this hidden field.

Examine line 39 carefully. We first identify the ChangeRequest field by the string

```
document.forms[0].ChangeRequest
```

JavaScript has its own object model. In that model, the page on which this script is being run is represented by the Document object. That object, in turn, has a number of collections, including the Forms collection. You can access each form by name (if you name the form) or by its position in the page, using a zero-based index. Thus, the first (and in this case only) form is document.forms[0]. Within that form reside all the elements. Here we access the ChangeRequest element by name. With that element, we can set its value as shown. We set it to the parameter passed to OnChangeRequest.

So far we've seen this parameter used only once, when we defined the form and set the parameter to "Search". Later, when we examine ProcessTag, we'll see that each control will call this method when clicked on.

If you ignore lines 40–45, then this function is quite simple. It sets the hidden field ChangeRequest to whatever the parameter is, and then it submits the form by calling the Submit() method on the form itself.

We'll return to this function and its sister function GetSelected() shortly, but for now we need to see the VB code that works with it.

Listing 6.2 is the code for the Respond method of EnhancedQueryForm.

Listing 6.2

```
0:   Private Sub EnhancedQueryForm_Respond()
1:
2:       Dim item As Variant
3:       For Each item In Request.Form
4:           Session(item) = Request.Form(item)
5:       Next
6:
7:       If Request.Form("ChangeRequest") = "Search" Then
8:           Set NextItem = ResultsFrameSet
9:       Else
10:          EnhancedQueryForm.WriteTemplate
11:      End If
12:
13:  End Sub
```

Even though there is not a lot of code here, some very critical work is being done. Recall from line 85 of the Listing 6.1 that when the form is submitted, it is submitted back to itself. This code runs when the form is submitted.

This code handles two conditions: Either we are searching or we are not. Let's look at the first condition. If we are searching, then we got here by pressing Submit. If so, then on line 84 of Listing 6.1, we will call OnChangeRequest with the parameter Search. This invokes the function on line 37 of Listing 6.1, and on line 39 the hidden field ChangeRequest will be given the value "Search". The form will then be submitted, calling EnhancedQueryForm_Respond.

On line 7 of Listing 6.2, the value of the ChangeRequest field is tested. Here we test it by examining the Form collection of the ASP Request object. This is how you examine any of the elements in a form. Because the value will be the string "Search", the If condition is fulfilled, and the NextItem property will be set to ResultsFrameSet. We won't chase this line of processing for now. Instead, let's consider what happens when the user clicks on one of the fields rather than submitting the form.

In this case, we are not searching but rather are requesting one of the JIT fields; thus, ChangeRequest will not hold Search but rather will hold the value of the field requested. The Else clause is invoked, and WriteTemplate is called.

We have a logical loop here that may be the source of some confusion. If Search is not in the ChangeRequest field, what is? We haven't seen this code yet, but we need to look at it now.

What Happens the First Time Through?

Note that in Listing 6.1 the hidden field ChangeRequest is initialized to Search. In the Respond method, we test this field, and if it is set to Search, we do not write the template but rather execute the search. How does this ever write the template? Why doesn't it search immediately?

The answer to this apparent conundrum is that the ChangeRequest item is *not* set to Search the first time through. The hidden field is not set until the page is drawn, and that doesn't happen until WriteTemplate is called. When we first hit Respond we haven't yet called WriteTemplate, the page hasn't been drawn, and the form object is empty. Thus, when the test on line 7 of Listing 6.2 is encountered:

```
7:      If Request.Form("ChangeRequest") = "Search" Then
```

the form has no "ChangeRequest" element, and thus it returns empty. This does not match Search. Consequently, the If statement fails, and WriteTemplate is invoked. WriteTemplate causes the associated HTML page (EnhancedQueryForm.htm) to be displayed, and the method ProcessTag is invoked whenever a tag is encountered.

Before we examine ProcessTag, however, let's back up and look at lines 2–5 of Listing 6.2.

```
2:      Dim item As Variant
3:      For Each item In Request.Form
4:          Session(item) = Request.Form(item)
5:      Next
```

This is a fairly conventional VB For...Each loop. The collection iterated over is the Form collection—the collection of controls from the submitted form. For each item in that collection, we'll make an entry in the Session object.

About the Session Object

The Session object is one of the five objects that ASP provides to your WebClass. This object provides the *state* that HTTP does not provide. There are, essentially, two ways to maintain state in a WebClass application: You can maintain state in the WebClass or you can maintain state in the Session object.

When I was in junior high school I read the classic novel *A Stranger in a Strange Land* by Robert Heinlein. In this book, an alien learns the ways of the Earth. At one point, he reports that he has learned two ways to tie his shoes. One is good for walking; the other is good for falling down.

Storing state in the Session object is good for walking. Storing it in the WebClass is good for falling down. Falling down in this case means slowing down your system and being unable to scale with large Web projects.

You store values in Session objects simply by assigning to them. Here we create a Session object for each item in the Request object's Form collection and store away the value currently in the form's object.

We'll use these values in the ProcessTag method.

Processing the Tags

Let's review. The user has clicked Search. We've stored all the values from the form in the Session object. However, because this is the first time through, there are no values, so we haven't stored a thing (yet). We check the ChangeRequest object in the form and find that it is empty (doesn't exist yet), and so we call WriteTemplate. We pump out the HTML shown in Listing 6.1, and when we run into tags, we call processTag. The first tag is shown on lines 92 and 93 of Listing 6.1:

```
92:            <td width="50%" bgcolor="#ccccff"><WC@SEARCHBYNAME>
93:            </WC@SEARCHBYNAME></td>
```

This invoked ProcessTag to handle this tag. Listing 6.3 shows the ProcessTag method.

 Note Even though I've shortened the VB lines wherever possible, some lines cannot be shortened without breaking them, so we've used the line continuation character (➡) to indicate that these lines should be typed on a single line.

Listing 6.3

```
0:   Private Sub EnhancedQueryForm_ProcessTag(ByVal TagName As _
1:       String, TagContents As String, SendTags As Boolean)
2:
3:       Dim theEmp As New employee
4:       Session("SearchOffset") = 0
5:
6:       If Session("ResetEvent") = True Then
7:           Session("SearchByName") = 0
8:           Session("SearchByOffice") = 0
9:           Session("SearchByHealthPlan") = 0
10:           Session("SomeTextField") = "Any Value"
11:           Session("SomeRadioButtons") = "Any Condition"
12:           Session("ResetEvent") = False
13:       End If
14:
```

```
15:        If Len(Session("SomeTextField")) = 0 Then _
16:            Session("SomeTextField") = "Any Value"
17:        If Len(Session("SomeRadioButtons")) = 0 Then _
18:            Session("SomeRadioButtons") = "Any Condition"
19:
20:        Select Case TagName
21:
22:        Case "WC@CLEAREVENT"
23:            TagContents = URLFor(EnhancedQueryForm, "Reset")
24:
25:        Case "WC@SearchByName"
26:
27:            If Request.Form("ChangeRequest") = "SearchByName" _
28:                Then
29:                Dim SearchByNameRS As Recordset
30:                Set SearchByNameRS = theEmp.GetAllEmployeeNames
31:                TagContents = _
32:                    "<input type = ""hidden"" name = ""SearchByNameDisplay""
➡value = """">"
33:                TagContents = TagContents & _
34:                    "<select name=""SearchByName""><option"
35:                If Session("SearchByName") = 0 Then TagContents _
36:                    = TagContents & " selected"
37:                TagContents = TagContents & _
38:                    " value=0 >Any Name</option>"
39:
40:                With SearchByNameRS
41:                    Dim idToMatch As Integer
42:                    If Len(Trim(Session("SearchByName"))) > 0 _
43:                        Then idToMatch = Session("SearchByName")
44:
45:                    While Not .EOF
46:                        TagContents = TagContents & _
47:                            "<option value = " & _
48:                            .Fields("EmployeeID")
49:
50:                        If idToMatch = .Fields("EmployeeID") _
51:                            Then
52:                            TagContents = TagContents & _
53:                                " selected >"
54:                        Else
55:                            TagContents = TagContents & ">"
56:                        End If
57:
58:                        TagContents = TagContents & CStr(sEmpty _
59:                            & .Fields("FirstName")) & " " & _
60:                            CStr(sEmpty & .Fields("LastName")) & _
61:                            "</option>"
62:                        .MoveNext
63:                    Wend
64:
65:                End With
```

continues

6

Listing 6.3—continued

```
66:
67:                TagContents = TagContents & "</select>"
68:          Else
69:
70:                If Not Session("SearchByName") = 0 And _
71:                    Len(Session("SearchByName")) > 0 Then
72:                    TagContents = TagContents & _
73:                        "<a href=""Javascript:OnChangeRequest(
➥'SearchByName')"">" _
74:                        & Session("SearchByNameDisplay") & _
75:                        "</a>"
76:                Else
77:                    Session("SearchByName") = 0
78:                    Session("SearchByNameDisplay") = "Any Name"
79:                    TagContents = TagContents & _
80:                        "<a href=""Javascript:OnChangeRequest(
➥'SearchByName')""><em>Any Name</em></a>"
81:                End If
82:
83:          End If
84:
85:      Case "WC@SearchByOffice"
86:
87:          If Request.Form("ChangeRequest") = "SearchByOffice" _
88:              Then
89:              TagContents = _
90:                  "<input type = ""hidden"" name = ""SearchByOfficeDisplay""
➥value = """">"
91:              Dim SearchByOfficeRS As Recordset
92:              Set SearchByOfficeRS = theEmp.GetOffices
93:              TagContents = TagContents & _
94:                  "<select multiple size = 5 name=""SearchByOffice""><option"
95:              If Session("SearchByOffice") = 0 Then _
96:                  TagContents = TagContents & " selected"
97:              TagContents = TagContents & _
98:                  " value=0 >Any Office</option>"
99:
100:              With SearchByOfficeRS
101:                  Dim ids As Variant
102:
103:                  If Len(Trim(Session("SearchByOffice"))) > 0 _
104:                      Then
105:                      ids = Split(Session("SearchByOffice"), _
106:                          ",")
107:                  Else
108:                      ids = Array(0)
109:                  End If
110:
111:                  While Not .EOF
112:                      TagContents = TagContents & _
113:                          "<option value = " & _
```

```
114:                                  .Fields("OfficeID")
115:                           Dim temp As Variant
116:                           temp = Filter(ids, .Fields("OfficeID"))
117:
118:                           If UBound(temp) > -1 Then
119:                               TagContents = TagContents & _
120:                                   " selected >"
121:                           Else
122:                               TagContents = TagContents & ">"
123:                           End If
124:
125:                           TagContents = TagContents & CStr(sEmpty _
126:                               & .Fields("OfficeName")) & _
127:                               "</option>"
128:                           .MoveNext
129:                       Wend
130:
131:               End With
132:
133:               TagContents = TagContents & "</select>"
134:           Else
135:
136:               If Session("SearchByOffice") > 0 Then
137:                   TagContents = TagContents & _
138:                       "<a href=""Javascript:OnChangeRequest(
➥'SearchByOffice')"">" _
139:                       & Session("SearchByOfficeDisplay") & _
140:                       "</a>"
141:               Else
142:                   Session("SearchByOffice") = 0
143:                   Session("SearchByOfficeDisplay") = _
144:                       "Any Office"
145:                   TagContents = TagContents & _
146:                       "<a href=""Javascript:OnChangeRequest(
➥'SearchByOffice')""><em>Any Office</em></a>"
147:               End If
148:
149:           End If
150:
151:       Case "WC@SearchByHealthPlan"
152:
153:           If Request.Form("ChangeRequest") = _
154:               "SearchByHealthPlan" Or _
155:               Len(Session("SearchByHealthPlan")) > 0 Then
156:               Dim SearchByHealthPlanRS As Recordset
157:               Set SearchByHealthPlanRS = _
158:                   theEmp.GetAllHealthPlans
159:           End If
160:
161:           If Request.Form("ChangeRequest") = _
162:               "SearchByHealthPlan" Then
163:               TagContents = TagContents & _
```

continues

Listing 6.3—continued

```
164:                    "<select name=""SearchByHealthPlan""><option"
165:               If Session("SearchByHealthPlan") = 0 Then _
166:                  TagContents = TagContents & " selected"
167:               TagContents = TagContents & _
168:                  " value=0 >Any Plan</option>"
169:
170:               With SearchByHealthPlanRS
171:                  If Len(Trim(Session("SearchByHealthPlan"))) _
172:                     > 0 Then idToMatch = _
173:                     Session("SearchByHealthPlan")
174:
175:                  While Not .EOF
176:                     TagContents = TagContents & _
177:                        "<option value = " & _
178:                        .Fields("HealthPlanID")
179:
180:                     If idToMatch = .Fields("HealthPlanID") _
181:                        Then
182:                        TagContents = TagContents & _
183:                           " selected >"
184:                     Else
185:                        TagContents = TagContents & ">"
186:                     End If
187:
188:                     TagContents = TagContents & CStr(sEmpty _
189:                        & .Fields("InsurancePlanName")) & _
190:                        "</option>"
191:                     .MoveNext
192:                  Wend
193:
194:               End With
195:
196:               TagContents = TagContents & "</select>"
197:            Else
198:
199:               If Not Session("SearchByHealthPlan") = 0 And _
200:                  Len(Session("SearchByHealthPlan")) > 0 Then
201:
202:                  With SearchByHealthPlanRS
203:                     .Filter = "HealthPlanID = " & _
204:                        Session("SearchByHealthPlan")
205:                     TagContents = TagContents & _
206:                        "<a href=""Javascript:OnChangeRequest(
➥'SearchByHealthPlan')"">" _
207:                        & .Fields("InsurancePlanName") & _
208:                        "</a>"
209:                  End With
210:
211:               Else
212:                  Session("SearchByHealthPlan") = 0
213:                  TagContents = TagContents & _
```

```
214:                              "<a href=""Javascript:OnChangeRequest(
➥'SearchByHealthPlan')"">" _
215:                              & "<em>Any Plan</em>" & "</a>"
216:              End If
217:
218:          End If
219:
220:      ' text field
221:      Case "WC@SomeTextField"
222:
223:          If Request.Form("ChangeRequest") = "SomeTextField" _
224:              Then
225:              TagContents = TagContents & _
226:                  "$ <input type=""text"""
227:              If Not Session("SomeTextField") = "Any Value" _
228:                  Then TagContents = TagContents & "value = " _
229:                  & Session("SomeTextField")
230:              TagContents = TagContents & _
231:                  " name=""SomeTextField"" size = ""6""> thousand"
232:          Else
233:
234:              If Not Session("SomeTextField") = "Any Value" _
235:                  And Len(Session("SomeTextField")) > 0 Then
236:                  TagContents = TagContents & _
237:                      "<a href=""Javascript:OnChangeRequest(
➥'SomeTextField')"">" _
238:                      & "$" & Session("SomeTextField") & _
239:                      " thousand." & "</a>"
240:              Else
241:                  Session("CapUnderMgmt") = "Any Value"
242:                  TagContents = TagContents & _
243:                      "<a href=""Javascript:OnChangeRequest(
➥'SomeTextField')""><em>Any Value</em></a>"
244:              End If
245:
246:          End If
247:
248:          If Len(Trim(TagContents)) = 0 Then TagContents = _
249:              "<a href=""Javascript:OnChangeRequest(
➥'SomeTextField')""><em>Any Value</em></a>"
250:
251:      ' radio buttons
252:      Case "WC@SomeRadioButtons"
253:
254:          If Request.Form("ChangeRequest") = _
255:              "SomeRadioButtons" Then
256:              TagContents = TagContents & _
257:                  "<br><input type=""Radio"" Name=""SomeRadioButtons""
➥Value=""Any Condition"""
258:              If Session("SomeRadioButtons") = "Any Condition" _
259:                  Then TagContents = TagContents & " Checked"
260:              TagContents = TagContents & ">Any Condition"
```

continues

Listing 6.3—continued

```
261:            TagContents = TagContents & _
262:               "<br><input type=""Radio"" Name=""SomeRadioButtons""
➡Value=""Condition One"""
263:            If Session("SomeRadioButtons") = "Condition One" _
264:               Then TagContents = TagContents & " Checked"
265:            TagContents = TagContents & ">Condition One<br>"
266:            TagContents = TagContents & _
267:               "<input type=""Radio"" Name=""SomeRadioButtons""
➡Value=""Condition Two"""
268:            If Session("SomeRadioButtons") = "Condition Two" _
269:               Then TagContents = TagContents & " Checked"
270:            TagContents = TagContents & ">Condition Two<br>"
271:            TagContents = TagContents & _
272:               "<input type=""Radio"" Name=""SomeRadioButtons""
➡Value=""Condition Three"""
273:            If Session("SomeRadioButtons") = _
274:               "Condition Three" Then TagContents = _
275:               TagContents & " Checked"
276:            TagContents = TagContents & _
277:               ">Condition Three<br>"
278:            TagContents = TagContents & _
279:               "<input type=""Radio"" Name=""SomeRadioButtons""
➡Value=""Condition Four"""
280:            If Session("SomeRadioButtons") = _
281:               "Condition Four" Then TagContents = _
282:               TagContents & " Checked"
283:            TagContents = TagContents & _
284:               ">Condition Four<br><br>"
285:      Else
286:
287:            If Not Session("SomeRadioButtons") = _
288:               "Any Condition" And _
289:               Len(Session("SomeRadioButtons")) > 0 Then
290:               TagContents = TagContents & _
291:                  "<a href=""Javascript:OnChangeRequest(
➡'SomeRadioButtons')"">" _
292:                  & Session("SomeRadioButtons") & "</a>"
293:            Else
294:               Session("SomeRadioButtons") = _
295:                  "Any Condition"
296:               TagContents = TagContents & _
297:                  "<a href=""Javascript:OnChangeRequest(
➡'SomeRadioButtons')""><em>Any Level</em></a>"
298:            End If
299:
300:         End If
301:
302:      End Select
303:
304:   End Sub
```

ProcessTag passes in three parameters: TagName, which is passed in by value, and TagContents and SendTags, both of which are sent in by reference to be set in the body of the method.

TagName contains the text you entered in the HTML form. Thus, when the HTML contains `<WC@SearchByName></WC@SearchByName>` the TagName contains the text "WC@SearchByName."

The TagContents is empty when you receive it, but this is what you fill with the HTML you want to substitute for the tag. Thus, where the HTML file says `<WC@SearchByName></WC@SearchByName>`, these tags will be erased and replaced by whatever you put in TagContents.

The final parameter is a Boolean value: SendTags. This determines whether the Tags (`<WC@SearchByName></WC@SearchByName>`) will be included in the substitution. The default is false, indicating that the tags are to be replaced rather than appended to. In every example in this book, we use the default (false).

> **Note**
>
> It is possible to send additional information to the ProcessTag method by including text between the opening and closing WC tags. This text is passed in as the starting value of TagContents. We don't use this technique in this book.

Continuing to Process the Tags

For now, let's skip over the first 18 lines of Listing 6.3 and begin with the `Select Case TagName` statement on line 20. This begins our processing of the TagName parameter. We look for matches to the tagName on lines 22, 25, 85, 151, 221, and 252. The Select statement is closed on line 302.

On line 22, we match a tag of `"ClearEvent"`. The code for this tag is shown in Listing 6.1 on lines 133–135. The ClearEvent tag is replaced by the code on line 23 of Listing 6.3. You've seen this idiom before: We create a URL for the EnhancedQueryForm (the page we're processing) with the event name Reset. This is substituted into line 133 of Listing 6.1 so that lines 133–135 become

```
133:        <a href=" URLFor(EnhancedQueryForm, "Reset")"> <img
134:        src="images/clearform.gif" width="97"  height="23"
135:        border="0" alt="Clear Form" ></a>
```

This is just what we want. The result is an anchor tag, which will invoke the EnhancedQueryForm's UserEvent method when clicked, as shown in Listing 6.4.

Listing 6.4

```
0:   Private Sub EnhancedQueryForm_UserEvent
0a:     (ByVal EventName As String)
1:
2:       Session("ResetEvent") = True
3:       Set NextItem = EnhancedQueryForm
4:
5:   End Sub
```

The effect of this function is to set the session variable "ResetEvent" to true and then to reprocess the form.

Of course, this tag cannot have been chosen yet because this is the first time we're drawing the page. What happens when this tag *has* been chosen? That is shown on lines 6–13: All the session variables are reset to their original condition. This will cause the entire form to be redrawn with the original values, as you'll see shortly.

Continuing with our analysis of Listing 6.3, we come to line 25 on which we process the SearchByName tag.

Displaying the Names

On line 25 we check whether the ChangeRequest hidden field has "SearchByName". If so, this is the field the user wants to modify. If not, then the user is modifying another field, and we have only to display the currently selected value. Because this is the first time through, we've not yet drawn the page, and so the user hasn't made a selection yet. Therefore, the If test on line 27 fails, and we process the Else clause on line 68. On lines 70 and 71, we check the value of the session variable "SearchByName". Again, we've not yet set this variable, so it has no value and no length, putting us into the Else clause on line 77. We set the SearchByName session variable to 0 and the SearchByDisplayName session variable to "Any Name".

We set the SearchByName session variable to 0 to indicate that Any Name is the current choice. We'll need this when we come back to this control.

We then fill in the TagContents with the HTML we want to output. This is an anchor—a link. The link is to JavaScript. When the user chooses this link, the JavaScript function OnChangeRequest is called with the parameter 'SearchByName'. Look at line 37 of Listing 6.1. The call to OnChangeRequest will have the effect of setting the hidden field ChangeRequest to SearchByName. This is just what we want.

Continuing with Listing 6.3, we complete the link on line 80 by putting in the text "Any Name" between emphasis tags (<em> and </em>), which causes the text to be written out in italics on most browsers.

On lines 85–150, we do virtually the same thing for the next field: SearchByOffice. Once again, the `Request.Form("ChangeRequest")` won't have a value because this is our first time through. We continue through the Else statements until we write out "Any Office."

This logic applies for each of the five fields. We now have displayed the screen as it appears in Figure 6.8.

Figure 6.8

The Search screen.

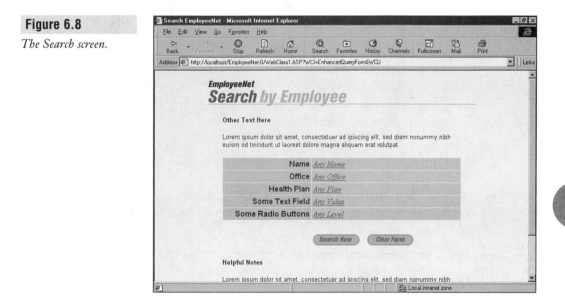

Handling the Any Name Selection

When the user clicks on the Any Name link, the list of employee names is displayed in a drop-down list. How is this done? Let's trace it through.

Recall that the code on line 80 of Listing 6.3 is the HTML we sent to the browser to draw the AnyName prompt and that it creates a link to the OnChangeRequest method, passing in SearchByName. This sets the hidden field ChangeRequest to SearchByName, as shown on line 39 of Listing 6.1. OnChangeRequest then submits the form, which calls the Respond method of EnhancedQueryForm, as shown in Listing 6.2.

Once again, all the form items would be copied to session variables. But, once again, there are no items in the form because the form consists of nothing but the links. None of the controls has been created yet.

A break point on line 7 of Listing 6.2 does show, however, that the hidden field "ChangeRequest" has a value, as shown in Figure 6.9.

Figure 6.9

Hidden field value.

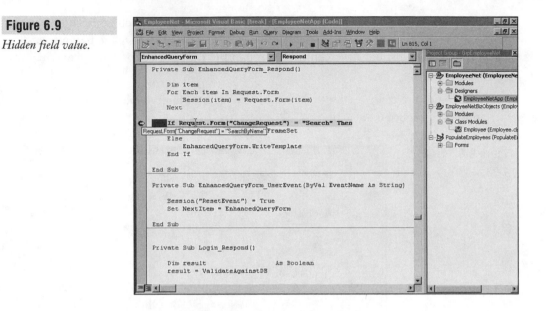

I've rested the cursor on the `Request.Form("ChangeRequest")`, and VB has graciously displayed its contents (Request.Form("ChangeRequest")="SearchByName", just as we would expect and hope.

Once again, WriteTemplate is called, and, once again, we are dropped in ProcessTag. This time, however, when we handle the WC@SearchByName tag, things progress somewhat differently.

This time the test on line 25 of Listing 6.3 succeeds. We now must create the drop-down list and fill it with the names of all the employees. To do this, we need a Recordset object and will declare it on line 29.

The next step is to allocate the Recordset object and then set it up with an appropriate SQL command to retrieve the records. In our earlier version, we did this from within the WebClass code.

The premise of Distributed interNet Applications, however, is that there ought to be a separation between the user interface layer (the WebClass) and the business layer. The user interface layer should not know anything at all about the design and layout of the database.

We solve this in the current version of EmployeeNet by creating an Employee business object.

Creating the Business Object—A (Very) Brief Excursion

If we were writing this in C++, this excursion would take between a chapter and an entire book to explain. Writing COM classes is not exactly easy in C++, even though it is far easier today than it was a few years ago. In VB though, it is embarrassingly simple. Here's what we do:

1. Stop running the project by pressing Stop.
2. Choose File/Add Project (note *Add*, not *New*).
3. Choose ActiveX DLL as the project type.
4. Rename the new project EmployeeNetBizObjects and rename the class module Employee.
5. Give Employee some methods.
6. Save the project and then return to the EmployeeNet project. Choose Project/References, and then add EmployeeNetBizObjects.

That's it. That's the end of this excursion. I told you it was easy.

The Business Object's GetAllEmployeeNames Method

We need a method that will return a recordset with all the names of all the employees. I originally wrote that method as shown in Listing 6.5.

Listing 6.5

```
0:   Public Function GetAllEmployeeNames() As Recordset
1:
2:       Dim sqlCmd As String
3:       sqlCmd = "Select employeeID, FirstName, LastName from Employee order by
➡LastName"
4:
5:       Dim rs As New Recordset
6:       rs.CursorType = adOpenStatic
7:       rs.CursorLocation = adUseClient
8:       rs.LockType = adLockBatchOptimistic
9:       Call rs.Open(sqlCmd, EMPLOYEE_NET_DSN)
10:       rs.ActiveConnection = Nothing
11:       Set GetAllEmployeeNames = rs
12:
13:  End Function
```

On line 3, I set up the SQL command, which will get the data I need from the Employee table. This pulls out the employee ID and first and last names of each employee, ordered alphabetically by last name.

The next few lines set up the Recordset object to be used as a disconnected recordset. This allows us to read through the data at our leisure, without holding open a connection to the database. Open connections are expensive: They use up resources and make it hard to grow your site past a few users. Disconnected recordsets are just what we need; they allow us to play with the data without annoying the Database server.

On line 6, we set the CursorType to OpenStatic. This is necessary for the disconnected recordset, but it means that, after we get the data, we won't see additions or deletions made by other users. That's fine! We just want a snapshot of the data, and that's what we'll get.

Line 7 sets the CursorLocation to adUseClient. Again, this is needed. The final requirement for disconnected recordsets is that we set the lock type to adLockBatchOptimistic. This means that the database will not keep a lock on the records. Because we won't be updating them, this doesn't affect us at all.

On line 9, we call open the recordset, passing in the SQL command we created on line 3 and a constant value EMPLOYEE_NET_DSN, which represents our ODBC system DSN.

> **Note**
> If you are unfamiliar with setting up system DSN files, talk with your system administrator or check the Microsoft Developer Network.

The call to Open fills the recordset with the data that match the SQL command; in this case, all the names of all the employees. Now that the recordset is full, we disconnect it from the database (hence the term *disconnected recordset*). We do this on line 10 by setting the ActiveConnection to Nothing. Finally, we return the recordset on line 11.

Making This More Efficient—A Brief Excursion

In the next section you'll see that we must call GetOffices when we want to populate the Offices database. I originally wrote GetOffices as shown in Listing 6.6.

Listing 6.6

```
0:  Public Function GetOffices() As Recordset
1:
2:      Dim sqlCmd As String
3:      sqlCmd = "Select distinct * from offices order by OfficeName"
4:      Dim rs As New Recordset
5:      rs.CursorType = adOpenStatic
6:      rs.CursorLocation = adUseClient
7:      rs.LockType = adLockBatchOptimistic
```

```
8:        Call rs.Open(sqlCmd, EMPLOYEE_NET_DSN)
9:        rs.ActiveConnection = Nothing
10:        Set GetAllEmployeeNames = rs
11:
12:   End Function
```

On line 3, I call "Select distinct," which ensures that only one copy of each record will be returned, with no duplicates.

There is a frightening similarity between this code and that for GetAllEmployeeNames. Every line was the same except the SQL command itself. Aha! This calls for factoring out this common code into a new method, Get Disconnected Recordset or GetDCRS(), as shown in Listing 6.7.

Listing 6.7

```
0:   Private Function GetDCRS(sqlCmd As String) As Recordset
1:
2:        Dim rs As New Recordset
3:        rs.CursorType = adOpenStatic
4:        rs.CursorLocation = adUseClient
5:        rs.LockType = adLockBatchOptimistic
6:        Call rs.Open(sqlCmd, EMPLOYEE_NET_DSN)
7:        rs.ActiveConnection = Nothing
8:        Set GetDCRS = rs
9:
10:   End Function
```

This greatly simplifies both GetAllEmployeeNames, shown in Listing 6.8, and GetOffices, shown in Listing 6.9.

Listing 6.8

```
0:   Public Function GetAllEmployeeNames() As Recordset
1:
2:        Dim sqlCmd As String
3:        sqlCmd = "Select employeeID, firstName, LastName from Employee order by
➥LastName"
4:        Set GetAllEmployeeNames = GetDCRS(sqlCmd)
5:
6:   End Function
```

Listing 6.9

```
0:   Public Function GetOffices() As Recordset
1:
2:        Dim sqlCmd As String
3:        sqlCmd = "Select distinct * from offices order by OfficeName"
4:        Set GetOffices = GetDCRS(sqlCmd)
5:
6:   End Function
```

As you can see, each of these now simply creates a SQL command, passes it to GetDCRS, and returns the result to the calling function.

Processing the List Box

As you may recall, we were all set to fill the list box, but we needed a recordset with that data.

The relevant portion of Listing 6.3 is reproduced here for your convenience:

```
25:        Case "WC@SearchByName"
26:
27:            If Request.Form("ChangeRequest") = "SearchByName" _
28:                Then
29:                Dim SearchByNameRS As Recordset
30:                Set SearchByNameRS = theEmp.GetAllEmployeeNames
31:                TagContents = _
32:                    "<input type = ""hidden"" name = ""SearchByNameDisplay""
➥value = """">"
33:                TagContents = TagContents & _
34:                    "<select name=""SearchByName""><option"
35:                If Session("SearchByName") = 0 Then TagContents _
36:                    = TagContents & " selected"
37:                TagContents = TagContents & _
38:                    " value=0 >Any Name</option>"
39:
40:                With SearchByNameRS
41:                    Dim idToMatch As Integer
42:                    If Len(Trim(Session("SearchByName"))) > 0 _
43:                        Then idToMatch = Session("SearchByName")
44:
45:                    While Not .EOF
46:                        TagContents = TagContents & _
47:                            "<option value = " & _
48:                            .Fields("EmployeeID")
49:
50:                        If idToMatch = .Fields("EmployeeID") _
51:                            Then
52:                                TagContents = TagContents & _
53:                                    " selected >"
54:                        Else
55:                                TagContents = TagContents & ">"
56:                        End If
57:
58:                        TagContents = TagContents & CStr(sEmpty _
59:                            & .Fields("FirstName")) & " " & _
60:                            CStr(sEmpty & .Fields("LastName")) & _
61:                            "</option>"
62:                        .MoveNext
63:                    Wend
64:
65:                End With
```

```
66:
67:                TagContents = TagContents & "</select>"
68:           Else
69:
70:                If Not Session("SearchByName") = 0 And _
71:                    Len(Session("SearchByName")) > 0 Then
72:                    TagContents = TagContents & _
73:                      "<a href=""Javascript:OnChangeRequest(
➥'SearchByName')"">" _
74:                        & Session("SearchByNameDisplay") & _
75:                        "</a>"
76:                Else
77:                    Session("SearchByName") = 0
78:                    Session("SearchByNameDisplay") = "Any Name"
79:                    TagContents = TagContents & _
80:                      "<a href=""Javascript:OnChangeRequest(
➥'SearchByName')""><em>Any Name</em></a>"
81:                End If
82:
83:           End If
```

> **Note**
>
> Statements in VB are very similar to those in JavaScript, Java, and C++, with just a few exceptions. First, no parentheses are needed. Second, VB uses the If, Then, Else, and End/If construction. If <some condition is true> Then <take some action> Else <take some other action> End If.
>
> If the Then keyword is on the same line as the If keyword, then the End If keyword is not needed.
>
> The truth that you are testing can be negated by the use of the keyword NOT. Thus,
>
> ```
> If not someCondition then TakeSomeAction
> ```
>
> The action will execute only if SomeCondition evaluates *false*. That is, if it is *not* true.
>
> Two conditions can be tested at once. We can test that condition one and condition two are *both* true using the AND keyword as we do on lines 70 and 71. We can also use the OR keyword to indicate that the body of the If statement ought to be executed if *either* statement is true.

On line 30, we call a method on the private module variable theEmp. This variable was initialized on line 3 of Listing 6.3:

```
3:      Dim theEmp As New employee
```

On line 30 we call GetAllEmployeeNames() on theEmp and the results are assigned to SearchByNameRS. Let's skip lightly over lines 31 and 32 for now and continue with lines 33 and 34. We fill TagContents with the HTML to produce a list box named SearchByName.

On line 35, we test whether Session("SearchByName") is equal to zero. Recall that when we drew the link with the text *Any Name*, we set this variable to zero. Here's what I wrote at that time:

We set the SearchByName session variable to 0 to indicate that Any Name is the current choice. We'll need this when we come back to this control.

And here we are, back at this control and happy to find that SearchByName is 0. This causes the If statement on line 35 to evaluate *true* and thus the contents Any Name are marked as selected in the list box (added on line 38).

Beginning on line 40, we iterate through the recordset, which contains all the names of all the employees. For each one, we set the value of the entry in the list box to the EmployeeID (lines 46 and 47).

We also want to see if this employee should be marked as selected. To do this, we assign to a temporary variable idToMatch the value in Session("SearchByName") (on line 43).

We then check this value against the current EmployeeID on line 50, marking it selected if we get a match (this time, we never do).

Finally, we set the display for the list box to the first and last names, separated by a space, and we iterate to the next record in the recordset (on line 62).

When we hit the last record, the While loop ends on line 63; then we close the list box code on line 67. We now have a list box to display to the user.

Handling the Offices Selection

The SearchByName drop-down menu presents us with a challenge. We want to fill this list box with each employee's name, but we need to stash away the employeeID, because this is what we'll use for our search. That's not a problem! We can save this ID in the value field for the list box. The problem comes later, when we want to display the current value for this field as a link (when the list box is gone).

The only value we'll get back from the list box is the value field—the employeeID. Unfortunately, this is not what we want to display. We need somehow to capture the employee's name as well as the ID.

There are two ways to solve this problem. First, we can use a hidden field on the form and stash away the name in the hidden field. The alternative is to query the database when we need the name.

We'll use both methods in this code to see how they work. For the employee's name, we'll save the display value (the actual text of the name) in a hidden field named SearchByNameDisplay.

The careful reader may note that we haven't created that hidden field in the HTML code. Correct! We need the hidden field only for a very short while: during the time we display the list box until another field is chosen or the form is submitted. Thus, we create the hidden field programmatically, during the processing of this tag. This way, the hidden field exists only as long as we need it.

Stashing Away the Display Name in a Hidden Field

On line 32 of Listing 6.3, we create a hidden field named SearchByNameDisplay. This field exists only while the drop-down is visible. When we process this form, we'll grab the name out of this hidden field and save it in a session variable. When we need the name, on line 74 of Listing 6.3, notice that we get it not from the hidden field but rather from the session variable.

How does it get into the session variable? Recall that every time we process the form, we run the code on lines 3–5 of Listing 6.2.

```
3:      For Each item In Request.Form
4:          Session(item) = Request.Form(item)
5:      Next
```

Every field on the form is saved in the session variables. As long as our hidden field has the value we need, we will automagically save it away in a session variable. Neat. The only problem is getting the display name for the selected fields *into* the hidden field.

As you may suspect, that is what JavaScript is for. Let's return to lines 17–47 of Listing 6.1, reproduced here for your convenience:

```
17:    function GetSelected(element)
18:    {
19:        value = "";
20:        for ( var i = 0; i< element.options.length; i++ )
21:        {
22:            if ( element.options[i].selected )
23:            {
24:                if ( value )
25:                    value += ", ";
26:                value += element.options[i].text;
27:            }
28:        }
29:        if ( ! value )
30:        {
31:            element.options[0].selected = true;
32:            value = element.options[0].text;
```

6

```
33:        }
34:        return value;
35:    }
36:
37:    function OnChangeRequest(whichRequest)
38:    {
39:        document.forms[0].ChangeRequest.value = whichRequest;
40:        if ( document.forms[0].SearchByName )
41:            document.forms[0].SearchByNameDisplay.value =
42:                GetSelected(document.forms[0].SearchByName);
43:        if ( document.forms[0].SearchByOffice )
44:            document.forms[0].SearchByOfficeDisplay.value =
45:                GetSelected(document.forms[0].SearchByOffice);
46:        document.forms[0].submit();
47:    }
```

Recall that each time the form is submitted, a call is made to OnChangeRequest, passing in the name of the element being requested. We've examined line 39 and seen how the hidden field ChangeRequest is set with that value.

Notice line 40. It says that if the element SearchByName exists, we are to set the field SearchByNameDisplay to a new value. This allows us to set this field only when it exists. The value it is set to is the result returned from calling GetSelected and passing in the list box SearchByName.

GetSelected is implemented on lines 17–35. We initialize a variable value to an empty string on line 19. We then iterate through the options array, which holds all the entries in the list box. For each one that is selected (as this might be a multiselect list box), we add that string to the variable value.

When GetSelected concludes, we have a comma-delimited list of the selected items. This list (or individual selection) is stashed away in the hidden field and then copied into a session variable.

Looking Up the Value

The alternative to stashing away the display field in a hidden field is to look up the value each time you need it. Let's take a look at SearchByHealthPlan, lines 151–218 of Listing 6.3.

```
151:        Case "WC@SearchByHealthPlan"
152:
153:            If Request.Form("ChangeRequest") = _
154:                "SearchByHealthPlan" Or _
155:                Len(Session("SearchByHealthPlan")) > 0 Then
156:                Dim SearchByHealthPlanRS As Recordset
157:                Set SearchByHealthPlanRS = _
158:                    theEmp.GetAllHealthPlans
159:            End If
160:
```

```
161:            If Request.Form("ChangeRequest") = _
162:                "SearchByHealthPlan" Then
163:                TagContents = TagContents & _
164:                    "<select name=""SearchByHealthPlan""><option"
165:                If Session("SearchByHealthPlan") = 0 Then _
166:                    TagContents = TagContents & " selected"
167:                TagContents = TagContents & _
168:                    " value=0 >Any Plan</option>"
169:
170:                With SearchByHealthPlanRS
171:                    If Len(Trim(Session("SearchByHealthPlan"))) _
172:                        > 0 Then idToMatch = _
173:                        Session("SearchByHealthPlan")
174:
175:                    While Not .EOF
176:                        TagContents = TagContents & _
177:                            "<option value = " & _
178:                            .Fields("HealthPlanID")
179:
180:                        If idToMatch = .Fields("HealthPlanID") _
181:                            Then
182:                            TagContents = TagContents & _
183:                                " selected >"
184:                        Else
185:                            TagContents = TagContents & ">"
186:                        End If
187:
188:                        TagContents = TagContents & CStr(sEmpty _
189:                            & .Fields("InsurancePlanName")) & _
190:                            "</option>"
191:                        .MoveNext
192:                    Wend
193:
194:                End With
195:
196:                TagContents = TagContents & "</select>"
197:            Else
198:
199:                If Not Session("SearchByHealthPlan") = 0 And _
200:                    Len(Session("SearchByHealthPlan")) > 0 Then
201:
202:                    With SearchByHealthPlanRS
203:                        .Filter = "HealthPlanID = " & _
204:                            Session("SearchByHealthPlan")
205:                        TagContents = TagContents & _
206:                            "<a href=""Javascript:OnChangeRequest(
➥'SearchByHealthPlan')"">" _
207:                            & .Fields("InsurancePlanName") & _
208:                            "</a>"
209:                    End With
210:
211:                Else
212:                    Session("SearchByHealthPlan") = 0
```

```
213:                        TagContents = TagContents & _
214:                           "<a href=""Javascript:OnChangeRequest(
➥'SearchByHealthPlan')"">" _
215:                           & "<em>Any Plan</em>" & "</a>"
216:              End If
217:
218:          End If
```

This code is similar to the code we saw for SearchByName, but this time no hidden field is created. Instead, the critical change is on line 207. Rather than the hidden field, the field InsurancePlanName is used. This is a field in a recordset. The recordset is created on line 156 and set on line 157 to get all the HealthPlan records. On line 203, we filter the results down to only those matching the particular HealthPlanID we're considering.

> **Note**
>
> It would be more efficient to just search for the matching health plan rather than to generate the larger recordset and use the filter. This way, however, I cannot only demonstrate the use of this ADO 2.0 feature, but I can also have only one set of code requesting the HealthPlan records, as shown on lines 156 and 157.

Which Way Is Better?

There is an argument to be made for the hidden field: By using it, we don't need to make a request to the database each time we want to display the names. The argument in favor of the database lookup is that it simplifies the code and eliminates the need for a lot of hard-to-get-right and even harder-to-debug client-side Java code.

The Other JIT Controls

You've seen how list boxes are filled. How do the other controls work? There aren't a lot of surprises here, but let's walk through a couple to touch all the bases.

Creating a Text Field

The code for the Text field begins on line 221 of Listing 6.3 and ends on line 249:

```
221:      Case "WC@SomeTextField"
222:
223:          If Request.Form("ChangeRequest") = "SomeTextField" _
224:              Then
225:              TagContents = TagContents & _
226:                  "$ <input type=""text"""
227:              If Not Session("SomeTextField") = "Any Value" _
228:                  Then TagContents = TagContents & "value = " _
229:                  & Session("SomeTextField")
```

```
230:                    TagContents = TagContents & _
231:                        " name="""SomeTextField"" size = ""6""> thousand"
232:              Else
233:
234:                  If Not Session("SomeTextField") = "Any Value" _
235:                      And Len(Session("SomeTextField")) > 0 Then
236:                      TagContents = TagContents & _
237:                          "<a href=""Javascript:OnChangeRequest(
➥'SomeTextField')"">" _
238:                          & "$" & Session("SomeTextField") & _
239:                          " thousand." & "</a>"
240:                  Else
241:                      Session("CapUnderMgmt") = "Any Value"
242:                      TagContents = TagContents & _
243:                          "<a href=""Javascript:OnChangeRequest(
➥'SomeTextField')""><em>Any Value</em></a>"
244:                  End If
245:
246:             End If
247:
248:             If Len(Trim(TagContents)) = 0 Then TagContents = _
249:                 "<a href=""Javascript:OnChangeRequest(
➥'SomeTextField')""><em>Any Value</em></a>"
```

If we are modifying this field, then the code on line 223 will return true, and we'll create a text field on line 226. We check the appropriate session variable on line 227 and fill the text field with the correct value if there is one.

If we are not editing the field, then we enter the Else statement on line 232. Again we check for the session variable and either create the URL with the appropriate text or use the standard "Any Value" text for the URL.

Implementing the Radio Buttons

The radio buttons are only slightly more complex. Their code begins on line 252 of Listing 6.3 and extends to line 300:

```
252:     Case "WC@SomeRadioButtons"
253:
254:         If Request.Form("ChangeRequest") = _
255:             "SomeRadioButtons" Then
256:             TagContents = TagContents & _
257:                 "<br><input type=""Radio"" Name=""SomeRadioButtons""
➥Value=""Any Condition"""
258:             If Session("SomeRadioButtons") = "Any Condition" _
259:                 Then TagContents = TagContents & " Checked"
260:             TagContents = TagContents & ">Any Condition"
261:             TagContents = TagContents & _
262:                 "<br><input type=""Radio"" Name=""SomeRadioButtons""
➥Value=""Condition One"""
263:             If Session("SomeRadioButtons") = "Condition One" _
```

```
264:                            Then TagContents = TagContents & " Checked"
265:                  TagContents = TagContents & ">Condition One<br>"
266:                  TagContents = TagContents & _
267:                     "<input type=""Radio"" Name=""SomeRadioButtons""
➥Value=""Condition Two"""
268:                  If Session("SomeRadioButtons") = "Condition Two" _
269:                     Then TagContents = TagContents & " Checked"
270:                  TagContents = TagContents & ">Condition Two<br>"
271:                  TagContents = TagContents & _
272:                     "<input type=""Radio"" Name=""SomeRadioButtons""
➥Value=""Condition Three"""
273:                  If Session("SomeRadioButtons") = _
274:                     "Condition Three" Then TagContents = _
275:                     TagContents & " Checked"
276:                  TagContents = TagContents & _
277:                     ">Condition Three<br>"
278:                  TagContents = TagContents & _
279:                     "<input type=""Radio"" Name=""SomeRadioButtons""
➥Value=""Condition Four"""
280:                  If Session("SomeRadioButtons") = _
281:                     "Condition Four" Then TagContents = _
282:                     TagContents & " Checked"
283:                  TagContents = TagContents & _
284:                     ">Condition Four<br><br>"
285:          Else
286:
287:                  If Not Session("SomeRadioButtons") = _
288:                     "Any Condition" And _
289:                     Len(Session("SomeRadioButtons")) > 0 Then
290:                     TagContents = TagContents & _
291:                        "<a href=""Javascript:OnChangeRequest(
➥'SomeRadioButtons')"">" _
292:                           & Session("SomeRadioButtons") & "</a>"
293:                  Else
294:                     Session("SomeRadioButtons") = _
295:                        "Any Condition"
296:                     TagContents = TagContents & _
297:                        "<a href=""Javascript:OnChangeRequest(
➥'SomeRadioButtons')""><em>Any Level</em></a>"
298:                  End If
299:
300:          End If
```

The trick here is that we must create a series of radio buttons, each with the same name, but each with its own value. We certainly could take these out of a database table, creating them dynamically. To do this we would simply substitute the value we get from the table for the value of each individual button.

On to the Search

What happens when the user presses Search Now? In this case, the ChangeRequest is filled with the value "Search". On line 8 of Listing 6.2, we see that the result is that NextItem is set to ResultsFrameSet.

```
7:        If Request.Form("ChangeRequest") = "Search" Then
8:            Set NextItem = ResultsFrameSet
```

This hands control of the application to the FrameSet, as is explained in Chapter 7.

Next Steps

Now that we have looked at how to gather the criteria for the search, it is time to consider how to query the database and display the results. That is the subject of Chapter 7.

Chapter 7

Searching the Database Using ADO and SQL

The user has filled in all the controls and pressed Search Now. What happens next? This chapter reviews how the information is passed to the frameset, how the search is accomplished, and how the results are displayed.

When You Press Search Now

Recall that each time you click on a control, JavaScript takes over, a hidden field is updated, and the form is submitted to itself. That means that the host is contacted and the EnhancedQueryForm Respond method is invoked, as shown in Listing 7.1.

Listing 7.1

```
0:   Private Sub EnhancedQueryForm_Respond()
1:
2:       Dim item As Variant
3:       For Each item In Request.Form
4:           Session(item) = Request.Form(item)
5:       Next
6:
7:       If Request.Form("ChangeRequest") - "Search" Then
8:           Set NextItem = ResultsFrameSet
9:       Else
10:          EnhancedQueryForm.WriteTemplate
11:      End If
12.
13:  End Sub
```

When the Search Now button is pressed, once again the form is submitted, but this time the ChangeRequest field is filled with the string "Search"; thus, the If statement on line 7 is true.

Remember that prior to line 7, on lines 3–5, the contents of the controls in the form were copied into session variables. Now, on line 8, NextItem is set to ResultsFrameSet.

Drawing the Frameset

Setting NextItem to ResultsFrameSet causes ResultsFrameSet's Respond method to be called, as shown in Listing 7.2.

Listing 7.2

```
0:   Private Sub ResultsFrameSet_Respond()
1:
2:        ResultsFrameSet.WriteTemplate
3:
4:   End Sub
```

The net effect is that frameset is sent to the browser. Listing 7.3 shows the HTML of the ResultsFrameSet document.

Listing 7.3

```
0:   <!DOCTYPE HTML PUBLIC "-//W3C//DTD HTML 4.0
0a:    Transitional//EN">
1:   <HTML><HEAD><TITLE>Untitled Document</TITLE>
2:   <META content="text/html; charset=iso-8859-1"
2a:    http-equiv=Content-Type>
3:   <META content="MSHTML 5.00.2314.1000" name=GENERATOR>
3a:      </HEAD>
4:   <FRAMESET cols=30%,70%><FRAME name=left
5:   src="WebClass1.ASP?WCI=ResultsIndexPage&amp;WCU">
5a:      <FRAME name=right
6:   src="WebClass1.ASP?WCI=BlankResult&amp;WCU">
6a:      </FRAMESET></HTML>
```

EXCURSION

HTML

A frameset defines a window with two or more frames. Typically the frames are visible and resizable. The definition of this frameset begins on line 4, with the tag FRAMESET. The frameset defines two columns: the first takes 30% of the width of the window; the second takes 70%.

This is followed by the definition of the two frames. The first, defined at the end of line 4, is named left and its source document, the document that will be displayed in the left frame, is WebClass1.ASP?WCI=ResultsIndexPage. This is ASP working with the WebClass to display the ResultsIndexPage in the left frame.

The second frame is defined starting on line 5. It is named right, and initially all that is displayed is BlankResult—a blank page.

The frameset will display the Results list in the left frame and a blank page in the right frame.

Flow of Control

When the frameset draws itself, it will draw the contents of each frame. This will, in turn, call the Respond method for each of the two pages. These in turn will call WriteTemplate, which renders the two pages.

It is important to note that the order in which these are called or rendered is not guaranteed. Thus, you must be careful to avoid dependencies between the two pages. If you treat them as independent entities, all will be well.

In our case, we'll start by writing the Results list to the left page and displaying a simple image in the right page, as shown in Figure 7.1.

Figure 7.1

The Results list.

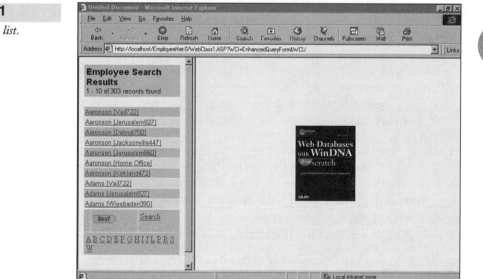

Searching the Database

How is this Results list generated? When the frameset is written, it indicates that the left frame is to be filled with ResultsIndexPage. This causes the ResultsIndexPage_Respond method to be invoked, as shown in Listing 7.4.

Listing 7.4

```
0:   Private Sub ResultsIndexPage_Respond()
1:
2:       Dim item
3:       Dim args()                      As String
4:       ReDim args(1, Session.Contents.Count - 1)
5:       Dim i                           As Integer
6:       i = 0
7:
8:       For Each item In Session.Contents
9:           args(0, i) = item
10:          args(1, i) = Session(item)
11:          i = i + 1
12:      Next
13:
14:      Dim emp                         As New employee
15:      Set rs = emp.Search(args, GetLtrsRS)
16:
17:      If Len(Trim(Session("SearchOffset"))) = 0 Then _
18:          Session("SearchOffset") = 0
19:      If Session("SearchOffset") > 0 Then rs.Move _
20:          (Session("SearchOffset"))
21:      Session("SearchOffset") = _
22:        Session("SearchOffset") + PAGESIZE
23:      If Session("SearchOffset") > rs.RecordCount Then _
24:          Session("SearchOffset") = rs.RecordCount
25:
26:      ResultsIndexPage.WriteTemplate
27:
28:  End Sub
```

The very first thing we need to do is create an array to hold all the session variables as name/value pairs. We will pass this array to our Business object, which will use the array to search the database.

What we really need is a two-dimensional array. The first dimension will hold all the names, and the second will hold all the values. Thus, Array(0,0) will hold the first name and Array(1,0) will hold its value. Array(0,1) will hold the second name, and Array(1,1) will hold the second value. Array(0,2) will hold the third name, and Array(1,2) will hold the third value. And so it continues.

Notice that the first index is always 0 or 1. The second index will count up to the total number of values held. We need to redimension the array so that the first index is 0 or 1 and the second is 0…Session.Contents.Count – 1. Session.Contents is the collection that holds all the session variables, and Count is the total number of variables in that collection. For example, if that number is 15, then the array will be from 0 to 14, or a total of 15 variables.

We accomplish this with the ReDim statement as shown on line 4. The second index is set to the total number of session variables less one (because we count from zero).

When we're done, the array looks like Figure 7.2.

Figure 7.2		0	1
A two-dimensional	0	Key 1	Value 1
array of keys and values.	1	Key 2	Value 2
	2	Key 3	Value 3
	3	Key 4	Value 4
	4	Key 5	Value 5

The net effect of lines 3–12 is that we've created a two-dimensional array. The first (0) element in each couple is a key; the second (1) element is the value. One way to make this explicit is to put a break point on line 15 and then open a watch window on args.

EXCURSION

Visual Basic

The Visual Basic debugger is a powerful tool, integrated into the VB development environment. A break point tells Visual Basic to run the program until the line on which you place the break point is reached, at which time processing is suspended and you are returned to the debugger.

A watch window allows you to examine an object. In this case, we'll examine args, to see what is held in each of its elements.

You can combine watch statements with break statements by setting a watch on a particular object to break when the object evaluates true, or when its value changes at all. This can be a great way to track down otherwise mysterious bugs in which values change when you don't expect them to.

I *strongly* recommend becoming familiar with every aspect of your debugger because it is your most important tool in developing applications. The power of the VB debugger contributes to my strong feeling that WebClasses offer a superior alternative to ASP, which has far weaker debugging options.

The result, as shown in Figure 7.3, is that we created a two-dimensional array, wherein the first dimension is filled with the keys and the second dimension is filled with the matching values.

7

Figure 7.3

The watch window.

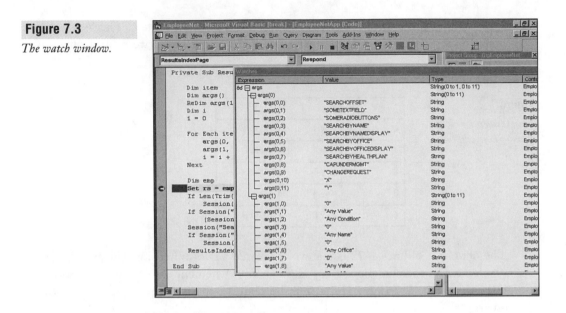

Creating a Business Object to Search

After we have built the array, we declare a new instance of the same employee Business object we saw used in Chapter 6.

On line 14, we call the employee's Search method. What do we want this method to do? We need two recordsets returned. First, we need a recordset with all the employees who match our search criteria. However, the spec also requires that we put up a list of letters at the bottom of the page so that the Human Resources manager can jump to the listings later in the alphabet (for example, jump to every employee whose last name begins with L). We need a recordset of all those letters.

> **Note**
>
> Note that rs and GetLtrsRS are defined at the module level so that their values can be shared across functions. I find that VB encourages this quasi-global approach to objects. However, I'm of two minds about my ambivalence toward this approach. You want to be careful to narrow the scope of objects so as to avoid nasty and unexpected side effects; nevertheless, they are ever so convenient.

We'll make the return value be the main recordset, and we'll pass in the second recordset by reference. The Search method will fill the first recordset and return it; it will fill in the second recordset and, because it was passed by reference (rather than by value), the calling method (in this case Respond) will have access to that recordset as well.

Note

If I were writing this method from scratch, I would probably pass both in by reference. I am doing it this way both because I first wrote it without the second recordset and because I wanted to demonstrate two ways to get a recordset back out of a called method.

EXCURSION

Visual Basic

Visual Basic supports two ways to pass parameters into methods: by value and by reference. If a parameter is passed by reference, changes to that parameter in the function are visible back in the calling function. If the parameter is passed by value, then a copy is made, and the changes are not visible in the calling method.

Objects are passed by reference as the default in VB. When you pass by reference, the address is passed in, and this is generally what you want: Addresses are smaller than objects, and you can access the object itself.

Passing by value has two possible benefits. First, because you are passing only a copy, the original object is protected from changes made in the called program. Second, and more important to our purposes here, if the Business object is on a different physical machine, then passing by reference means that, every time you touch the referred-to object, you must make a round trip across the network, which can be terribly inefficient.

To pass by value, just add the keyword ByVal:

```
Private Sub AddEmployee_ProcessTag(ByVal TagName As String, _
    TagContents As String, SendTags As Boolean)
```

In this example, TagName is passed in by value, and TagContents and SendTags are passed in by reference. Because we will fill TagContents, it could *not* be passed in by value and must be passed in by reference; otherwise, we would be filling a copy that wouldn't do us any good at all.

The Search method, therefore, takes two parameters: the two-dimensional array we created holding all the key/value pairs representing the session variables and the second recordset created to hold the initials of the matching employees.

All this is shown on line 15 of Listing 7.4:

```
15:    Set rs = emp.Search(args, GetLtrsRS)
```

rs and GetLtrsRS are declared at the top of the module:

```
Private rs               As Recordset
Private GetLtrsRS        As Recordset
```

rs stands for recordset and GetLtrsRS stands for Get Letters Recordset.

7

EXCURSION

Visual Basic

Declaring these variables to be Private indicates that they are visible only to functions in this module. The alternative is to declare the variable using `dim` or to explicitly declare it to be public, in which case it is visible to procedures in all modules.

It is good programming practice to limit the visibility of variables and objects as much as possible. This "data hiding" decouples your modules from one another and allows you greater flexibility because small changes in one module should not be able to break any other module. To the extent that variables are hidden and accessed through other objects, you are free to change them (for example, store them in a database or change their type) without breaking other functions that use them indirectly.

Examining the Business Object Search in Detail

When line 15 of Listing 7.4 is executed, control passes to the Search method of our Business object. The complete method is shown in Listing 7.5.

Listing 7.5

```
0:   Public Function Search(args() As String, GetLtrsRS As _
1:       Recordset) As Recordset
2:
3:       Dim myDict          As New Scripting.Dictionary
4:       myDict.CompareMode = vbTextCompare
5:       Dim i As Integer
6:
7:       For i = LBound(args, 2) To UBound(args, 2)
8:           Call myDict.Add(args(0, i), Replace(args(1, i), "'", _
9:               "''"))
10:      Next i
11:
12:      Dim sqlCmd          As String
13:      Dim GetLtrs         As String
14:      Dim MidPart         As String
15:      Dim joinPhrase      As String
16:      joinPhrase = ""
17:      MidPart = ""
18:      sqlCmd = "Select * from employee "
19:      GetLtrs = _
20:          "Select distinct substring(employee.LastName,1,1) " _
21:          & "as ltrs from employee "
22:  ' always need this information for display
23:      joinPhrase = joinPhrase & _
24:          " inner join offices on employee.officeID = " _
25:          & "offices.officeid "
26:      joinPhrase = joinPhrase & _
27:          "inner join address on offices.officeaddress = " _
28:          & "address.addressid "
```

```
29:
30:         If myDict("SEARCHBYOFFICE") <> 0 Then
31:             MidPart = MidPart & "offices.officeID in (" & _
32:                 myDict("SEARCHBYOFFICE") & ") and "
33:         End If
34:
35:         If myDict("SEARCHBYHEALTHPLAN") <> 0 Then
36:
37:             If InStr(joinPhrase, "EmployeeHealthPackage") = 0 Then
38:                 joinPhrase = joinPhrase & _
39:                     "inner join EmployeeHealthPackage on " _
40:                     & "EmployeeHealthPackage.EmployeeID = " _
41:                     & "employee.EmployeeID"
42:             End If
43:
44:             MidPart = MidPart & _
45:                 "(EmployeeHealthPackage.HealthPlanID = " & _
46:                 myDict("SEARCHBYHEALTHPLAN") & " or " & _
47:                 "EmployeeHealthPackage.DentalPlanID = " & _
48:                 myDict("SEARCHBYHEALTHPLAN") & ") and "
49:         End If
50:
51:         If myDict("SEARCHBYNAME") <> 0 Then MidPart = MidPart & _
52:             "Employee.EmployeeID = " & myDict("SEARCHBYNAME") & _
53:             " and "
54:
55:         If Len(Trim(myDict("ResultsStartWith"))) > 0 Then
56:             MidPart = MidPart & "employee.LastName Like '" & _
57:                 myDict("ResultsStartWith") & "%' and "
58:         End If
59:
60:         sqlCmd = sqlCmd & joinPhrase & " where " & MidPart & _
61:             "1 = 1 order by employee.LastName"
62:         GetLtrs = GetLtrs & joinPhrase & " where " & MidPart & _
63:             "1 = 1 order by substring(employee.LastName,1,1)"
64:         Dim rs              As Recordset
65:         Set rs = GetDCRS(sqlCmd)
66:     ' log for debugging
67:         Dim lf              As New LogFile
68:         Dim theKey          As Variant
69:         Dim theField        As Variant
70:         Dim outputString    As String
71:         outputString = " Dictionary has: "
72:
73:         For Each theKey In myDict
74:             outputString = outputString & theKey & "=" & _
75:                 myDict.Item(theKey) & ", "
76:         Next theKey
77:
78:         lf.WriteToLog (outputString)
79:         outputString = " SQLString: " & sqlCmd
80:         lf.WriteToLog (outputString)
```

continues

Listing 7.5—continued

```
81:        outputString = "  ** First 10 Results (Trimmed): "
82:        lf.WriteToLog (outputString)
83:        outputString = " "
84:        Dim counter          As Integer
85:        counter = 0
86:
87:        With rs
88:
89:            While Not .EOF And counter < 10
90:
91:                For Each theField In rs.Fields
92:                    outputString = outputString & theField.Name _
93:                        & "=" & Trim(theField.Value) & ", "
94:                Next
95:
96:                lf.WriteToLog (outputString)
97:                outputString = " "
98:                counter = counter + 1
99:                .MoveNext
100:           Wend
101:
102:       End With
103:
104:       If Not rs.BOF Then rs.MoveFirst
105:       lf.WriteToLog (outputString)
106:       Set GetLtrsRS = GetDCRS(GetLtrs)
107:       Set Search = rs
108:
109: End Function
```

We start this method by converting the array received as a parameter into a Visual Basic dictionary. The dictionary is declared on line 3 and filled on lines 7–10.

EXCURSION

Visual Basic

A dictionary is a collection in which a key is tied to a value. Once in the dictionary, given a key, you can retrieve the value in much the same way that you can retrieve a definition from a dictionary given a word.

This matches our planned use of these name/value pairs nicely and makes manipulation of this information easy and straightforward, as we'll see shortly.

You add items to a dictionary with the Add method, passing in two arguments—the key and the value. Note on line 8 that I massage the value before entering it with this code:

```
Replace(args(1, i), "'", _"''"))
```

This is a common idiom when using VB to interact with a database. Replace takes three arguments: a string, what to look for, and what to replace it with. In this case, I pass in the value (of the name/value pair) and replace every instance of a single quote with two single quotes. Thus, if we start with this pair (LastName, O'Leary), we end up with a dictionary entry with a key of LastName and a value of O''Leary. When we pass this to SQL Server, it recognizes the double quote as a single quote.

This is necessary because the name will be marked off with single quotes like this:

```
"Select * from firms where LastName = 'O''Leary'"
```

Were it not for the double single quotes, SQL Server would think that the first quote ended the Last Name:

```
"Select * from firms where LastName = 'O'Leary'"
```

and it wouldn't know what to do with `Leary'`.

Conditional Search Strings

The rest of this method is given over to solving the following problem: Depending on what fields are filled in, we need to build a Select statement that will return the appropriate records.

As a simple first approach, we could assemble a SQL statement for each possible combination. Thus, if we have a name to search for, we have SQL code with the name. If we have an office, we have a different SQL statement for the office; if we have a health plan, we search for that.

If, however, we have both an office and a health plan, we'll need yet a different search plan. This could get complicated pretty quickly. Just imagine the combinatorial explosion when we have, for example, 12 different controls (for example, name, office, health plan, investment schedule, number of years of service).

Clearly we need conditional logic to "build" the SQL query as we go. This turns out to be a little tricky. With a reasonably well-designed database, not all the information is in a single table. For example, to find all employees in a given office, you need to join the Employee table to the Offices table. More interestingly, if we are to display the city of the office in which a given employee works, we must also join in the Address table.

EXCURSION
Joining Tables

In SQL programming, it is common to "join" together two or more tables. Think of your first table as having all its columns aligned side by side. The second table is joined alongside, creating a new, wider table with some or all of the columns of each.

When you join two tables, say Employees and Offices, you must tell SQL which column to join them *on*. In this case, we want to join the Employees table to the Offices table where the employees.officeID field matches the offices.officeID field. That way, we match the correct office to each employee.

Second, we must qualify the join as one of five *types*: cross, inner, left, right, and full.

An inner join specifies that SQL should return rows only when there is a match in both tables. That is, if an employee has an office ID but there is no matching office, don't show that employee. If there is an office with no matching employee, don't show that office. The syntax for this join is

```
Select * from employee e inner join offices o on e.officeID = o.officeID
```

Note that I've used an alias for both tables, using e for employee and o for offices. This just makes typing somewhat easier.

Suppose that you want all the employees, regardless of whether there is a matching office or not, but you want only offices with employees. The left join gives you what you need:

```
Select * from employee e left join offices o on e.officeID = o.officeID
```

Similarly, the right join would show a record for every office, with matching employees if found. The full join says that all rows from either table should be returned, using null if there are no data. The cross join creates the cross-product (or Cartesian product) of both tables. For each record in the first table, *all* the records in the second table are joined. This creates a huge (huge!) recordset.

The vast majority of joins are inner joins and, failing that, left joins. The others are used less often, but they do have their uses.

It is common to join multiple tables together, as we'll see in Chapter 8.

Similarly, if we are searching for a health plan, we must join in the EmployeeHealthPackage table.

What makes this tricky is that we do *not* want to join these tables unless we are searching for criteria within them. For example, let's say we have a table in which an employee might appear more than once. We do not want to search that table unless we are going to have a qualifying Where clause, or we may well see multiple results returned for employees who have multiple records within the table.

Let's take a quick example from the AssetAllocation table. Here's how it works. Each employee has a portfolio, which is represented by an entry in the Portfolio table (one entry per employee). In addition, each employee may have one or more funds. Each fund is represented by an entry in the AssetAllocation table.

Look at Figure 7.4. Notice that Employee 3871 is listed as Jesse Levine. You'll find an entry for this employeeID in the Portfolio table (upper-right corner), with portfolioID 3300. Now look at the AssetAllocation table in the upper-left corner. There are three entries for portfolioID 3300: one each for funds 1, 2, and 3.

Now, let's try a search. First we'll try

```
select * from employee where employeeID = 3871.
```

Figure 7.4

Relating tables.

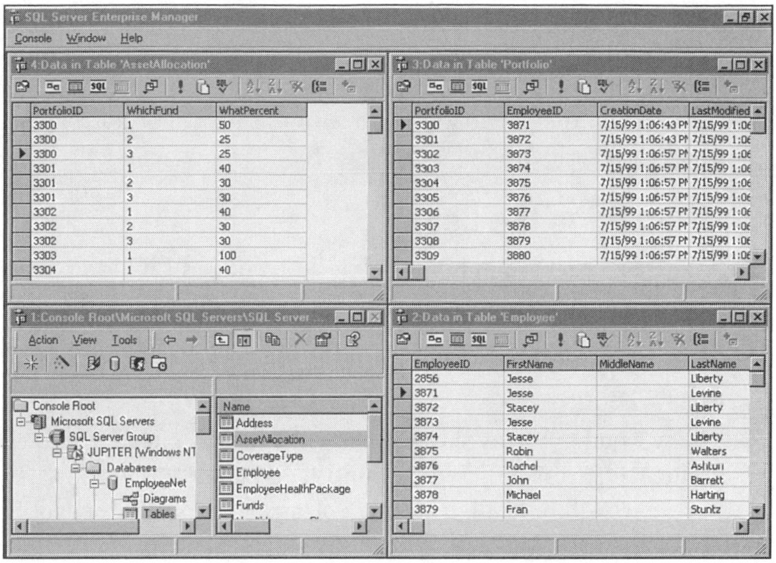

This returns one record, as we'd expect. Let's join in the Portfolio table:

```
select * from employee e
join portfolio p on  p.employeeID =  e.employeeID
where e.employeeID = '3871'.
```

This code says: "Select all the fields you get back (`select *`) from employee joined to portfolio (make one wide table of both) finding every record in which there is a match between the employeeID field in portfolio (p) and the employeeID field in employee (e), but only where the employeeID field in employee is 3871."

Once again, we get one record. No problem! Now let's add the AssetAllocation table:

```
select * from employee e
join portfolio p on p.employeeid = e.employeeid
join assetallocation a on a.portfolioid = p.portfolioid
where e.employeeID = '3871'.
```

This time, however, we get three results because there are three records with the employeeID of 3871 and the matching portfolioIDs in the Portfolio and AssetAllocation tables.

If we were searching for every employee who participates in a particular fund, we could use this join to great advantage. For example, if we wanted to find any employee who had fund 1, we might inquire:

```
select * from employee e
join portfolio p on p.employeeID = e.employeeID
join assetallocation a on a.portfolioID = p.portfolioID
where whichFund = 1.
```

This asks SQL for every field from the Employee, Portfolio, and AssetAllocation tables for each employee whose Portfolio and AssetAllocation tables indicate participation in fund 1. Specifically, we want to join up an employee with his portfolio record and the portfolio record with the asset allocation record, and then find only those with whichFund is equal to 1.

Examining the Code

With this background in mind, follow along as I build up the SQL statement. We'll ignore the details of GetLtrsRS for now and focus on the sqlCmd statement.

On line 12, I declare the sqlCmd string, and on line 18 I assign to it "Select * from employee ".

Now I build up two phrases that will later be concatenated with this SQL statement. The MidPart is declared on line 14, and joinPhrase is declared on line 15. The MidPart will hold all my Where clauses; the joinPhrase will hold all the joins as I need them.

Because I know I will include information about which office each employee works in and the address of that office, and because each employee works in only one office, I add the Offices join on line 24 and the Address join on line 27. If no search criteria are selected in the Search dialog box, the tests on lines 30, 35, and 51 will fail. In that case, on line 60, I proceed to add to the SQLCmd string (`"Select * from employee"`) the join phrase (inner join offices on `employee.officeID = offices.officeID` inner join address on `offices.officeaddress = address.addresid`). Then I'll concatenate the word `where` and end with whatever is in MidPart (in this case it will be blank) and the phrase `"1 = 1"` (we'll discuss this shortly) ending with `"order by employee.LastName"`.

Thus, the minimal search is

```
Select * from employee
inner join offices on employee.officeID = offices.officeID
inner join address on offices.officeaddress = address.addresid
where 1 = 1 order by employee.LastName
```

Adding in Search Clauses

If, on the other hand, the user has chosen an office, then the session variable `"SearchByOffice"` would have a value, in which case that value would have been copied into the two-dimensional array and thence to the dictionary. In that case, the If statement on line 30 would evaluate true, and MidPart would be modified as shown on lines 31 and 32:

```
30:        If myDict("SEARCHBYOFFICE") <> 0 Then
31:            MidPart = MidPart & "offices.officeID in (" & _
32:                myDict("SEARCHBYOFFICE") & ") and "
```

EXCURSION

SQL

The In clause used on line 31 says that any of the comma-delimited values in the parentheses may be used to match. Rather than saying `where a = b or a = c or a = d`, we
just say `where a in (b,c,d)`.

Let's assume that SearchByOffice has the values 156 and 158 (the user having chosen
two offices). This would modify the search string to, for example,

```
Select * from employee inner join offices on employee.officeID =
offices.officeID inner join address on offices.officeaddress = address.addresid
where offices.officeID in ( 156, 158 ) and 1 = 1 order by employee.LastName

Select * from employee
inner join offices on employee.officeID = offices.officeID
inner join address on offices.officeaddress = address.addresid
where offices.officeID in ( 156, 158 ) and
1 = 1 order by employee.LastName
```

It is clear now why we use the 1 = 1 phrase. This way all the midPart statements can
safely end with "and "; when we're done adding phrases the 1 = 1 is tacked on, and
since 1 does equal 1, it does no harm.

If the user also wants to search for a health plan, then we must include the
EmployeeHealthPackage table into our search. We see this code from lines 35 to 49:

```
35:        If myDict("SEARCHBYHEALTHPLAN") <> 0 Then
36:
37:            If InStr(joinPhrase, "EmployeeHealthPackage") = 0 Then
38:                joinPhrase = joinPhrase & _
39:                    "inner join EmployeeHealthPackage on " _
40:                    & "EmployeeHealthPackage.EmployeeID = " _
41:                    & "employee.EmployeeID"
42:            End If
43:
44:            MidPart = MidPart & _
45:                "(EmployeeHealthPackage.HealthPlanID = " & _
46:                myDict("SEARCHBYHEALTHPLAN") & " or " & _
47:                "EmployeeHealthPackage.DentalPlanID = " & _
48:                myDict("SEARCHBYHEALTHPLAN") & ") and "
49:        End If
```

Line 37 checks if we've included this table yet and, if not, it adds it to the inner join
string. In either case, the MidPart string is then modified to include the ID of the

health plan the user has chosen. Because we can't know if a health plan or a dental plan is chosen, we search for either. The SQL statement is now

```
Select * from employee
inner join offices on employee.officeID = offices.officeID
inner join address on offices.officeaddress = address.addresid
inner join EmployeeHealthPackage on
EmployeeHealthPackage.EmployeeID = employee.EmployeeID
where offices.officeID in ( 156, 158 ) and
(EmployeeHealthPackage.HealthPlanID = 7 or
EmployeeHealthPackage.DentalPlanID = 7) and
1 = 1 order by employee.LastName
```

As you can see, we add in the phrases we need, maintaining a legal SQL statement in any case.

Getting the Initials

The specification calls for finding the first letter of the last names of all the matching employees. We'll do this work in parallel with building the SQL statement, as the search is essentially identical.

On line 19, immediately after initializing the SQL statement, we initialize GetLtrs:

```
18:        sqlCmd = "Select * from employee "
19:        GetLtrs = _
20:           "Select distinct substring(employee.LastName,1,1) " _
21:           & "as ltrs from employee "
```

EXCURSION

SQL

The As clause in a Select statement changes the *name* assigned to the column returned. If I say `select EmployeeID as EmployeeNumber` from employee…, the recordset will return with that field named EmployeeNumber rather than EmployeeID.

GetLtrs will use the same MidPart and joinPhrase as does sqlCmd. The only other difference is that rather than ordering by the last name, we'll order by the first letter of the last name:

```
60:        sqlCmd = sqlCmd & joinPhrase & " where " & MidPart & _
61:           "1 = 1 order by employee.LastName"
62:        GetLtrs = GetLtrs & joinPhrase & " where " & MidPart & _
63:           "1 = 1 order by substring(employee.LastName,1,1)"
```

As you can see, we successfully reuse the code for generating the SQL command in the code for generating the list of letters. The advantage of this approach is that we present to the user only those letters that will match at least one record.

EXCURSION

SQL

Substring is a SQL command that returns (as you might guess) a substring from a larger string. You pass in the larger string, the offset to begin extracting, and how many letters to get. In this case, we begin at the first letter and order by the first letter.

Logging the Search

Debugging this kind of application can be very difficult: You are firing off searches and seeing results. How do you know exactly what is being sent to the database? I find it useful to log the contents of the session variables, the SQL command, and the results so that I can review all three when something goes wrong.

The code to do this is quite simple. It starts by creating a new class module named LogFile. Give that class a single method: WriteToLog, as shown in Listing 7.6.

Listing 7.6

```
0:   Public Function WriteToLog( _
1:       theString As String, Optional isError As Boolean = False) _
2:        As Boolean
3:       Dim output As String
4:       Dim rightNow As Date
5:       rightNow = Time
6:       output = rightNow & ": " & theString
7:       Dim objfso As New Scripting.FileSystemObject
8:       Dim LogFile As TextStream
9:       If isError Then
10:          Set LogFile = objfso.OpenTextFile _
11:             ("d:\logfiles\EmployeeErrorLog.txt", _
12:                 ForAppending, True)
13:      Else
14:          Set LogFile = objfso.OpenTextFile _
15:              ("d:\logfiles\EmployeeLog.txt",  _
16:                 ForAppending, True)
17:      End If
18:
19:      LogFile.WriteLine (output)
20:      LogFile.WriteBlankLines (1)
21:      LogFile.Close
22:  End Function
```

This simple method takes two parameters: the string you want to write to the log and an optional second parameter indicating whether you are logging an error (rather than routine logging). The method itself returns a Boolean indicating success or failure.

7

On line 6, we create a time stamp and add to that the string passed in. On lines 9–17, we determine whether to open EmployeeErrorLog.txt (line 11) or EmployeeLog.txt, depending on that second optional parameter.

After the file is open, the time-stamped string is written out to the file on line 19. We then write a blank line and close the file. It's simple.

With this in hand, we're ready to log the session variables, the SQL statement, and the first ten records in the resultset.

Returning to Listing 7.5, we start the logging by creating a string of all the session variables on lines 73–76. Here is an example:

```
3:14:35 PM:  Dictionary has: SEARCHOFFSET=0, SOMETEXTFIELD=Any Value,
SOMERADIOBUTTONS=Any Condition, SEARCHBYNAME=0, SEARCHBYNAMEDISPLAY=Any Name,
SEARCHBYOFFICE=0, SEARCHBYOFFICEDISPLAY=Any Office, SEARCHBYHEALTHPLAN=0,
CAPUNDERMGMT=Any Value, CHANGEREQUEST=Search, X=53, Y=13, ResultsStartWith=,
```

As you can see, each entry in the dictionary (and thus each session variable) is written out as a name/value pair. This string is written to the log on line 78.

Next, on lines 79 and 80 we write out the SQL command itself as shown here:

```
3:14:35 PM:  SQLString: Select * from employee  inner join offices on
employee.officeID = offices.officeID inner join address on
offices.officeaddress = address.addressID  where 1 = 1 order by
employee.LastName
```

Finally, lines 81–105 write out the first ten results. The first two are shown here:

```
3:14:35 PM:   ** First 10 Results (Trimmed):
3:14:35 PM:  EmployeeID=3893, FirstName=Mike, MiddleName=, LastName=Aaronson,
Title=Mr., Suffix=, HomeAddress=3578, OfficeID=244, MailAddress=3578,
OfficeID=244, OfficeName=Vail722, OfficeAddress=3555, Manager=2856,
AddressID=3555, AddressLine1=722 COAST Ave., AddressLine2=, City=Vail,
State=AK, ZipCode=, Phone1=4585452646, Phone2=8332152538, Fax1=4167671829,
Fax2=0073411107,
3:14:35 PM:  EmployeeID=3934, FirstName=Larry, MiddleName=, LastName=Aaronson,
Title=Ms., Suffix=, HomeAddress=3619, OfficeID=243, MailAddress=3619,
OfficeID=243, OfficeName=Jerusalem927, OfficeAddress=3554, Manager=3872,
AddressID=3554, AddressLine1=927 BAKER St., AddressLine2=, City=Jerusalem,
State=AS, ZipCode=, Phone1=6200372242, Phone2=3042857935, Fax1=0649196314,
Fax2=2910359548,
```

Creating the Recordset

We are now ready to submit the SQL statement to the database and to return the disconnected recordset to ResultsIndexPage's Respond method. On line 65, we call GetDCRS passing in sqlCmd.

 **Note**

GetDCRS, which stands for Get Disconnected Recordset, is a private (helper) function I wrote. This function encapsulates all the code to take a SQL statement and return a disconnected recordset—a recordset that you can use like any other but that is no longer connected to the database, as discussed in Chapter 6.

We then log the search as described earlier, and on line 106 we set GetLtrsRS to the result of calling in GetDCRS with GetLtrs.

Both recordsets are returned to Respond on line 15 of Listing 7.4. Lines 17–24 set the SearchOffset session variable. We'll return to this code later, but the point of SearchOffset is to keep track as we page through the Results list. For now, it is set to zero, and on line 26 we call WriteTemplate.

This, of course, displays the results and calls ProcessTags for the tags in the HTML file. The job of the HTML file is to list each matching employee name, followed by the next and previous buttons and then an alphabetical list of the first letters of the last names of the matching employees. The HTML is shown in Listing 7.7.

Listing 7.7

```
0:   <html>
1:   <head>
2:   <title>Search Results</title>
3:   <meta http-equiv="Content-Type"
4:   content="text/html; charset=iso-8859-1">
5:   </head>
6:
7:   <body bgcolor="#ffffff">
8:
9:   <table width="100%" border="0" cellspacing="1" cellpadding="4">
10:     <tr valign="top">
11:       <td bgcolor="#CCCCFF">
12:       <font face="Arial, Helvetica, sans-serif"
13:   size="+1"><b>Employee Search Results</b></font>
14:   <font face="Arial, Helvetica, sans-serif"><br>
15:         <font size="2"><WC@HOWMANYFOUND></WC@HOWMANYFOUND>
16:   </font></font></td></TR>
17:   </TABLE>
18:
19:
20:   <table width="100%" border="0" cellspacing="1"
21:   cellpadding="2"><WC@RESULTS></WC@RESULTS>
22:
23:
24:   </table>
25:
26:
```

continues

Listing 7.7—continued

```
27:
28:   <table width="100%" border="0" cellspacing="1"
29:   cellpadding="4">
30:     <tr>
31:       <td bgcolor="#CCCCFF"><WC@PREV></WC@PREV> </td>
32:       <td bgcolor="#CCCCFF"><WC@Next></WC@NEXT> </td>
33:       <td bgcolor="#CCCCFF">
34:         <p><WC@EditQuery></WC@EditQuery></p>
35:         <p></p>
36:   </td>
37:     </tr>
38:     <tr>
39:       <td colspan="3" bgcolor="#CCCCFF" >
40:       <WC@Folders></WC@Folders>
41:   </td>
42:     </tr>
43:   </table>
44:   <p> </p>
45:   </body>
46:   </html>
```

Three tables are created in this page. Each has a zero-sized (invisible) border, and each is used to control the layout of the final display page.

The first table, lines 9–17, is used to create the header and has the WebClass tag HowManyFound—we'll use this tag to report on the total number of matching records.

The second table, lines 20–21, will be filled with the list of matching employees, each set as a link to the details page.

The final table, lines 28–43, will be used to hold three buttons (Previous, Next, and Edit Query) as well as the alphabetic list of initials (WC@Folders).

Listing 7.8 shows the ProcessTag method used to parse and respond to these tags.

Listing 7.8

```
0:   Private Sub ResultsIndexPage_ProcessTag _
1:     (ByVal TagName As String, _
2:     TagContents As String, SendTags As Boolean)
3:
4:     Dim item
5:     Const ODDROW = "#CCCCFF"
6:     Const EVENROW = "#CCCCCC"
7:     Dim color            As String
8:
9:     Select Case TagName
10:
11:       Case "WC@HOWMANYFOUND"
12:
```

```
13:        If Len(Trim(Session("ResultsStartWith"))) > 0 Then
14:          TagContents = "[<b>" & _
15:             Session("ResultsStartWith") & "</b>]: "
16:        End If
17:
18:        If rs.RecordCount > PAGESIZE Then
19:          TagContents = TagContents & _
20:          Session("SearchOffset") - 9 & " - "
21:          TagContents = TagContents & _
22:             Session("SearchOffset") & _
23:             " of " & CStr(rs.RecordCount) & _
24:             " records found.<br>"
25:        Else
26:          TagContents = TagContents & _
27:           CStr(rs.RecordCount) & " record"
28:          If rs.RecordCount > 1 Then _
29:             TagContents = TagContents & "s"
30:          TagContents = TagContents & " found.</b><br>"
31:        End If
32:
33:        If Len(Trim(Session("ResultsStartWith"))) > 0 Then
34:          TagContents = TagContents & _
35:             "<a href=""" & URLFor(ResultsIndexPage, "All") _
36:             & """ Target=left>See Results" _
37:             & " For All Letters</A><br>"
38:        End If
39:
40:      Case "WC@Results"
41:        Dim i            As Integer
42:        Dim theName         As String
43:        i = 0
44:        TagContents = TagContents & "<br>"
45:        Session("SearchRecordCount") = rs.RecordCount
46:
47:        While i < PAGESIZE And Not rs.EOF
48:          theName = Trim(rs!LastName)
49:          If Len(theName) > MAX_DISPLAY_NAME Then theName = _
50:             Left(theName, MAX_DISPLAY_NAME - 1) & "..."
51:          If (i / 2 = Int(i / 2)) Then color = _
52:            ODDROW Else color = EVENROW
53:          TagContents = TagContents & "<tr> <td bgcolor=" & _
54:            color
55:          TagContents = TagContents & _
56:             "><font face=""Arial, Helvetica, " _
57:             & " sans-serif"" Size = ""2""> "
58:          TagContents = TagContents & _
59:             "<a href=""" & URLFor(ResultOutput, _
60:             CStr(rs!EmployeeID)) & """ Target=right>" _
61:             & theName & "  [" & rs!OfficeName & _
62:             "]</A></FONT></TD></TR>"
63:          i = i + 1
64:          rs.MoveNext
```

continues

Listing 7.8—continued

```
65:          Wend
66:
67:       Case "WC@Prev"
68:
69:          If Session("SearchOffset") > PAGESIZE Then
70:            TagContents = _
71:               "<a href=""" & URLFor(ResultsIndexPage, _
72:               "Previous") & """ Target=left>" _
73:               & "<IMG src=""images/prev.gif"" border=0> </A> "
74:          Else
75:       TagContents = "        
➥   "
76:          '<font color=""#C0C0C0"">Previous</font>"
77:          End If
78:
79:       Case "WC@Next"
80:
81:          If Session("SearchOffset") < Session _
82:            ("SearchRecordCount") _
83:            Then
84:            TagContents = _
85:               "<a href=""" & _
86:               URLFor(ResultsIndexPage, "Next") _
87:               & """ Target=left>" _
88:               & " <IMG src=""images/next.gif"" border=0> </A> "
89:          Else
90:       TagContents = "        
➥   "
91:          '<font color=""#C0C0C0"">Previous</font>"
92:          End If
93:
94:       Case "WC@EditQuery"
95:          TagContents = TagContents & _
96:            "<a href=""" & _
97:            URLFor(EnhancedQueryForm) & _
98:            """ Target=_top>Search</A>"
99:
100:       Case "WC@Folders"
101:          Dim ltrString      As String
102:
103:          With GetLtrsRS
104:
105:            While Not .EOF
106:               ltrString = GetLtrsRS!ltrs
107:               TagContents = TagContents & _
108:                 "<a href=""" & _
109:                 URLFor(ResultsIndexPage, ltrString) _
110:                 & """ Target=left>" _
111:                 & ltrString & "</A> "
112:               .MoveNext
113:            Wend
```

```
114:
115:            End With
116:
117:      End Select
118:
119: End Sub
```

On lines 5 and 6, we set up the background colors for the alternating rows. This creates a ledger-like effect, which makes it easy to distinguish one row from another, as shown in Figure 7.1.

EXCURSION

Visual Basic

A constant declaration, as shown on line 5, is much like a variable, except that the value never changes. From line 5 onward, therefore, the name ODDROW will evaluate to the string "#CCCCFF", which is a color used by the browser.

On line 11, we match the HowManyFound tag, which is the sole occupant of the topmost hidden table. We fill this with the number of records found. This number varies depending on whether we're displaying a particular initial (for example, the user clicked on the letter D) or the entire record set.

We test the session variable "ResultsStartWith" on line 13 to see if we're displaying a particular initial. The first time through, of course, we are not, so this If statement will fail.

On lines 18–24, we test to see if the total number of records found (rs.RecordCount) is greater than the predefined constant PAGESIZE (which I've set to 10). If so, then we'll have more than one page of records, and so we must determine what the current offset is (are we looking at the first page or a later page?). For the first page, the offset has been set to 10 (see line 22 of Listing 7.4). We subtract 9 (leaving 1) and mark the page as 1–10 of however many records were found altogether.

EXCURSION

ADO

RecordCount returns the total number of records held in an ADO Recordset object.

Let's skip over lines 33–38 because they deal with processing the initials; we'll return to this topic shortly.

7

On line 40, we handle the WC@Results tag. Recall that this tag is the sole occupant of the middle hidden table. Our job is to fill this table with the results from the list and to make each result a link to the details page.

Our first action, on line 45, is to stash away the total count of records in the session variable "SearchRecordCount". We will now create the rows of alternating background color and list them out one by one.

We create on line 47 a While loop, which will continue to iterate while two conditions are true. The first condition is that we've not yet added all ten results (While i < PAGESIZE). The second condition is that we've not yet reached the end of the recordset (And Not rs.EOF).

Even though these conditions are unmet, we need to extract the last name of each employee. Because we have limited display space, we'll check the length of the last name. If it is longer than a predefined limit MAX_DISPLAY_NAME, then we'll reduce its length by 1 and add ellipses (...) to the end.

EXCURSION
Visual Basic

The VB Trim function returns the string with all leading and trailing spaces removed.

Len returns the length of the string.

Left returns the first n characters of the string, where n is the second parameter and the string is the first parameter. Thus, if MAX_DISPLAY_NAME is equal to 10, then Left(theName, MAX_DISPLAY_NAME - 1) will return the first 9 characters of theName.

Int takes a fractional or decimal number and returns an integer (whole number) value. It does this by "lopping off" the fractional part, turning 9.9 into 9 (not 10!). Thus, if i is 7 then i/2 would be 3.5, but Int(i/2) would return 3.

You may increment a variable by adding to it. Thus, if i is 3, then i = i + 1 sets i to 4 (C++ would just write ++i).

Now that we have the last name (or the first part of the last name), we are ready to display it. First, we need to set the correct background color. We do this by testing whether i is an odd or even number on line 51:

```
51:          If (i / 2 = Int(i / 2))
```

Note

An alternative technique for finding out if a number is even or odd is to use the modulus operator. The modulus operator is best explained by thinking back to how you were taught to divide in third grade: 17 divided by 2 is 8, remainder 1. The modulus operator returns the remainder, if any.

> Even numbers are evenly divisible by 2, so
>
> Result = i mod 2
>
> will cause the result to be zero if the number is odd and 1 if it is odd. For example, 37 mod 2 returns 1.

After we know whether or not i is an even number, we can set the background color, as shown on line 52.

We now create the row and column (lines 53 and 54), and we're ready to put in the contents. Remember that we want this to be a link, so we create the anchor tag on line 59 and use our old friend URLFor to create the link. The target will be ResultOutput (the details page), and the event to pass in to ResultOutput's UserEvent method is the particular employee's EmployeeID.

EXCURSION

Visual Basic

CStr takes a nonstring value (in this case an integer) and turns it into a string. Thus, if the EmployeeID is 127, this will create the string "127".

We set the target for this URL to right, the right frame of the frameset. Finally, we set the display value to the employee's name, with his associated OfficeName in brackets (which is why Search, considered earlier, had to include the Office table).

Finally, on line 63, we increment the counter i and get the next record in the recordset on line 64.

Next and Previous Button Display

Drawing the Next and Previous buttons is straightforward, except that we need to decide whether they should be visible. The logic is shown on line 69. If the current offset is greater than a PAGESIZE, then we know that we are on at least the second page of results and we can display the Previous button. We do this by creating another link, again using URLFor, but this time targeting the very page we are on: ResultsIndexPage, passing in "Previous" to the UserEvent method.

The same logic applies for Next, except this time we want to see if we're at the last page.

The EditQuery tag indicates that the user wants to return to the query page, and we create a straightforward link to that page. Note that there is no second parameter in this URLFor, indicating that no value will be passed to EnhancedQueryForm's UserEvent page. None is needed.

The final tag is `WC@Folders`. We will substitute the links to the alphabetic lists of initials by using the GetLtrsRS recordset returned by Search.

Each record in GetLtrsRS is processed in turn. For each one, we create a link using URLFor and passing in the letter itself as the event.

Handling the User Events

Previous, Next, and Folders all call the UserEvent of the ResultsIndexPage, as shown in Listing 7.9.

Listing 7.9

```
0:   Private Sub ResultsIndexPage_UserEvent _
1:   (ByVal EventName As String)
2:       Select Case EventName
3:       Case "Previous"
4:           If Session("SearchOffset") > PAGESIZE Then
5:               Session("SearchOffset") = _
6:                   Session("SearchOffset") - 20
7:           End If
8:
9:       Case "Next"
10:          'No action to take, increment is automatic
11:       Case "All"
12:           Session("ResultsStartWith") = ""
13:           Session("SearchOffset") = 0
14:
15:       Case Else
16:               If Len(Trim(EventName)) = 1 Then
17:                   Session("ResultsStartWith") = EventName
18:                   Session("SearchOffset") = 0
19:               End If
20:       End Select
21:       Set NextItem = ResultsIndexPage
22:
23:   End Sub
```

We test for each of the events, including Next, although, as shown on line 10, there is nothing to do in the case of Next. Because the SearchOffset is automatically incremented each time we draw the page, Next works without further intervention. It is listed here to make the code easier to understand and thus to maintain.

In the case of Previous, we must decrement the SearchOffset value by 20 (not 10) because we have already advanced it by 10, and decrementing by the same 10 would just redisplay the same page we've already seen.

The processing of the request for an individual letter is shown on lines 16–19. All that is involved is resetting the SearchOffset to zero and setting the session variable ResultsStartWith to the letter in question.

At the end of Listing 7.9, we set NextItem to ResultsIndexPage. This, of course, calls Respond, which in turn calls back into Search.

This time through Search, we note that we're searching for a particular initial, as shown on lines 55–58 of Listing 7.5, reproduced here:

```
55:        If Len(Trim(myDict("ResultsStartWith"))) > 0 Then
56:            MidPart = MidPart & "employee.LastName Like '" & _
57:                myDict("ResultsStartWith") & "%' and "
58:        End If
```

Note that we now narrow the search for names that begin with the letter we stashed away in this session variable.

EXCURSION

SQL

The Where clause can search for exact matches or wildcard matches. You create a wild-card match by using the keyword Like (rather than =) and the wildcard character %, which operates much as * does when searching for files from the command prompt.

Thus, the Select statement

```
Select * from employees where LastName like 'C%'
```

will find every employee whose last name begins with C.

Searching by Letter

When we return to process tags, the recordset will contain only the employees whose last names match the requested initial.

This will return us to line 13 in Listing 7.8, where the If statement will evaluate true and we'll print out the letter we've searched for.

```
13:        If Len(Trim(Session("ResultsStartWith"))) > 0 Then
14:            TagContents = "[<b>" & _
15:                Session("ResultsStartWith") & "</b>]: "
16:        End If
```

Because we are now searching by letter, we must also print out the option to see all the results for all the letters. This is handled on lines 33–38:

```
33:        If Len(Trim(Session("ResultsStartWith"))) > 0 Then
34:            TagContents = TagContents & _
35:                "<a href=""" & URLFor(ResultsIndexPage, "All") _
```

```
36:                  & """ Target=left>See Results" _
37:                  & "For All Letters</A><br>"
38:            End If
```

Again, this time the If statement will evaluate true, and we'll create a link to ResultsIndexPage with the event name "All", which we see handled on lines 11–13 of Listing 7.9.

```
11:      Case "All"
12:            Session("ResultsStartWith") = ""
13:             Session("SearchOffset") = 0
```

That closes the loop on how we display these records in the left pane of the Results frameset.

Next Steps

Look at the URL we created on lines 58–62 of Listing 7.8:

```
58:            TagContents = TagContents & _
59:             "<a href=""" & URLFor(ResultOutput, _
60:              CStr(rs!EmployeeID)) & """ Target=right>" _
61:              & theName & "  [" & rs!OfficeName & _
62:              "]</A></FONT></TD></TR>"
```

The effect of clicking on one of these links will be to call the ResultOutput's UserEvent method, passing in the EmployeeID. In Chapter 8, we look at how the details page is displayed.

Chapter 8

Creating the Details Page

Now that we have displayed all the matching employees, we want to be able to click on an individual employee and display the details of his employment record.

Designing the Output

One of the significant advantages of WebClasses is that they are fairly easy to work with, both for you and for the designer. You can hand the user interface designer a sketch of the kinds of information you want to capture and receive a design with tags in place, ready for you to fill in the data.

In short, WebClasses offer a clean division between HTML and design on the one hand and tags and data on the other. For this project, I handed Maethee a series of screen shots that showed the kind of data I wanted to display. An example is shown in Figure 8.1.

Maethee turned this screen into a professional-looking design without needing to know or worry about how I'd get the data into or out of the database. I was able to fold in his design for the individual pages in less than an hour! The results are shown in Figure 8.2.

The important thing to note here, however, is that my code did not change *at all*. I still process the same tags, in exactly the same way. The tags are simply placed in a more elegant HTML document. Consequently, the results are far better, but the underlying implementation is *identical*.

Figure 8.1

A rough view of the data.

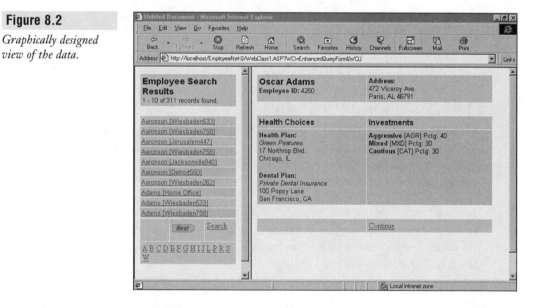

Figure 8.1

A rough view of the data.

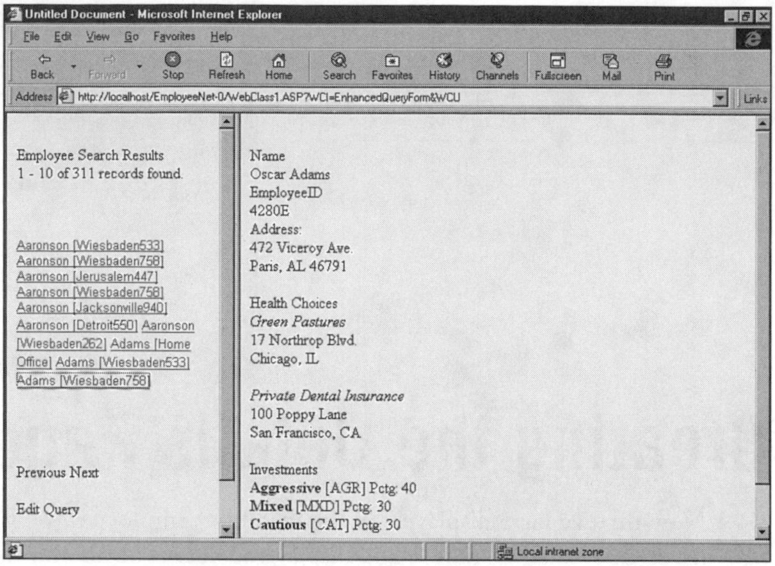

Figure 8.2

Graphically designed view of the data.

Displaying the Details

Whatever the design of the output document, we still need to display a great deal of information about each employee. This includes the employee's contact information, health insurance choices, and investment decisions.

The Output Template

Processing this page begins with the ResultOutput template, illustrated in Figure 8.3.

Figure 8.3

Template for displaying results.

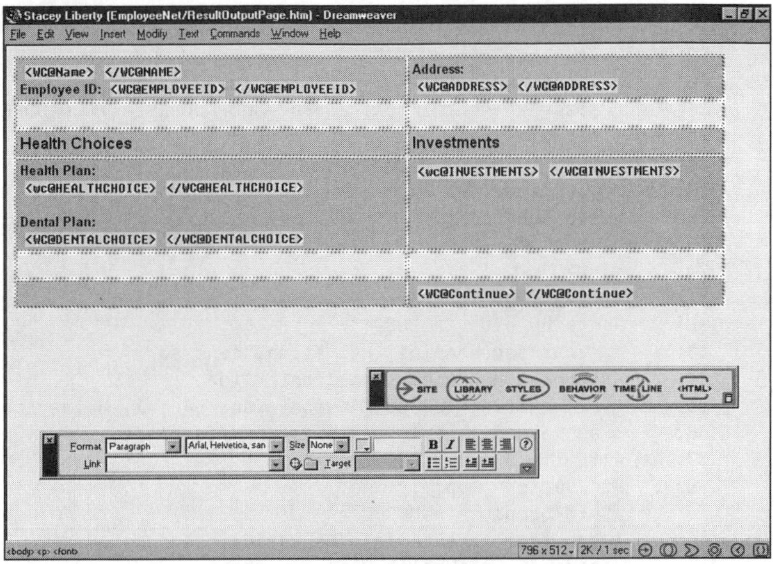

As you can see, the template creates a table, and there are tags for each of the significant pieces of information we'll supply from the database.

Listing 8.1 shows the HTML for this page.

Listing 8.1

```
0:  <html>
1:  <head>
2:  <title>Stacey Liberty</title>
3:  <meta http-equiv="Content-Type"
4:  content="text/html;
5:  charset=iso-8859-1">
6:  </head>
7:  <body bgcolor="#FFFFFF">
8:  <table width="95%" border="0"
9:  cellspacing="1"
10:   cellpadding="4">
11:    <tr valign="top">
12:      <td bgcolor="#CCCCFF">
13:      <font face="Arial, Helvetica, sans-serif"
14:      size="+1"><b><WC@Name></WC@NAME>
15:
16:      </b></font>
17:      <font face="Arial, Helvetica, sans-serif"
```

continues

8

Listing 8.1—continued

```
18:      font size="2">
19:      <br><b>Employee ID: </b><WC@EMPLOYEEID></WC@EMPLOYEEID>
20:
21:      </font></td>
22:      <td bgcolor="#CCCCFF">
23:      <font face="Arial, Helvetica, sans-serif"
24:      size="2"><b>Address:</b><br><WC@ADDRESS></WC@ADDRESS>
25:      </font></td>
26:   </tr>
27:   <tr valign="top">
28:      <td> </td>
29:      <td> </td>
30:   </tr>
31:   <tr valign="top">
32:      <td bgcolor="#CCCCFF">
33:      <font face="Arial, Helvetica, sans-serif">
34:      <b>Health Choices</b></font></td>
35:      <td bgcolor="#CCCCFF"><font face="Arial, Helvetica,
36:      sans-serif"><b>Investments</b></font></td>
37:   </tr>
38:   <tr valign="top">
39:      <td bgcolor="#CCCCCC">
40:      <p><font face="Arial, Helvetica, sans-serif"
41:      size="2"><b>Health Plan:</b><br>
42:      <wc@HEALTHCHOICE></WC@HEALTHCHOICE>
43:      </font></p>
44:      <p><font face="Arial, Helvetica,
45:      sans-serif" size="2">
46:      <b>Dental Plan:</b><br>
47:      <WC@DENTALCHOICE></WC@DENTALCHOICE>
48:      </font><font face="Arial, Helvetica,
49:      sans-serif"></font></p>
50:      </td>
51:      <td bgcolor="#CCCCCC"><font face="Arial,
52:      Helvetica, sans-serif"
53:      size="2"><wc@INVESTMENTS></WC@INVESTMENTS>
54:
55:      </font></td>
56:   </tr>
57:   <tr>
58:      <td> </td>
59:      <td> </td>
60:   </tr>
61:   <tr bgcolor="#CCCCFF">
62:      <td> </td>
63:      <td><WC@Continue></WC@Continue></td>
64:   </tr>
65: </table>
66: <p> </p>
67: <p> </p>
68: <p><font face="Arial, Helvetica, sans-serif"><br>
```

```
69:    <br>
70:    </font></p>
71:  </body>
72:  </html>
```

This is straightforward HTML. There is fairly careful control over size, font style, and color, but there are no surprises here. The tags allow us to plug in the very same data from the earlier screens.

What Is Difficult?

When you first start working with WebClasses, it seems as if manipulating the relationship between the HTML and the data will be the difficult part. After you've written a few pages, however, you'll quickly realize that the difficult part is manipulating the data—not the WebClass.

This is as it should be. The application takes advantage of a sophisticated database design. Getting exactly the data you need, efficiently and quickly, is and ought to be the difficult part of the process.

Recall from Chapter 7 that when each employee is listed in the left pane, the following code from Listing 7.8 is used:

```
"<a href=""" & URLFor(ResultOutput, CStr(rs!EmployeeID))
& """ Target=right>" _
& theName & "  [" & rs!OfficeName
& _"]</A></FONT></TD></TR>"
```

The URLFor creates a link, and clicking on that link brings you to the ResultOutput page. In fact, the effect is to call UserEvent on ResultOutput, passing in the chosen record's EmployeeID as the parameter.

Listing 8.2 shows the UserEvent method of ResultOutput.

Listing 8.2

```
0:  Private Sub ResultOutput_UserEvent _
1:    (ByVal employee As String)
2:
3:      Session("EmployeeID") = employee
4:      Set NextItem = ResultOutput
5:
6:  End Sub
```

This routine does nothing more than stash the employeeID passed in as a parameter in a session variable (creatively named EmployeeID) and then set NextItem to ResultOutput. As you know, this calls the Respond method of ResultOutput, shown in Listing 8.3.

Listing 8.3

```
0:  Private Sub ResultOutput_Respond()
1:
2:      Dim theEmp    As New employee
3:      Set DetailsRS = theEmp.GetByID(Session("EmployeeID"))
4:
5:      ResultOutput.WriteTemplate
6:
7:  End Sub
```

Once again, this is fairly simple code. We declare an instance of the employee business object and call its GetByID method, passing in the EmployeeID we stored in the UserEvent method. We then call WriteTemplate to write out the HTML, and this will call ProcessTags. Before we look at how the data are used, let's start by examining GetByID, as shown in Listing 8.4.

Listing 8.4

```
0:  Public Function GetByID(myID As Integer) As Recordset
1:
2:      Dim rs                      As New Recordset
3:      Dim sqlStmnt                As String
4:      Dim objConn                 As New Connection
5:      objConn.Provider = "msdatashape"
6:      objConn.Open _
7:          "DataProvider = sqloledb; data source = " _
8:          & "EmployeeNet; initial catalog = " _
9:          & "EmployeeNet"
10:
11:         sqlStmnt = "Shape{{Call dbo.spEmployeeGetByID" _
12:         & "(" & CStr(myID) & ")}} as Employee " _
13:         & "APPEND({Select AssetAllocation.PortfolioID, " _
14:         & "AssetAllocation.WhatPercent, Funds.FundName, " _
15:         & "Funds.FundSymbol from AssetAllocation inner " _
16:         & "join funds on AssetAllocation.WhichFund = " _
17:         & "Funds.FundID} as AssetAllocation " _
18:         & "RELATE 'portfolioID' to 'portfolioID') " _
19:         & "as AssetAllocation" _
20:
21:      rs.CursorType = adOpenStatic
22:      rs.CursorLocation = adUseClient
23:      rs.LockType = adLockBatchOptimistic
24:      Call rs.Open(sqlStmnt, objConn)
25:      rs.ActiveConnection = Nothing
26:      Set GetByID = rs
27:
28:  End Function
```

The purpose of this code is to fill a recordset with all the information we require about a particular employee. This code divides neatly into two principal aspects. The first is a call to a stored procedure spEmployeeGetByID. The second is a call to create an ADO shaped recordset.

We'll consider the stored procedure first because it is more in line with what we've looked at already. After we see how this works, we'll return to the shaped recordset.

EXCURSION

SQL

A stored procedure is a precompiled series of SQL statements.

Each time a SQL statement is submitted to SQL Server, it must be compiled. During the compile, SQL Server generates a query plan to determine the most efficient way to search the database.

When a stored procedure is created, it is compiled once and then saved. Each time you call the stored procedure, SQL Server uses the query plan it has already built, rather than regenerating it. The net effect is that the stored procedure runs far more quickly than it would if you submitted the SQL statements programmatically each time.

You create a stored procedure in Enterprise Manager by right-clicking on the Stored Procedure entry under your database and choosing New Stored Procedure, as shown in Figure 8.4.

Figure 8.4

Creating a stored procedure.

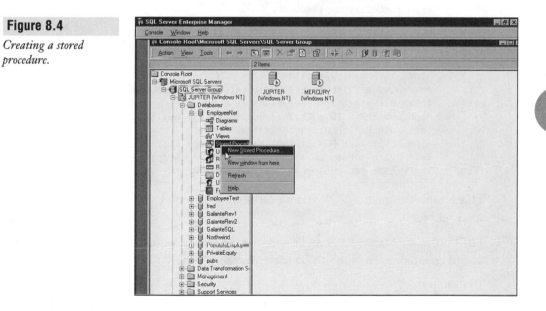

Stored procedures can take parameters. You identify the parameter in the Create clause with the @ symbol, providing the data type. You can then use the parameter later in the stored procedure; SQL Server will resolve the parameter at runtime to generate a valid SQL statement.

Examining the Stored Procedure

The stored procedure we'll use for retrieving the relevant information about employees is shown in Listing 8.5.

Listing 8.5

```
0:   CREATE PROCEDURE spEmployeeGetByID @employeeid int
1:   AS  Select employee.*, address.*,
2:       employeeHealthPackage.HealthPlanID,
3:       employeeHealthPackage.DentalPlanID,
4:       employeeHealthPackage.HealthCoverageType,
5:       employeeHealthPackage.DentalCoverageType,
6:       employeeHealthPackage.MyCost,
7:       hiph.InsurancePlanName as HealthPlanName,
8:       hiph.InsCoName as InsCo_H,
9:       hiph.InsCoAddr1 as InsCoAddress1_H,
10:      hiph.InsCoAddr2 as InsCoAddress2_H,
11:      hiph.InsCoCity as InsCoCity_H,
12:      hiph.InsCoState as InsCoState_H,
13:      hipD.InsurancePlanName as HealthPlanName_D,
14:      hipD.InsCoName as InsCo_D,
15:      hipD.InsCoAddr1 as InsCoAddress1_D,
16:      hipD.InsCoAddr2 as InsCoAddress2_D,
17:      hipD.InsCoCity as InsCoCity_D,
18:      hipD.InsCoState as InsCoState_D,
19:       portfolio.portfolioid from employee
20:       left join portfolio on
21:      portfolio.employeeID = employee.employeeid
22:       left join employeeHealthPackage
23:      on employeeHealthPackage.employeeid = employee.employeeid
24:      left join HealthInsurancePlans as HIPH on
25:      hiph.healthPlanID = EmployeeHealthPackage.HealthPlanID
26:      left join HealthInsurancePlans as HIPD on
27:      hipd.healthPlanID = EmployeeHealthPackage.DentalPlanID
28:      left join Address on address.addressid = employee.homeaddress
29:      where employee.EmployeeID =  @employeeID
```

This intimidating bit of SQL is not nearly as complicated as it looks. Let's take it apart bit by bit.

The best way to analyze a complicated stored procedure such as this is also the best way to create one, building it slowly step by step in the Query Analyzer.

To fire up the Query Analyzer, open Enterprise Manager, navigating to the EmployeeNet database, and then click on Tools/SQL Server Query Analyzer, as shown in Figure 8.5.

This brings up the SQL Server Query Analyzer (as you might expect!) in another window (as perhaps you might *not* expect), as shown in Figure 8.6. It turns out that the SQL Server Query Analyzer is an independent, albeit related, program.

Figure 8.5

Using the Query Analyzer.

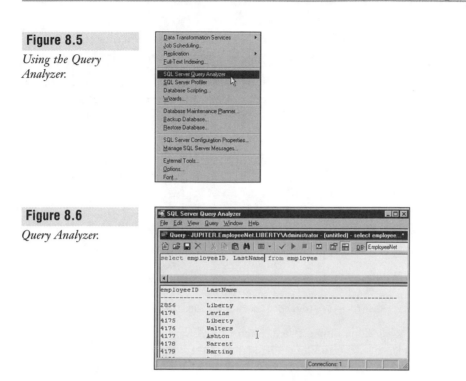

Figure 8.6

Query Analyzer.

You can enter any SQL statement into this window. Its syntax will be checked, and the results will appear in the bottom pane.

Let's start by entering the stored procedure into the Query Analyzer. The first task is to turn this stored procedure into a query. To do that, we need to make a few adjustments.

First, delete everything before the word Select, eliminating the command to create a stored procedure. Second, scroll down to the bottom of the command and change @EmployeeID to **4175**. This supplies a specific ID to search for. Execute the query. It runs quickly, and quite a bit of information is returned about Employee 4175. Note that much of this information is from multiple tables.

Now let's look at this query step by step. Line 1 selects everything from employee and address. Lines 2–6 select from the EmployeeHealthPlanPackage.

The next few lines get confusing unless you step back and think about what problem we're trying to solve. Recall that our design created a table called HealthInsurancePlans, which contains information about health plans and dental plans. We'd like to be able to differentiate between these two records.

We solve this by creating aliases for the columns, depending on whether they contain information about health plans or dental plans. We want to merge paired rows.

For example, a given employee's health plan will appear in one record, whereas his dental plan will be in another. It would be convenient if the recordset that is returned allowed us to view both records as if they were in the same row, with appropriately named columns.

We can accomplish this by joining the HealthInsurancePlans table into our Select statement *twice*. The first time we'll join it on the HealthPlanID and then give it the alias HIPH, as shown on lines 24 and 25.

```
24:     left join HealthInsurancePlans as HIPH on
25:     hiph.healthPlanID = EmployeeHealthPackage.HealthPlanID
```

The second time we'll join *the same tables* on the dentalPlanID and use the alias HIPD, as shown on lines 26 and 27.

```
26:     left join HealthInsurancePlans as HIPD on
27:     hipd.healthPlanID = EmployeeHealthPackage.DentalPlanID
```

We now have the same table joined twice. Each time different records are joined in based on the On clause (for example, on `hipd.healthPlanID = EmployeeHealthPackage.DentalPlanID`).

We now want to create columns for both the health plan's address information and the dental plan's address information. This is done on lines 8–18.

Note on line 8 that we can use the alias hiph even though we don't create it until line 24. SQL is not procedural; it considers the statement all-of-a-piece.

To get a better handle on this procedure, let's strip it down to the essentials. Listing 8.6 simplifies the Select statement, eliminating all the address information.

Listing 8.6

```
0:  Select employee.*,
1:      employeeHealthPackage.HealthPlanID,
2:      employeeHealthPackage.DentalPlanID,
3:      hiph.InsurancePlanName as HealthPlanName,
4:      hipD. InsurancePlanName as HealthPlanName_D
5:      from employee
6:      left join employeeHealthPackage
7:      on employeeHealthPackage.employeeid = employee.employeeid
8:      left join HealthInsurancePlans as HIPH on
9:      hiph.healthPlanID = EmployeeHealthPackage.HealthPlanID
10:      left join HealthInsurancePlans as HIPD on
11:      hipd.healthPlanID = EmployeeHealthPackage.DentalPlanID
12:      where employee.EmployeeID = 4175
```

The results of this Select statement are shown in Listing 8.7.

Listing 8.7

```
0:   EmployeeID      FirstName      MiddleName      LastName      Title      Suffix
1:   4175            Stacey                         Liberty       Ms.
2:
3:   HomeAddress     OfficeID       MailAddress     HealthPlanID      DentalPlanID
4:   3871            156            3871            3                 7
5:
6:   HealthPlanName       HealthPlanName_D
7:   HMOGreen             HMODental
```

Now we can see clearly! By joining the HealthInsurancePlans on those records for which the employee's DentalPlanID matched the healthPlanID in the table, we could create HIPD, the dental choice. HealthPlanName_D is a column in the recordset created by extracting the InsurancePlanName from this aliased table!

The results of running the full query are pretty much the same, except that all the address details have been added back in, as shown in Listing 8.8.

Listing 8.8

```
0:   EmployeeID      FirstName      MiddleName      LastName      Title      Suffix
1:   4175            Stacey                         Liberty       Ms.
2:
3:   HomeAddress     OfficeID       MailAddress     AddressID      AddressLine1
4:   3871            156            3871            3871           390 Baker St.
5:
6:   AddressLine2       City           State       ZipCode     Phone1        Phone2
7:                      Jerusalem      AS          41426       5196531747    5802013105
8:
9:   Fax1            Fax2           HealthPlanID    DentalPlanID    HealthCoveragetype
10:  6580164317      9507444230     3               7               1
11:
12:  DentalCoverageType      MyCost         HealthPlanName      InsCo_H
13:  1                       NULL           HMOGreen            Green Pastures
14:
15:  InsCoAddress1_H         InsCoAddress2_H         InsCoCity_H      InsCoState_H
16:  17 Northrop Blvd.       NULL                    Chicago          IL
17:
18:  HealthPlanName_D        InsCo_D          InsCoAddress1_D    InsCoAddress2_D
19:  HMODental               HMO Dental Plan  50 Main Street     Mail Stop R17
20:
21:  InsCoCity_D     InsCoState_D               portfolioid
22:  Acton           MA                         3604
```

Shaped Recordsets

The data returned by the stored procedure is fairly flat and traditional. Each employee has an address and a health and dental plan. We acquire this information by a complicated but straightforward series of joins from the Employee table to the EmployeeHealthPackage table and thence to the details about each insurance package found in the HealthInsurancePlans table. The result is a large recordset with a field for each piece of data.

Some of the data in the Employee record are not flat, however; they are hierarchical. Each employee, for example, has one or more assets in his portfolio. He may have 100% of his investments in a single fund, or he may have distributed his investments in three funds.

We can find the totality of the funds with a second query, by asking for all the rows that match this employee's portfolio. An alternative, however, is to make a single ADO call, requesting a single shaped recordset in return.

A shaped recordset can be thought of as a recordset in which at least one of the columns is itself a recordset. Imagine a table in which one column is itself a table. Within that inner table are various columns, some of which may themselves be tables. It is like falling into a mirror, tumbling into tables within tables.

We saw the implementation of a shaped recordset on lines 11–19 of Listing 8.4:

```
11:          sqlStmnt = "Shape{{Call dbo.spEmployeeGetByID" _
12:          & "(" & CStr(myID) & ")}} as Employee " _
13:          & "APPEND({Select AssetAllocation.PortfolioID, " _
14:          & "AssetAllocation.WhatPercent, Funds.FundName, " _
15:          & "Funds.FundSymbol from AssetAllocation inner " _
16:          & "join funds on AssetAllocation.WhichFund = " _
17:          & "Funds.FundID} as AssetAllocation " _
18:          & "RELATE 'portfolioID' to 'portfolioID') " _
19:          & "as AssetAllocation" _
```

The syntax for a shaped recordset is intimidating. Here's how it works. The keyword Shape signals that you are creating a shaped recordset. The syntax is

```
Shape { parent command } [ as table_alias ]
Append ( {child Command } [ as child_table_alias ]
Relate parent_table_column to child_table_column ) [ as column name]
```

So, for example, you might write

```
Shape { select * from employee }
Append ( { select * from address }
Relate employee.employeeID to address.employeeID ) as address
```

This would create a shaped recordset in which the employee record would have an additional field (address), which would itself be a recordset of addresses (this does not apply to the current design, but would work if a given employee had multiple addresses).

> **Note** The optional table aliases are not terribly useful, but the column name is critical. It is the name of the column in the resulting recordset, which represents the shaped subrecords.

In the case shown in Listing 8.4, the parent command is the stored procedure spEmployeeGetByID, which we explored earlier in this chapter. The child command is the following complicated string:

```
Select AssetAllocation.PortfolioID, AssetAllocation.WhatPercent,
Funds.FundName, Funds.FundSymbol from AssetAllocation inner join
funds on AssetAllocation.WhichFund = funds.fundID
```

We should, of course, use a stored procedure for this command as well, although I haven't bothered because it is a simple Select statement.

These two recordsets are related to each other in the Relate statement, where the parent command's portfolioID value is related to the child command's portfolioID.

The net result of this statement is to join the two commands so that each record shown in Listing 8.8 has an additional column named AssetAllocation. That column actually contains a recordset with the results of the child command. Specifically, that column's recordset has the fund allocation for that employee!

Shaped Recordset Providers

To use the shaped recordset, you must tell your ADO connection object that the provider you are using is msdatashape. You haven't had to worry about the connection object (let alone the provider) until now, but using a connection is straightforward. The syntax for creating the connection and opening it is shown on lines 5–9 in Listing 8.4.

Using the Shaped Recordset to Display the Details Page

Recall that we entered the GetByID method by calling it from ResultOutput's Respond method (line 3 of Listing 8.3). At that time we passed in the EmployeeID.

On line 12 of Listing 8.4 that ID is passed in to the stored procedure, which is the parent command of the shaped recordset we created on lines 11–19.

We return to Listing 8.3, reproduced here for your convenience.

```
0:  Private Sub ResultOutput_Respond()
1:
2:      Dim theEmp    As New employee
3:      Set DetailsRS = theEmp.GetByID(Session("EmployeeID"))
4:
5:      ResultOutput.WriteTemplate
6:
7:  End Sub
```

The result of all this work is a recordset, which is returned to the Respond method and stored in the module-level recordset DetailsRS.

Respond ends by calling WriteTemplate, which sends the HRML to the browser and then calls ProcessTags to process the tags in the HTML, as shown in Listing 8.9.

Listing 8.9

```
0:  Private Sub ResultOutput_ProcessTag(ByVal TagName As String, _
1:  TagContents As String, SendTags As Boolean)
2:
3:  Dim rsAssets         As Recordset
4:
5:  Select Case TagName
6:
7:     Case "WC@EmployeeID"
8:        TagContents = CStr(DetailsRS.Fields("EmployeeID"))
9:
10:     Case "WC@Name"
11:        TagContents = CStr(DetailsRS.Fields("FirstName")) & _
12:          CStr(" " & DetailsRS.Fields("MiddleName") & " ") & _
13:          CStr(DetailsRS.Fields("LastName"))
14:
15:     Case "WC@Address"
16:        TagContents = CStr(DetailsRS.Fields("AddressLine1"))
17:        If Len(CStr(DetailsRS.Fields("AddressLine2"))) > 0 Then
18:          TagContents = TagContents & _
19:          "<BR>" & CStr(DetailsRS.Fields("AddressLine2"))
20:        End If
21:        TagContents = TagContents & _
22:          "<BR>" & CStr(DetailsRS.Fields("City")) & ", "
23:        TagContents = TagContents & _
24:          CStr(DetailsRS.Fields("State")) & " " & _
25:          CStr(DetailsRS.Fields("ZipCode")) & "<br>"
26:
27:     Case "WC@HealthChoice"
28:        TagContents = "<em>" & CStr(sEmpty & DetailsRS!InsCo_H) _
29:          & "</em><br>" & CStr(sEmpty _
30:          & DetailsRS!InsCoAddress1_H)
31:        TagContents = TagContents & "<BR>" & CStr(sEmpty & _
32:          DetailsRS!InsCoCity_H) & ", " & CStr(sEmpty & _
33:          DetailsRS!InsCoState_H) & "<br>"
```

```
34:
35:        Case "WC@DentalChoice"
36:           TagContents = "<em>" & CStr(sEmpty & DetailsRS!InsCo_D) _
37:              & "</em><br>" & CStr(sEmpty _
38:              & DetailsRS!InsCoAddress1_D)
39:           TagContents = TagContents & "<BR>" & CStr(sEmpty & _
40:              DetailsRS!InsCoCity_D) & ", " & CStr(sEmpty & _
41:              DetailsRS!InsCoState_D) & "<br>"
42:
43:        Case "WC@Investments"
44:           Set rsAssets = DetailsRS.Fields("AssetAllocation").Value
45:
46:           With rsAssets
47:
48:              While Not .EOF
49:                 TagContents = TagContents & "<b>" & CStr(sEmpty & _
50:                    .Fields("FundName")) & "</b> [" & CStr(sEmpty & _
51:                    .Fields("FundSymbol")) & "]"
52:                 TagContents = TagContents & " Pctg: "
53:                 TagContents = TagContents & CStr(sEmpty & _
54:                    .Fields("WhatPercent")) & "<br>"
55:                 .MoveNext
56:              Wend
57:
58:           End With
59:
60:        Case "WC@Continue"
61:           TagContents = TagContents & _
62:              "<a href=""" & URLFor(Login) & _
63:              """ Target=_top>Continue</A><br>"
64:     End Select
65:
66:  End Sub
```

8

 Note

> I access field names with two styles: rs.Fields("FieldName") and
> rs!FieldName. The latter is obsolete and "deprecated" by Microsoft, but old
> habits die hard. I've left them in the book so that you'll get used to seeing both
> styles because that is what you'll run into in real-world code. (I did it on purpose,
> honest, I swear!)

Displaying the EmployeeID (line 8) and the name (lines 11–13) is straightforward. The address lines 16–25 are only slightly more complicated. Even the health and dental choices (lines 28–41) are easily displayed; each field is accessed through its (virtual) column in the recordset.

However, we see the power of the shaped recordset when we display the investments. On line 44, we assign the module-level rsAssets recordset to a particular column in the DetailsRS recordset using the syntax shown. Essentially, this code accesses the AssetAllocation field from detailsRS and then accesses that field's value member, which is in fact a recordset.

On lines 46–58, we iterate through this subrecordset, extracting the specifics of the employee's particular allocation of funds.

Trouble in Paradise

What a wicked cool technique. Amaze your friends, impress your neighbors, be a hero in your neighborhood! But don't look *too* closely. There is an ugly little secret about shaped recordsets that I'm almost afraid to tell you.

It turns out that the shape provider performs *no* optimization. In fact, the parent statement and child statement are not joined on the server; they are joined *on the client*. This means that both statements are executed independently.

In our case, this is no problem. Imagine, if you will, however, the following database design where each health insurance company has a series of offices. Perhaps the larger insurance companies have an office in each of 200 major cities. Within these offices are employees. We'll have two tables: personnel (which tells you who the managers are) and people (which has the data on every person in the system).

We want to build a page for our application that lists each of the insurance companies and then, for each company, each of its offices and all the managers in these offices.

We could build a recordset along the lines shown in Listing 8.10.

Listing 8.10

```
0:  sqlStmnt = "Shape{ Select * from InsuranceCos where " _
1:  & " InsuranceCos.InsCoID = '" & Trim(theInsCoID) & "' }  " _
2:  & "Append ((Shape{select * f1rom offices order " _
3:  & "by officeType desc }  " _
4:        & "APPEND({Select * from people inner join personnel " _
5:        & "on personnel.personID = people.personID} " _
6:        & "RELATE 'officeID' to 'officeID') as  people)" _
7:  & "RELATE 'InsCoID' to 'InsCoID') as offices"
```

This is somewhat more complex than the shaped recordset we saw earlier in that it has a parent-child-grandchild relationship. The parent Select statement is on line 1; the child is created by the Append statement on line 2. Notice that line 2 also includes the Shape statement.

The grandchild is created in the Append statement on line 4, which appends to the child related by the fields on line 6. The child is finished off by the Relate statement on line 7.

Note   This code does *not* relate to the Employee database but is provided here to help explain the limitations of shaped recordsets.

Let's further assume that the first Select statement

```
Select * from InsuranceCos where  InsuranceCos.InsCoID =
  '" & Trim(theInsCoID) & "'
```

returns exactly one record and that the second Select statement

```
select * from offices order by officeType
```

returns all 200 offices. Then, the third Select statement

```
Select * from people inner join personnel on
personnel.personID = people.personID
```

returns all 2,000 personnel (from all the offices combined). Thus, we get back 2,201 records. Unfortunately, all we need is the 21 offices that match this insurance company and the 200 people who work in these offices. Thus, we are getting 2,201 records to display 221.

In some applications, the numbers are much worse. I recently worked on a project in which the shaped recordset would return 25,000 records when all I needed was 12. Not great.

The answer, in that case, was to break the single Shape statement into a series of individual Select statements. For example, we could break the Shape statement in Listing 8.10 into the statements shown in Listing 8.11.

8

Listing 8.11

```
0:   select * from InsuranceCos where
1:       InsuranceCos.InsCoID = theInsCoID
2:
3:   select * from offices where
4:       offices.InsuranceCOID = theInsCoID
5:
6:   select * from people
7:       inner join personnel on personnel.personID =
8:       people.personID where people.InsuranceCOID = theInsCoID
```

Shaped recordsets definitely have their use, but you need to keep an eye on the performance trade-off. I'll be interested to see if subsequent versions of ADO solve this problem.

Next Steps

The database is the workhorse of the entire application, and it can be a significant factor in the overall performance of your Web site. In the next chapter, we look at what you can do to optimize your use of the database.

Chapter 9

Database Optimization

Now that the search and display pages are up and working, it's time to optimize their performance. Although the round-trip from the server to the client in a Web application is typically far more time-consuming than even the slowest search, improving the performance of the database can have a dramatic impact on the user's experience. We look at how indexing your tables and querying your profiles can dramatically improve performance.

It Starts with Analysis

SQL Server provides a number of tools designed to help you understand the performance of your database and to tune that performance.

The best place to begin is with the SQL Server Profiler. Open Enterprise Manager, choose the EmployeeNet database, and click on Tools/SQL Server Profiler, as shown in Figure 9.1.

Figure 9.1

Using SQL Server Profiler.

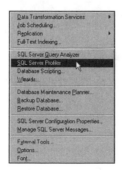

When the Server Profiler opens, choose Tools/Create Trace Wizard..., which will open the Trace Wizard. Click Next after reading the preliminary dialog box and choose the server on which the database resides. There are a number of precanned traces available from this wizard. Before proceeding, click on the Problem drop-down and review the options. Let's choose the default, "Find the worst performing queries," as shown in Figure 9.2. Click Next.

Figure 9.2

Creating a trace.

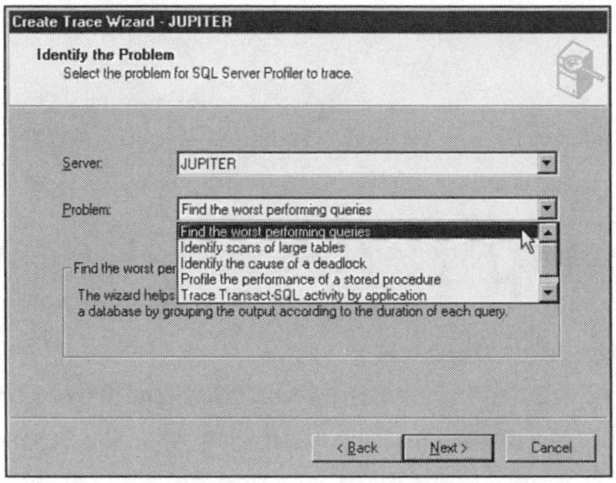

Choose the EmployeeNet database and delete all values from the Minimum Duration text box, as shown in Figure 9.3. Click Next.

Figure 9.3

Choosing the database.

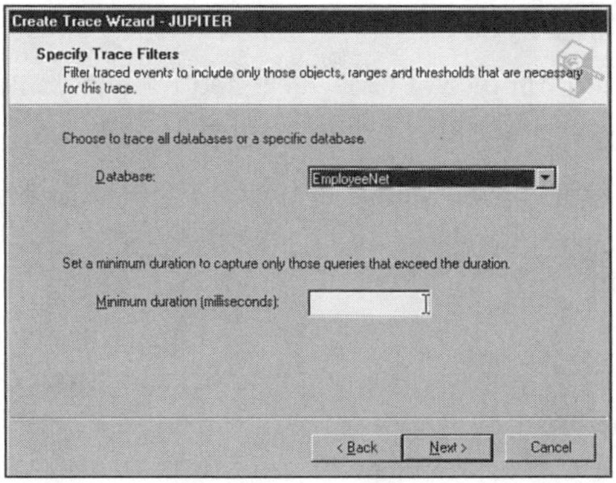

Choose Trace All Options and click Next. On the final dialog screen, name your trace and click Finish. This opens the Profiler with your defined profile, as shown in Figure 9.4.

Click on the Properties button (or choose File/Properties) to open the Properties dialog box. Look through the options and then click on the Data Columns tab. This allows you to manipulate the information that will be presented. Click on Duration and then Down to move the Duration field out of the Groups section (which would group your results by duration) and back down to the columns section so that your results will not be grouped. Remove SQL and NT User Name as well as Application Name, but add in Reads and Writes, as shown in Figure 9.5.

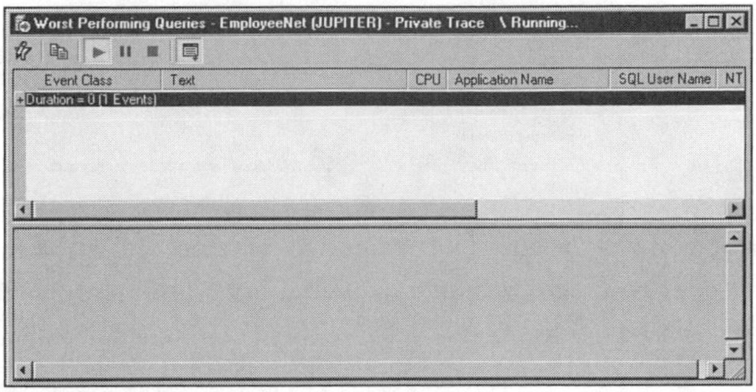

Figure 9.4

The Profiler.

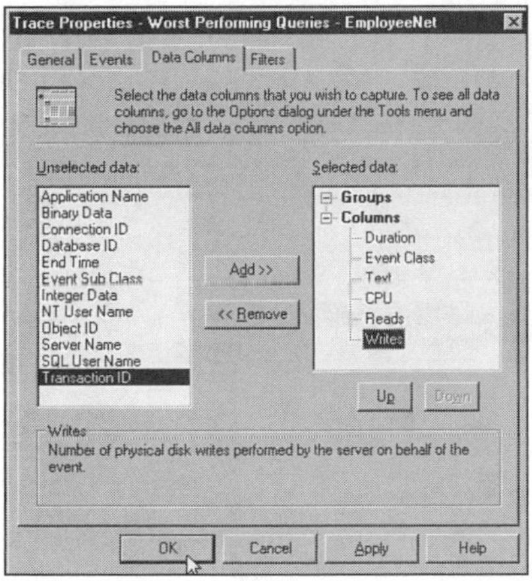

Figure 9.5

Modifying the columns.

SQL Server Profiler alerts you that the trace changes will not take effect until you stop and restart the trace. Click OK and then click the Stop This Trace button (the red square) followed by the Start This Trace button (the green arrow).

Your new trace is started and ready to track the performance of your queries. Launch EmployeeNet and click on Search to bring up the Search dialog box. Now switch back to the analyzer; the results are shown in Figure 9.6.

There are two things to note about this output. First, we see that a query was executed twice—the first time it ran in 10 milliseconds, and the second time it took no measurable amount of CPU time to run.

Figure 9.6

Examining the results.

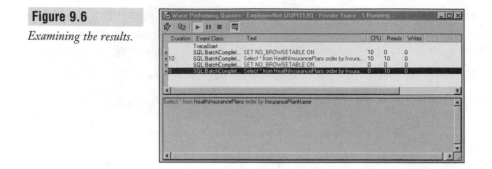

Why is this running at all? That's a good question. There is no need for this search to run in order to create the query form. This search should not be running yet. Something must be wrong.

Let's put a break point in the ProcessTags method for this page on SearchByHealthPlan, as shown in Figure 9.7.

Figure 9.7

Setting the break point.

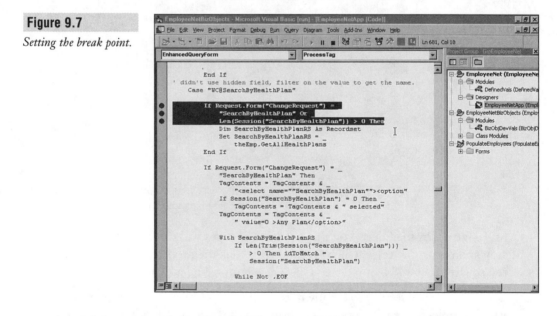

A quick inspection shows that the If statement is evaluating true, and we're entering the code in which we call GetAllHealthPlans—and thus search the database. Placing the cursor on the variable `Session("SearchByHealthPlan")` shows that this variable has the value 0 (rather than begin empty!), as shown in Figure 9.8. Thus, `Len(Session("SearchByHealthPlan"))` evaluates to 1 rather than to 0, and the code is doing just what we asked, but not at all what we want.

Figure 9.8

Examining the length.

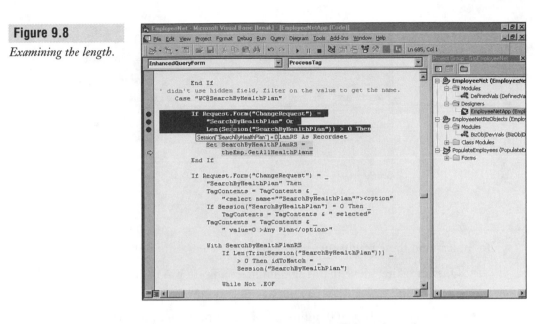

The fix is easy! Let's change the If statement to test if the value of Session("SearchByHealthPlan") is zero, rather than the length. If you stop and restart the query tracer and rerun the program, you'll find that there are no searches completed when you view the Search dialog box.

This wasn't why we used the SQL Server Profiler in the first place, but it did help us find a bug in our code!

 Note   In order to provide more realistic data for this search, I'll use the Populate Employee module I wrote to fill the database with 10,000 dummy Employee records. We'll consider this quick and dirty data-generating program in Chapter 10.

9

Having added 10,000 employees and fixed our code, let's look at a full query of the database. Restart the application, and leaving all the default choices (for example, Any Name or Any Office), choose Search Now. After a bit of a pause, the results are displayed, Records 1–10 of 10,303. Let's switch back to the SQL Server Profiler to see what we've learned, as shown in Figure 9.9.

The duration of a search is measured in milliseconds (1/1000 of a second). We want to focus our attention on the most problematic searches.

Figure 9.9

Examining the profile.

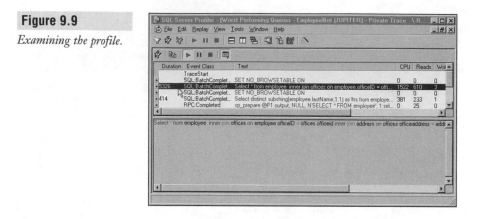

To understand these results, here are some quick rules of thumb:

- Queries taking more than 1,000 milliseconds are problems that must be solved.
- Queries taking less than 100 milliseconds are fine.
- Queries taking 100–500 milliseconds are suspect, and those taking 500–1,000 milliseconds are almost certainly problems.

These are not hard and fast rules but rather quick and dirty guidelines to help you get started.

The Select statement took over 5 seconds (5,326 milliseconds is 5.326 seconds)! That clearly is a problem, but to understand this problem in context we need to take a look at a number of smaller, simpler searches. Let's run some quick benchmark tests before we delve into how the tool might help.

For example, return to the search window and click on the Name drop-down. Uh oh! This searches for every one of the 10,303 employee names. This generates the search

```
Select employeeID, firstName, LastName from Employee order by LastName
```

which the profiler reports takes 1,083 milliseconds. Clearly this is too slow for a simple search of a single table, but it's not anything like the amount of time it took to run the more complicated search to find the resultset.

 **Note**

If you try this test, you'll find that your browser times out before the list box can be filled. Our method of examining each record before adding it to the drop-down simply does not scale to 10,000 entries.

Tools

These searches are taking too long because until now we have (properly!) ignored all issues about optimization of the database. Now that we have things working, however, and we have enough data in place to matter, it is time to at least begin the process of tuning the database.

Full database optimization is a topic well beyond the scope of this book. What I'll show you in the next few pages is how you get started. Please check the reading list in the appendix for resources that can help you beyond what is provided here.

There are steps, which I will discuss shortly, that I'd normally take before running the Index Tuning Wizard. Why not take your best shot at optimizing the database before asking for automated help? To clarify the power of the built-in help, however, I'll run the Index Tuning Wizard before taking any further steps.

Before using this wizard, however, we'll want to build up a file from the SQL Server Profiler. We must also edit the Profile characteristics to be useful to the Index Tuning Wizard.

Return to your Profiler and click the Edit Profile button, as shown in Figure 9.10.

Figure 9.10

Editing the profile.

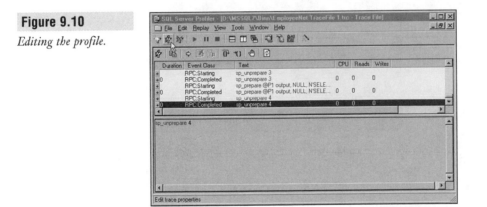

This opens the Trace Properties window. Click on the Trace Name drop-down and choose the trace you've been working with, as shown in Figure 9.11.

Navigate to the Events tab and open up the TSQL list in the left window, adding RPC:Completed, RPC:Start, SQL:BatchCompleted, and SQL:BatchStart if they are not already in the right window, as shown in Figure 9.12.

Save your changes and then stop and restart the trace. Now you are ready to create a Workload Profile.

Figure 9.11

Editing the properties.

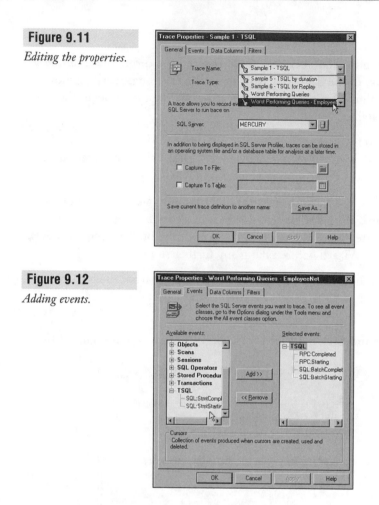

Figure 9.12

Adding events.

Building Up a Workload File

Return to EmployeeNet. Let's try to use every table in various ways. Click on various options, run a variety of searches (based on employee name, office, health plan, and so on), and then page through the results. Be sure to display individual records, click on various letters of the alphabet to narrow the search, and so forth.

Then, from within SQL Server Profiler, save the file. We'll need it in just a moment.

To get started, click on Tools/Index Tuning Wizard..., as shown in Figure 9.13.

The opening dialog box tells you the steps for tuning your indices (indexes), as shown in Figure 9.14.

Figure 9.13

We're off to see the wizard....

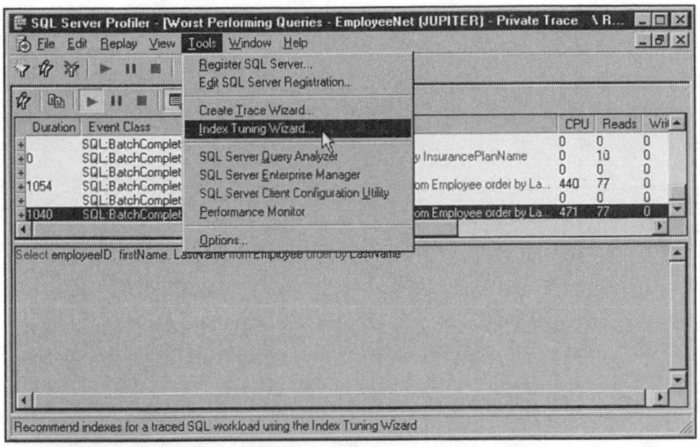

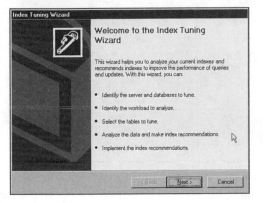

Figure 9.14

Follow the yellow brick road.

EXCURSION

Indexes

Any given table has a specific order in which the records are stored. For example, the Employee table might be stored in order of EmployeeID or date of hire. If we want to search on a particular field, say LastName, then SQL Server must find the matching record. If the table is sorted by EmployeeID, SQL Server must search through every record to find the one we want.

An index is a special table that sorts on a field you think you might search, for example, Last Name. Typically, such an index table would be much smaller than the full Employee table: All that would be in the index would be the last names (in alphabetic order) with record numbers pointing back into the Employee table. Now, when you ask to find *Liberty*, SQL Server is free to go to the Last Name index table, quickly (very quickly!) find the matching record, use the pointer back into the full Employee table, and retrieve the record that matches the name.

Indexes can greatly increase the performance of searching. However, every time you add a record to the table, you must now also add a row to the index, and every time you delete a record from the main table, you must delete the entry in the index. Thus, even though indexes greatly speed up searching, they can slow down insertions and deletions.

There are two check boxes on the next dialog box, as shown in Figure 9.15. The Keep All Existing Indexes check box ensures that the optimizer does not drop any indices that you've painstakingly built but reduces the efficiency of the automated process. We'll turn it off.

Figure 9.15

Perform thorough analysis.

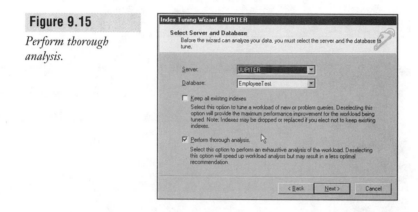

The Perform Thorough Analysis check box turns on a more robust analysis, which takes longer but is more effective. We'll select this option. After you've made these changes and selected the appropriate server and database, click Next.

The final dialog box asks if you have already saved a workload file. We did, just before we began this exercise, so we'll choose the first option, as shown in Figure 9.16.

Figure 9.16

Using the workload file.

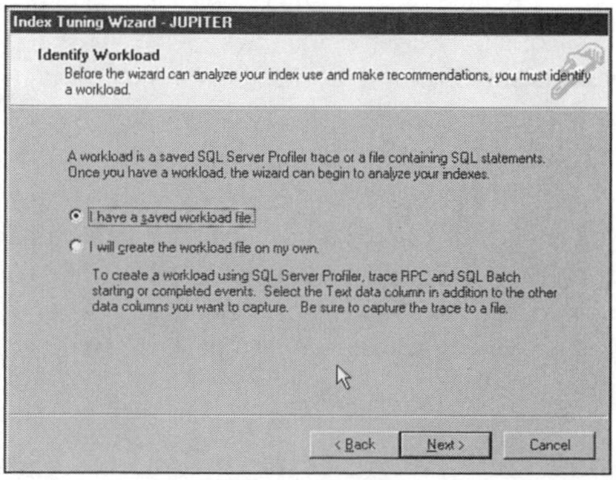

Click Next and fill in the name of the file you saved. You can navigate to it by clicking on the button to the right of the fill-in field, as shown in Figure 9.17.

Figure 9.17

Filling in the name.

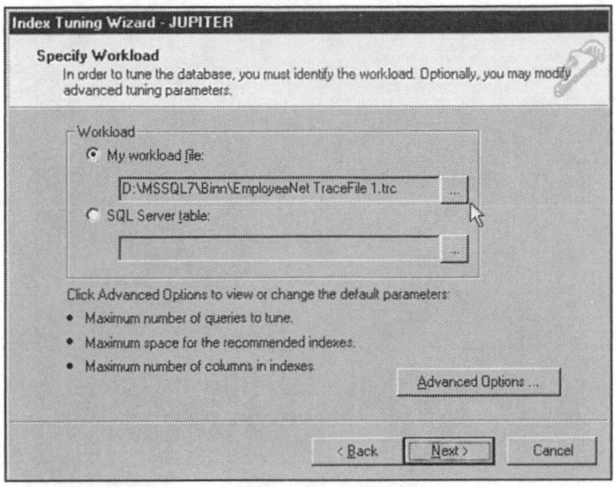

Click Next and ensure that all the tables from the EmployeeNet application are included except for dbo.sysTableComments, which is used for the SQueaL application that we haven't reviewed yet. Your dialog box should look similar to that in Figure 9.18.

Figure 9.18

Selecting tables.

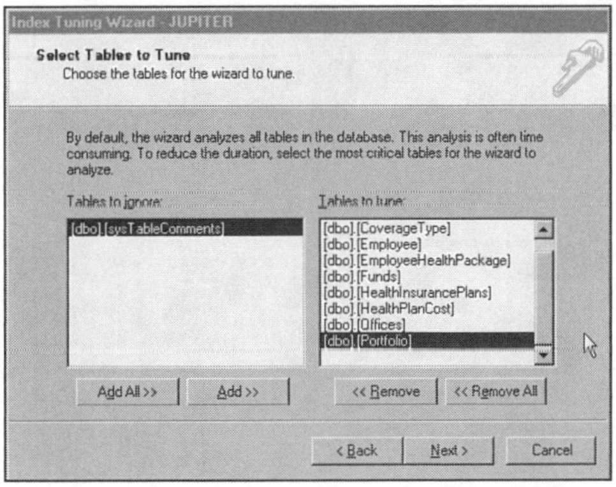

You will see a series of dialog boxes like the one shown in Figure 9.19 while the Index Tuning Wizard works. This process can take a few moments.

When the wizard completes its work, you'll be presented with a dialog box with recommendations, as shown in Figure 9.20.

Click Next. The wizard will offer to execute a script that will implement the recommended changes! Click on Apply Changes, and choose Execute Recommendations Now, as shown in Figure 9.21.

Figure 9.19

Pay no attention to the man behind the curtain.

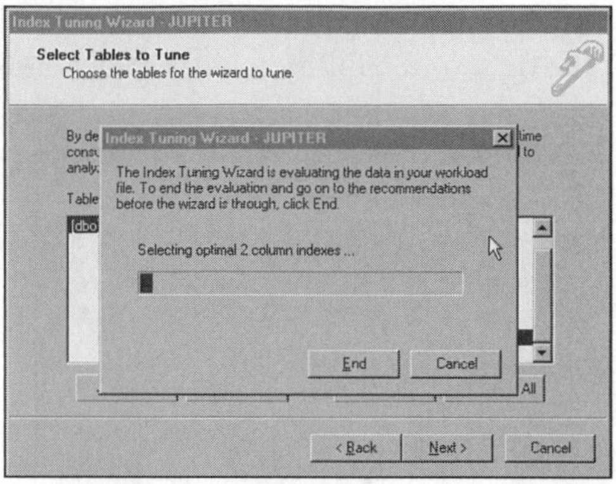

Figure 9.20

Index recommendations.

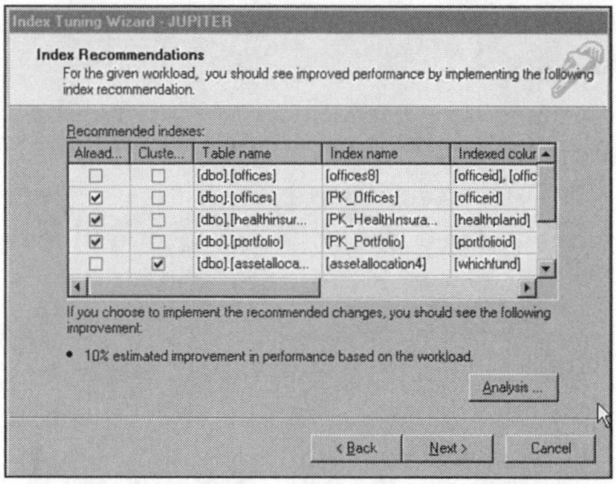

Figure 9.21

Applying the changes.

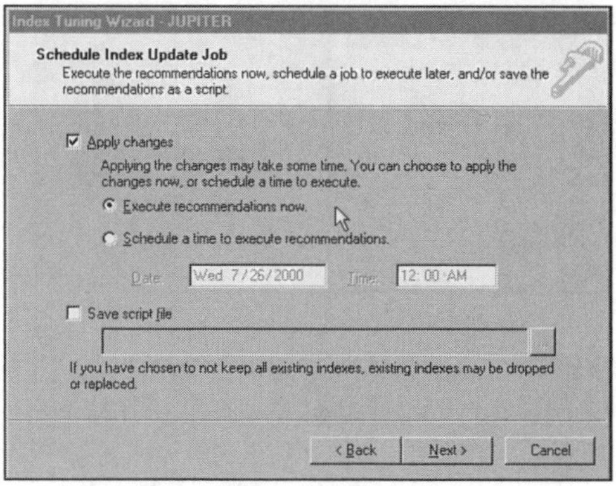

Click Next. The wizard builds the indexes it has recommended. You should find that your database is noticeably more responsive.

Standard Tuning Mechanisms

As I suggested earlier, you can take a number of steps even before subjecting your system to analysis. Alternatively, you can do the analysis first and then supplement the work of the wizard by following these guidelines. Again, what I'm about to suggest is not exhaustive, but it is a good start.

Set Priorities

The first question to ask yourself when designing and then again when optimizing your database is: Do you care more about fast additions to the database or fast searches?

If, as is the case here, additions are infrequent and often made only by a limited number of people, whereas searches are more frequent, then you may want to optimize for quick searches. On the other hand, if you have a system in which data are frequently added but seldom searched, then you may make very different decisions.

Indexes speed up searches but they slow down inserts. That general rule is too simple to be completely accurate, but it is a good starting point. In the Employee database, we want a lot of indexes. We do a lot of searching and we don't mind the cost of slightly slower inserts.

Nulls

There is a temptation to allow many columns to accept null values. Why not? You never know when it will be inconvenient to have to supply a value. We talked earlier about not doing this because you want the database to ensure the integrity and correctness of your data. There is also an efficiency reason to disallow nulls. Null columns slow down searches. This, of course, must be traded off against columns with very infrequent data, in which case the presence of null values may save a lot of space (and therefore time searching) in the database.

Clustered Indexes

SQL Server loves clustered indexes. In fact, unless there is a very good reason, you should make sure *every* table has a clustered index. The problem is, however, that each table can have at most *one* such clustered index and so you must choose wisely.

I said previously that every table is in a specific order and that you create indexes to overcome this limitation. Each index is a separate table, ordered by the column you want to optimize. When you create a clustered index, you tell SQL Server how to order the original table itself. Thus, if you create a clustered index in Employee on LastName, then the table is *physically* organized in last name order. This is wonderfully fast and avoids the creation of a second index table, but of course every table can have at most one clustered index (after all, it can't physically be ordered on more than one column at the same time!).

Note that a clustered index, or any index, *can* be on a combination of columns. In other words, you can index on last name and first name, as long as that is a single index. Thus, you can sort within last name (Abby Jones before Bruce Jones) but not separately on last name and first name.

The first and most important rule is not to create a clustered index on any monotonically increasing key such as an identity column. Doing so saves you little time in searching and creates tremendous stress on the system when adding records. If you cluster on a sequencing value such as the identity column, you force every new record to the end of the table, which can create a "hot spot" of contention in the database. (Don't say hot spot around my dog. He is a Golden Retriever, and hot spots are the bane of a Golden's life. They are also the bane of the life of a Database Administrator (DBA), although we rarely shave the DBA's hair off when we find one. On second thought, however, it may not be a bad idea.)

Hot spot—An area of the disk that is constantly in demand.

Contention—When two or more programs are trying to access the same area of the disk or of memory, they "contend" for that area and one will have to wait, slowing down performance.

Golden Retriever—Four legs in service to a stomach.

For each table, decide which column will be searched most frequently and make that column a clustered index. Watch your searches fly.

Clustered indexes are especially powerful when you use queries with the Group-By, Order-By, or Where clause. Because that includes most of your queries, this insight may be of only limited value, but typically one query stands out as especially important, and we target the cluster to satisfying that all-important query.

Short Keys

All other things being equal (and when are they ever?), indexes on short keys will zip along faster than indexes on longer keys.

Note   Shorter keys are faster because more indexes will fit on each "page" in the B-tree that SQL Server will build. Thus, you'll require fewer reads from disk. If this is Greek to you, don't worry—just keep your keys short and let SQL Server sweat the details.

Selectivity

An index in which every key value is unique has perfect selectivity, measured as 1. An index in which every key value is exactly the same has a selectivity of 0 and is totally useless. You measure the selectivity by dividing the number of distinct keys in an index by the number of rows in the index. The closer to 1 the more efficient the index and the faster it will run.

Be Careful How You Join

Queries that join two tables may do so in either of two ways (table a joins b or table b joins a). With 4 tables, there are 24 possible permutations (that is 4! or 4 factorial). With 16 tables there are nearly 21 trillion such permutations. SQL Server must create a plan for your query. If you join lots of tables, building that plan will be a difficult exercise. (If you start exploring permutations one at a time, and you explore one permutation every second, you'll finish a little over 663,000 years later.)

The current wisdom is that you ought to limit yourself to joining no more than 4–6 tables, although Microsoft does say it can handle up to 16. I can only assume it is not using the brute force method.

You can tell the Query Optimizer how you'd like the tables to be joined, if you think you know more than it does. However, such arcane behavior is well beyond the scope of this book and is left as an exercise for the confident reader.

Time Is Money

When building a Web application, you cannot ignore database optimization, but frankly the database is usually not the problem. When you consider how long a round-trip takes from the client machine to your server and thence to the database and back, the couple hundred milliseconds for a search are almost certainly insignificant. That said, adding indexes and optimizing queries (especially using stored procedures) can have a profound impact on the performance of your system.

9

Next Steps

In Chapter 10, we look at how we get data into the system, building the forms and validating the data for user input. Until now, all the data has been known to be valid, but once users start entering their own data, watch out!

Data Entry

Until now, we worked under the assumption that there are data in the database for us to search. How is that information added? In this chapter, we explore both the data entry pages used by the Human Resources department and the tiny applet I created to populate the database for this book.

Applet—A tiny application. Java applets are embedded in HTML and run in your browser. I mean nothing so fancy here; an applet here is just a small application.

Data Entry Forms

In a sense, there is nothing new in data entry that you haven't seen before. After all, a data entry form is not all that different from a search form. The key difference is this: During data entry we must ensure that the information provided is valid. In other words, we must do data validity checking.

It is here that the middle tier—the business tier—has more to say. In searching, the business object (Employee) was really acting more as a data-level object—mediating between the user interface and the database. Now that we are considering data entry, however, the rules of the business must be enforced to ensure that, if an employee is added, all of the appropriate data are gathered.

Where to Check the Input

Even though the business object must be responsible for ensuring the integrity of the data, you must keep in mind that the business object is running on the server. If you check each field only on the server, you require a round-trip from client to server for the check and then back to the client for the correction. That can slow down your site and annoy your users.

The answer is to employ client-side scripting to do the first-round level of error-checking. The client-side script can ensure that all required fields have a value, that phone numbers are ten digits, and so forth. After the fundamentals have been ensured, you can do a final round of business-specific checking on the server before adding the data to the database.

Therefore, we'll set out to accomplish the following tasks:

1. Draw the form and wait for user input.
2. Validate the format and basic content of the data using client-side scripting.
3. Validate the business requirements have been met by presenting the results to the business object.
4. Add the data to the database.

Creating the Form

The form we will create is a fairly straightforward and common HTML form. This time we won't bother with Just-In-Time controls because we have few drop-downs and each has little information in it. Figure 10.1 illustrates the form I have in mind.

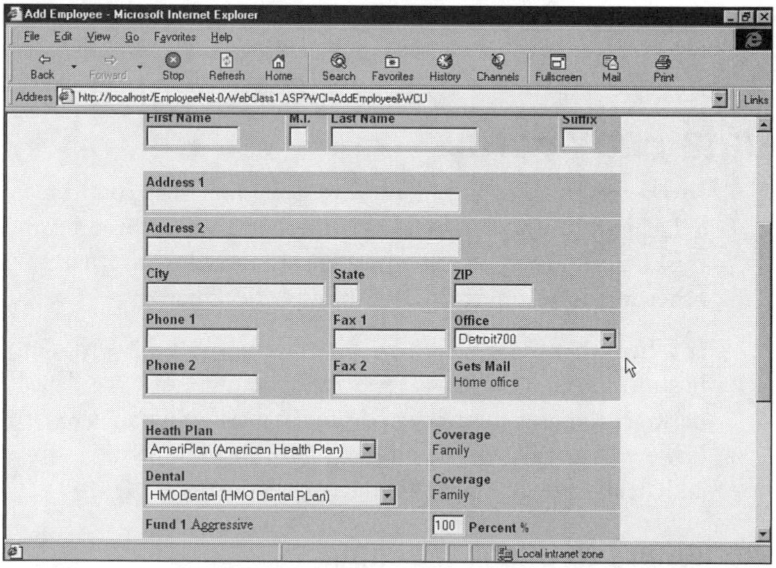

Figure 10.1

Data entry form excerpt.

Note

Because of the limitations of the screen capture software, you can see only a fraction of the screen in this picture. On a 1024 × 768 monitor, virtually the entire form is visible at one time.

My editor points out that current UI design guidelines generally recommend designing for 800 × 600, but the EmployeeNet target audience will all have higher-resolution monitors, so we decided to take a great leap forward. Besides, 800 × 600 hurts my eyes.

Creating this form is not terribly difficult. Figure 10.2 shows the form opened in DreamWeaver. For the purpose of this demonstration, much of the explanatory text on the form has been replaced by Greeking (Lorem ipsum dolor sit amet, consectetuer ad ipiscing elit…).

Figure 10.2

Data entry form in DreamWeaver.

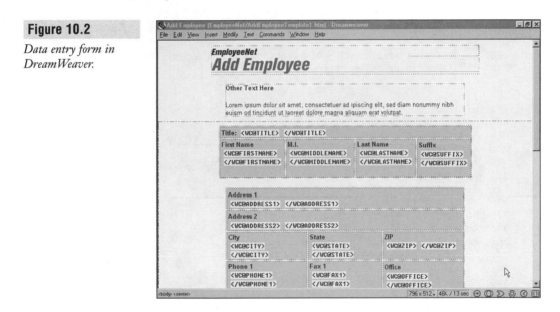

The important thing to note, however, is that none of the data entry fields is in the form, even though this text and the prompts are provided as part of the form. Instead, we find tags, which we'll substitute for in the ProcessTags method. Listing 10.1 shows the HTML associated with this page.

Listing 10.1

```
0:  <HTML>
1:  <HEAD>
2:
3:  <SCRIPT LANGUAGE="JavaScript" SRC="AddEmpCheck.js"></SCRIPT>
4:  <script language="JavaScript">
5:
6:  function SetTheFocus(where)
```

continues

10

Listing 10.1—continued

```
 7:  {
 8:      // do we have this element at all?
 9:      if ( document.forms[0].elements[where] )
10:      {
11:          // is an array
12:          if ( document.forms[0].elements[where].length )
13:              document.forms[0].elements[where][0].focus();
14:          else                      // not an array
15:              document.forms[0].elements[where].focus();
16:      }
17:
18:  }
19:
20:  function CheckVals()
21:  {
22:      return ( validateAddEmployee(document.frmAddEmp) &&
23:      fixupFields(document.frmAddEmp) )
24:
25:  }
26:  </script>
27:
28:
29:  <title>Add Employee</title>
30:  <meta http-equiv="Content-Type" content="text/html;
31:  charset=iso-8859-1">
32:  </head>
33:
34:  <body bgcolor="#ffffff">
35:  <center>
36:    <table width="560" border="0" cellspacing="0"
37:      cellpadding="0">
38:      <tr>
39:        <td width="413">
40:          <A href="WebClass1.ASP?WCI=Login&amp;WCU" >
41:          <IMG alt=EmployeeNet border=0 height=23
42:          src="images/p2_logo.gif"
43:          width=413></a></td>
44:        <td align="right"> </td>
45:      </tr>
46:      <tr>
47:        <td colspan="2"><IMG alt="Add Employee"
48:          border=0 height=37
49:          src="images/addemployee_t.gif" width=560 ></td>
50:      </tr>
51:    </table>
52:    <br>
53:    <table width="500" border="0" cellspacing="0"
54:      cellpadding="0">
55:      <tr>
56:        <td>
57:          <p><font face="Arial, Helvetica, sans-serif"><b>
```

```
58:              <font size="2">Other Text
59:              Here </font></b></font></p>
60:             <p><font face="Arial, Helvetica, sans-serif" size="2">
61:              Lorem ipsum dolor sit amet, consectetuer ad ipiscing
62:              elit, sed diam nonummy nibh euism od tincidunt ut
63:              laoreet dolore magna aliquam erat volutpat.</font></p>
64:           </td>
65:         </tr>
66:       </table>
67:
68:       <form method="post" action="" onSubmit="return CheckVals()"
69:         name="frmAddEmp" >
70:        <table width="500" border="0" cellspacing="1"
71:              cellpadding="3">
72:         <tr valign="top" bgcolor="#cccccc">
73:          <td colspan="4"><b><font face="Arial, Helvetica,
74:               sans-serif" size="2">Title:</font>
75:             </b><WC@TITLE></WC@TITLE>   </td>
76:         </tr>
77:         <tr valign="top" bgcolor="#cccccc">
78:          <td width="30%"><font face="Arial, Helvetica,
79:               sans-serif" size="2"><b>First
80:            Name</b><br><WC@FIRSTNAME></WC@FIRSTNAME>
81:
82:            </font></td>
83:          <td><font face="Arial, Helvetica, sans-serif" size="2">
84:               <b>M.I.</b><br><WC@MIDDLENAME></WC@MIDDLENAME>
85:
86:            </font></td>
87:          <td><font face="Arial, Helvetica, sans-serif" size="2">
88:               <b>Last Name</b><br><WC@LASTNAME></WC@LASTNAME>
89:
90:            </font></td>
91:          <td><font face="Arial, Helvetica, sans-serif" size="2">
92:               <b>Suffix</b></font><br><WC@SUFFIX></WC@SUFFIX>
93:
94:           </td>
95:         </tr>
96:       </table>
97:       <br>
98:       <table width="500" border="0" cellspacing="1"
99:               cellpadding="3">
100:         <tr valign="top" bgcolor="#cccccc">
101:          <td colspan="3"><font face="Arial, Helvetica,
102:            sans-serif" size="2"><b>Address
103:            1</b></font><br><WC@ADDRESS1></WC@ADDRESS1>
104:
105:           </td>
106:         </tr>
107:         <tr valign="top" bgcolor="#cccccc">
108:          <td colspan="3"><font face="Arial, Helvetica,
109:            sans-serif" size="2"><b>Address
```

continues

10

Listing 10.1—continued

```
110:          2</b></font><br><WC@ADDRESS2></WC@ADDRESS2>
111:
112:          </td>
113:      </tr>
114:      <tr valign="top" bgcolor="#cccccc">
115:       <td><b><font face="Arial, Helvetica, sans-serif"
116:         size="2">City<br><WC@CITY></WC@CITY>
117:
118:          </font></b></td>
119:       <td><b><font face="Arial, Helvetica, sans-serif"
120:         size="2">State<br><WC@STATE></WC@STATE>
121:
122:          </font></b></td>
123:       <td><b><font face="Arial, Helvetica, sans-serif"
124:         size="2">ZIP<br><WC@ZIP></WC@ZIP>  </font></b></td>
125:      </tr>
126:      <tr valign="top" bgcolor="#cccccc">
127:       <td><b><font face="Arial, Helvetica, sans-serif"
128:         size="2">Phone 1<br><WC@PHONE1></WC@PHONE1>
129:
130:          </font></b></td>
131:       <td><b><font face="Arial, Helvetica, sans-serif"
132:         size="2">Fax 1<br><WC@FAX1></WC@FAX1>
133:
134:          </font></b></td>
135:       <td><font face="Arial, Helvetica, sans-serif"
136:         size="2"><b>Office</b></font><br>
137:            <WC@OFFICE></WC@OFFICE>
138:
139:       </td>
140:      </tr>
141:      <tr valign="top" bgcolor="#cccccc">
142:       <td>
143:         <p><b><font face="Arial, Helvetica, sans-serif"
144:            size="2">Phone 2</font></b><br>
145:          <b><font face="Arial, Helvetica, sans-serif"
146:            size="2"><WC@PHONE2></WC@PHONE2>
147:
148:          </font></b> </p>
149:       </td>
150:       <td><b><font face="Arial, Helvetica, sans-serif"
151:         size="2">Fax 2<br><WC@FAX2></WC@FAX2>
152:
153:          </font></b></td>
154:       <td><font face="Arial, Helvetica, sans-serif"
155:         size="2"><b>Gets Mail</b><br>
156:         Home office</font></td>
157:      </tr>
158:      </table>
159:      <br>
160:      <table width="500" border="0" cellspacing="1"
```

```
161:          cellpadding="3">
162:      <tr bgcolor="#cccccc">
163:       <td width="60%"><b><font face="Arial, Helvetica,
164:        sans-serif" size="2">Heath
165:        Plan<br><WC@HEALTHPLAN></WC@HEALTHPLAN>
166:
167:        </font></b></td>
168:       <td><b><font face="Arial, Helvetica, sans-serif"
169:        size="2">Coverage<br>
170:        </font></b><font face="Arial, Helvetica, sans-serif"
171:           size="2">
172:           <WC@HEALTHPLANCOVERAGE></WC@HEALTHPLANCOVERAGE>
173:
174:        </font></td>
175:      </tr>
176:      <tr bgcolor="#cccccc">
177:       <td width="60%"><b><font face="Arial, Helvetica,
178:        sans-serif" size="2">Dental</font></b>
179:        <br><WC@DENTALPLAN></WC@DENTALPLAN>
180:
181:        </td>
182:       <td><b><font face="Arial, Helvetica,
183:           sans-serif" size="2">Coverage<br>
184:        </font></b><font face="Arial, Helvetica,
185:           sans-serif" size="2">
186:           <WC@DENTALPLANCOVERAGE></WC@DENTALPLANCOVERAGE>
187:
188:        </font></td>
189:      </tr>
190:      <tr bgcolor="#cccccc">
191:       <td width="60%"><b><font face="Arial, Helvetica,
192:        sans-serif" size="2">Fund
193:        1 </font></b><WC@FUND1></WC@FUND1></td>
194:       <td><b><font face="Arial, Helvetica, sans-serif"
195:        size="2"><WC@FUND1PCT></WC@FUND1PCT>
196:        Percent
197:        %</font></b></td>
198:      </tr>
199:      <tr bgcolor="#cccccc">
200:       <td width="60%"><b><font face="Arial, Helvetica,
201:        sans-serif" size="2">Fund
202:        2 </font></b><WC@FUND2></WC@FUND2></td>
203:       <td><b><font face="Arial, Helvetica, sans-serif"
204:        size="2"><WC@FUND2PCT></WC@FUND2PCT>
205:        Percent
206:        %</font></b></td>
207:      </tr>
208:      <tr bgcolor="#cccccc">
209:       <td width="60%"><b><font face="Arial, Helvetica,
210:        sans-serif" size="2">Fund
211:        3 </font></b><WC@FUND3></WC@FUND3></td>
212:       <td><b><font face="Arial, Helvetica, sans-serif"
```

continues

Listing 10.1—continued

```
213:          size="2"><WC@FUND3PCT></WC@FUND3PCT>
214:          Percent
215:          %</font></b></td>
216:        </tr>
217:      </table>
218:      <p>
219:        <input type="image" src="images/add_btn.gif" width="97"
220:          height="23" border="0" alt="Add! ">
221:              
222:          <a href="javascript:document.frmAddEmp.reset()">
223:          <img alt=Clear border=0 height=23
224:          src="images/clearform.gif" width=97></a></p>
225:
226:    </form>
227:
228:    <br>
229:    <table width="500" border="0" cellspacing="0"
230:      cellpadding="0">
231:      <tr>
232:        <td>
233:        <p><font face="Arial, Helvetica, sans-serif">
234:        <b><font size="2">Other Prompts
235:          Here </font></b></font></p>
236:        <p><font face="Arial, Helvetica, sans-serif"
237:          size="2">Lorem ipsum dolor
238:          sit amet, consectetuer ad ipiscing elit, sed diam
239:          nonummy nibh euism od tincidunt ut laoreet dolore
240:          magna aliquam erat volutpat. Lorem ipsum dolor sit
241:          amet, consectetuer ad ipiscing elit, sed diam
242:          nonummy nibh euism od tincidunt ut laoreet dolore
243:          magna aliquam erat volutpat.</font>
244:        </p>
245:        </td>
246:      </tr>
247:    </table>
248:    <p> </p>
249:  </center>
250:
251:  </body>
252:  </html>
```

Line 3 is new and interesting. It declares a script in the JavaScript language and then sets SRC equal to a file name (AddEmpCheck.js). This is an include file; it causes the Java interpreter to read the file AddEmpCheck.js just as if we had typed it in here. (AddEmpCheck.js is covered in detail later in the book.)

This code and the code in lines 4–26 are used for client-side data validation. We consider this code in Chapter 11, so we'll skip over it for now.

On lines 29–32, we finish out the heading for this page, and then on line 34 we begin the body of the page. On line 40, we see an anchor tag to the opening page (Login) tied to an image. The image is in the file p2_logo.gif in the images subdirectory under the virtual directory in which EmployeeNet runs, as shown in Figure 10.3.

Figure 10.3

EmployeeNet

The logo.

We have effectively created a hot image on which the user can click to return to the opening page. On line 47, we add another image, addemployee_t.gif, as shown in Figure 10.4.

Figure 10.4

Add Employee

Clickable image.

These images work together as a single image, as illustrated in Figure 10.1.

Lines 60–63 fill in the Greeking discussed earlier, and line 68 creates the Post method for the form. Note that this Post method has associated with it an event: OnSubmit. This event will be called when the form is submitted, and it will return the value returned from CheckVals(). CheckVals is the JavaScript routine we'll use in Chapter 11 to provide client-side validation of the data. If CheckVals succeeds (returns true), then the form is submitted. Finally, on line 69, we name the form: "frmAddEmp".

Starting on line 70 and running through line 217, we fill a table with the prompts and WebClass tags we'll use in the ProcessTags method for this page.

At the bottom of the page, on lines 219–224, we create the Reset button, which also has an event associated with it, so that this button will invoke the Reset method. What we're doing here is simply connecting this *image* of a button to the same Reset method that would be called if we created a Reset button.

The Respond Method

When this page is invoked, the Respond method is called first, as you saw previously. The Respond method is shown in Listing 10.2.

Listing 10.2

```
0:  Private Sub AddEmployee_Respond()
1:      Dim theEmp              As New employee
```

continues

Listing 10.2—continued

```
2:
3:        If Request.Form.Count < 1 Then
4:            Set HealthPlanRS = theEmp.GetAllHealthPlans
5:            Set officesRS = theEmp.GetOffices()
6:            Set FundRS = theEmp.GetFunds
7:            AddEmployee.WriteTemplate
8:        Else
9:            Dim item
10:           Dim i                    As Integer
11:           Dim args()               As String
12:           ReDim args(1, Request.Form.Count - 1)
13:
14:           For Each item In Request.Form
15:               args(0, i) = item
16:               args(1, i) = Request.Form(item)
17:               i = i + 1
18:           Next
19:
20:           Session.Contents("EmployeeID") = _
21:           theEmp.AddEmployee(args)
22:
23:           If Session.Contents("EmployeeID") > 0 Then
24:               Set NextItem = ResultOutput
25:           Else
26:               AddEmployee.WriteTemplate
27:           End If
28:
29:       End If
30:
31:   End Sub
```

The first time through the form has not been drawn yet, so the count of elements in the form is zero and the If statement on line 3 succeeds.

The GetAllHealthPlans method is invoked on line 4. The code for this is shown in Listing 10.3.

Listing 10.3

```
0:   Public Function GetAllHealthPlans() As Recordset
1:
2:       Dim sqlCmd                   As String
3:       sqlCmd = _
4:           "Select * from HealthInsurancePlans "
5:       sqlCmd = sqlCmd & _
6:           "order by InsurancePlanName"
7:       Set GetAllHealthPlans = GetDCRS(sqlCmd)
8:
9:   End Function
```

This method does nothing more than set up a SQL statement (`Select * from HealthInsurancePlans order by InsurancePlans`), which returns every entry in the HealthInsurancePlans table in alphabetical order. The last line passes this SQL command to GetDCRS, which creates a disconnected recordset.

Returning to Listing 10.2, line 5 calls GetOffices. GetOffices is almost the same as GetAllHealthPlans, except that the SQL command is

`"Select distinct * from offices order by OfficeName"`

Finally, line 6 of Listing 10.2 calls GetFunds, which is just like the previous two methods, except that the SQL command is `"Select * from funds order by FundName"`. On line 7, we write out the template, using the HTML shown in Listing 10.1. This invokes the ProcessTag method, shown in Listing 10.4.

Listing 10.4

```
0:   Private Sub AddEmployee_ProcessTag(ByVal TagName As String, _
1:       TagContents As String, SendTags As Boolean)
2:       Dim theEmp                As New employee
3:       Select Case TagName
4:
5:           Case "WC@FirstName"
6:               TagContents = TagContents & _
7:                   "<input name=""FirstName"" size=""12"" onFocus=""
➥promptEntry(strFirstName)""  onChange=""checkString(this,strFirstName)"""
8:               If Len(Trim(Session("FirstName"))) > 0 Then TagContents = _
9:                   TagContents & _
10:                  "value=""" & Trim(Session("FirstName")) & """"
11:              TagContents = TagContents & ">"
12:
13:          Case "WC@MiddleName"
14:              TagContents = TagContents & _
15:                  "<input name=""MiddleName"" size=""1"" onFocus=""
➥promptEntry(strMiddleName)"" onBlur=""blankEntry()"" onChange=""
➥checkString(this,strMiddleName)"""
16:              If Len(Trim(Session("MiddleName"))) > 0 Then TagContents = _
17:                  TagContents & _
18:                  "value=""" & Trim(Session("MiddleName")) & """"
19:              TagContents = TagContents & ">"
20:
21:          Case "WC@LastName"
22:              TagContents = TagContents & _
23:                  "<input name=""LastName"" size=""20"" onFocus=""
➥promptEntry(strLastName)"" onBlur=""blankEntry()""  onChange=""
➥checkString(this,strLastName)"""
24:              If Len(Trim(Session("LastName"))) > 0 Then TagContents = _
25:                  TagContents & _
26:                  "value=""" & Trim(Session("LastName")) & """"
27:              TagContents = TagContents & ">"
```

10

continues

Listing 10.4—continued

```
28:
29:        Case "WC@Title"
30:            TagContents = TagContents & _
31:                "<input name=""Title"" size=""3"" onFocus=""
➥promptEntry(strTitle)"" onBlur=""blankEntry()"" "
32:            If Len(Trim(Session("Title"))) > 0 Then TagContents = _
33:                TagContents & _
34:                "value=""" & Trim(Session("Title")) & """"
35:            TagContents = TagContents & ">"
36:
37:        Case "WC@Suffix"
38:            TagContents = TagContents & _
39:                "<input name=""Suffix"" size=""3"" onFocus=""
➥promptEntry(strSuffix)"" onBlur=""blankEntry()"" "
40:            If Len(Trim(Session("Suffix"))) > 0 Then TagContents = _
41:                TagContents & _
42:                "value=""" & Trim(Session("Suffix")) & """"
43:            TagContents = TagContents & ">"
44:
45:        Case "WC@Address1"
46:            TagContents = TagContents & _
47:                "<input name=""Address1"" size=""45"" onFocus=""
➥promptEntry(strAddress1)"" onBlur=""blankEntry()"" onChange=""
➥checkString(this,strAddress1)"""
48:            If Len(Trim(Session("Address1"))) > 0 Then TagContents = _
49:                TagContents & _
50:                "value=""" & Trim(Session("Address1")) & """"
51:            TagContents = TagContents & ">"
52:
53:        Case "WC@Address2"
54:            TagContents = TagContents & _
55:                "<input name=""Address2"" size=""45"" onFocus=""
➥promptEntry(strAddress2)"" onBlur=""blankEntry()"" "
56:            If Len(Trim(Session("Address2"))) > 0 Then TagContents = _
57:                TagContents & _
58:                "value=""" & Trim(Session("Address2")) & """"
59:            TagContents = TagContents & ">"
60:
61:        Case "WC@City"
62:            TagContents = TagContents & _
63:                "<input name=""City"" size=""25"" onFocus=""
➥promptEntry(strCity)"" onBlur=""blankEntry()"" onChange=""
➥checkString(this,strCity)"""""
64:            If Len(Trim(Session("City"))) > 0 Then TagContents = _
65:                TagContents & _
66:                "value=""" & Trim(Session("City")) & """"
67:            TagContents = TagContents & ">"
68:
69:        Case "WC@State"
70:            TagContents = TagContents & _
```

```
71:                     "<input name="""State"" size=""2"" onFocus=""
➥promptEntry(strState)"" onBlur=""blankEntry()"" onChange=""
➥checkString(this,strState)"""""
72:               If Len(Trim(Session("State"))) > 0 Then TagContents = _
73:                    TagContents & _
74:                    "value=""" & Trim(Session("State")) & """"
75:               TagContents = TagContents & ">"
76:
77:          Case "WC@Zip"
78:               TagContents = TagContents & _
79:                    "<input name=""ZipCode"" size=""10"" onFocus=""
➥promptEntry(strZip)"" onBlur=""blankEntry()"" onChange=""
➥checkZIPCode(this,false)"""
80:               If Len(Trim(Session("ZipCode"))) > 0 Then TagContents = _
81:                    TagContents & _
82:                    "value=""" & Trim(Session("ZipCode")) & """"
83:               TagContents = TagContents & ">"
84:
85:          Case "WC@Phone1"
86:               TagContents = TagContents & _
87:                    "<input name=""Phone1"" size=""15"" onFocus=""
➥promptEntry(strPhone)"" onBlur=""blankEntry()"" onChange=""
➥checkUSPhone(this,false)"""
88:               If Len(Trim(Session("Phone1"))) > 0 Then TagContents = _
89:                    TagContents & _
90:                    "value=""" & Trim(Session("Phone1")) & """"
91:               TagContents = TagContents & ">"
92:
93:          Case "WC@Phone2"
94:               TagContents = TagContents & _
95:                    "<input name=""Phone2"" size=""15"" onFocus=""
➥promptEntry(strPhone)"" onBlur=""blankEntry()"" onChange=""
➥checkUSPhone(this,true)"""
96:               If Len(Trim(Session("Phone2"))) > 0 Then TagContents = _
97:                    TagContents & _
98:                    "value=""" & Trim(Session("Phone2")) & """"
99:               TagContents = TagContents & ">"
100:
101:          Case "WC@Fax1"
102:               TagContents = TagContents & _
103:                    "<input name=""Fax1"" size=""15"" onFocus=""
➥promptEntry(strFax)"" onBlur=""blankEntry()"" onChange=""
➥checkUSPhone(this,true)"""
104:               If Len(Trim(Session("Fax1"))) > 0 Then TagContents = _
105:                    TagContents & _
106:                    "value=""" & Trim(Session("Fax1")) & """"
107:               TagContents = TagContents & ">"
108:
109:          Case "WC@Fax2"
110:               TagContents = TagContents & _
```

10

continues

Listing 10.4—continued

```
111:                    "<input name=""Fax2"" size=""15"" onFocus=""
➥promptEntry(strFax)"" onBlur=""blankEntry()"" onChange=""
➥checkUSPhone(this,true)"""
112:               If Len(Trim(Session("Fax2"))) > 0 Then TagContents = _
113:                    TagContents & _
114:                     "value=""" & Trim(Session("Fax2")) & """"
115:               TagContents = TagContents & ">"
116:
117:          Case "WC@OFFICE"
118:               TagContents = "<select name=""OfficeID""><option "
119:
120:               With officesRS
121:                    .MoveFirst
122:
123:                    While Not .EOF
124:
125:                         If Session("OfficeID") = Trim(CStr(sEmpty & _
126:                             .Fields("officeName"))) Then
127:                              TagContents = TagContents & _
128:                                  "<option selected "
129:                         Else
130:                              TagContents = TagContents & "<option "
131:                         End If
132:
133:                         TagContents = TagContents & " Value = " & _
134:                             .Fields("OfficeID") & ">"
135:                         TagContents = TagContents & CStr(sEmpty & _
136:                             .Fields("officeName"))
137:                         TagContents = TagContents & "</option>"
138:                         .MoveNext
139:                    Wend
140:
141:          End With
142:
143:          TagContents = TagContents & "</select>"
144:
145:          Case "WC@GetsMail"
146:               TagContents = TagContents & "Home Office"
147:
148:          Case "WC@HealthPlan"
149:               TagContents = "<select name=""HealthPlan""><option "
150:
151:               With HealthPlanRS
152:                    .MoveFirst
153:
154:                    While Not .EOF
155:
156:                         If .Fields("TypeOfInsurance") = 1 Then
157:
158:                              If Session("HealthPlan") = _
159:                                  .Fields("HealthPlanID") Then
```

```
160:                                    TagContents = TagContents & _
161:                                        "<option selected "
162:                                Else
163:                                    TagContents = TagContents & "<option "
164:                                End If
165:
166:                                TagContents = TagContents & " Value = " & _
167:                                    .Fields("HealthPlanID") & ">"
168:                                TagContents = TagContents & CStr(sEmpty & _
169:                                    .Fields("InsurancePlanName")) & " ("
170:                                TagContents = TagContents & CStr(sEmpty & _
171:                                    .Fields("InsCoName")) & ") "
172:                                TagContents = TagContents & "</option>"
173:                            End If
174:
175:                            .MoveNext
176:                        Wend
177:
178:                    End With
179:
180:                    TagContents = TagContents & "</select>"
181:
182:                Case "WC@HealthPlanCoverage"
183:                    TagContents = "Family"
184:
185:                Case "WC@DentalPlan"
186:                    TagContents = "<select name=""DentalPlan""><option "
187:
188:                    With HealthPlanRS
189:                        .MoveFirst
190:
191:                        While Not .EOF
192:
193:                            If .Fields("TypeOfInsurance") = 2 Then
194:
195:                                If Session("DentalPlan") = _
196:                                    .Fields("HealthPlanID") Then
197:                                    TagContents = TagContents & _
198:                                        "<option selected "
199:                                Else
200:                                    TagContents = TagContents & "<option "
201:                                End If
202:
203:                                TagContents = TagContents & " Value = " & _
204:                                    .Fields("HealthPlanID") & ">"
205:                                TagContents = TagContents & CStr(sEmpty & _
206:                                    .Fields("InsurancePlanName")) & " ("
207:                                TagContents = TagContents & CStr(sEmpty & _
208:                                    .Fields("InsCoName")) & ") "
209:                                TagContents = TagContents & "</option>"
210:                            End If
211:
```

continues

Listing 10.4—continued

```
212:                    .MoveNext
213:               Wend
214:
215:          End With
216:
217:          TagContents = TagContents & "</select>"
218:
219:      Case "WC@Fund1"
220:          FundRS.Filter = "FundID = 1"
221:          TagContents = FundRS!FundName
222:
223:      Case "WC@Fund2"
224:          FundRS.Filter = "FundID = 2"
225:          TagContents = FundRS!FundName
226:
227:      Case "WC@Fund3"
228:          FundRS.Filter = "FundID = 3"
229:          TagContents = FundRS!FundName
230:
231:      Case "WC@Fund1Pct"
232:          TagContents = TagContents & _
233:              "<input name=""Fund1Pct"" size=""3"" maxlength=""3"""
234:
235:          If Len(Trim(Session("Fund1Pct"))) > 0 Then
236:              TagContents = TagContents & _
237:                  "value=""" & Trim(Session("Fund1Pct")) & """"
238:          Else
239:              TagContents = TagContents & "value = ""100"""
240:          End If
241:
242:          TagContents = TagContents & ">"
243:
244:      Case "WC@Fund2Pct"
245:          TagContents = TagContents & _
246:              "<input name=""Fund2Pct"" size=""3"" maxlength=""3"""
247:
248:          If Len(Trim(Session("Fund2Pct"))) > 0 Then
249:              TagContents = TagContents & _
250:                  "value=""" & Trim(Session("Fund1Pct")) & """"
251:          Else
252:              TagContents = TagContents & "value = ""0"""
253:          End If
254:
255:          TagContents = TagContents & ">"
256:
257:      Case "WC@Fund3Pct"
258:          TagContents = TagContents & _
259:              "<input name=""Fund3Pct"" size=""3"" maxlength=""3"""
260:
261:          If Len(Trim(Session("Fund3Pct"))) > 0 Then
262:              TagContents = TagContents & _
```

```
263:                        "value=""" & Trim(Session("Fund1Pct")) & """"
264:                Else
265:                    TagContents = TagContents & "value = ""0"""
266:                End If
267:
268:                TagContents = TagContents & ">"
269:
270:            Case "WC@Fund4Pct"
271:                TagContents = TagContents & "<input name=""Fund4Pct"""
272:
273:                If Len(Trim(Session("Fund4Pct"))) > 0 Then
274:                    TagContents = TagContents & _
275:                        "value=""" & Trim(Session("Fund1Pct")) & """"
276:                Else
277:                    TagContents = TagContents & "value = ""0"""
278:                End If
279:
280:                TagContents = TagContents & ">"
281:
282:            Case "WC@DentalPlanCoverage"
283:                TagContents = "Family"
284:        End Select
285:
286:  End Sub
```

Line 3 begins the Select statement for each of the controls for the form. The first one encountered is the First Name fill-in. We set the size to 12, indicating a width great enough to hold 12 characters, and we set three events: OnFocus, OnBlur, and OnChange. OnFocus will be invoked when the user puts the cursor into this text box, and OnBlur will be invoked when the cursor is moved out of the text box (blur is unfocused, get it?). OnChange will be invoked whenever the value in the text box is changed, but only at the moment the text box is to lose focus.

Each of these calls a short JavaScript. We'll examine these scripts in Chapter 11.

On line 7, we assign to the value of the text box whatever we have in the associated session variable. That way, if we return to this page, the existing value will be shown.

Very similar logic is applied to the subsequent text boxes until we come to line 117. Our task here is to fill the Offices drop-down with all the offices currently on record in the system.

To do this, we iterate through the officeRS recordset. If the current value being added matches the value stashed away in the session variable OfficeID, then this value was selected, and we mark it accordingly.

On line 145, we have not yet implemented the option for the user to indicate whether the employee receives his mail at home or the office, so we hard wired "Home Office" in the text as an indication that we'll be offering this choice soon.

10

On lines 148–178, we fill the HealthPlan drop-down in much the same way that we filled Offices, and we do the same for the DentalPlan drop-down in the following lines.

Lines 219–229 are interesting. We have a recordset with all the funds that have two fields of interest: FundName and FundID. On line 220, we filter that recordset for only those records that have FundID set to 1. Then on line 221, we access the FundName of the first matching record. This will be the FundName for the record with FundID set to 1.

On line 224, we then refilter the same recordset for those records where Fund is set to 2. Note that this filtering is being accomplished on a *disconnected* recordset—we no longer have a connection to the database!

Adding the Employee

In Chapter 11, we consider the JavaScript that tests the validity of the data entry at client side. Let's assume for now that this testing was completed and that the user is able to submit a completed form, filled with the data about a new employee, as shown in Figure 10.5.

Figure 10.5

Clicking Add.

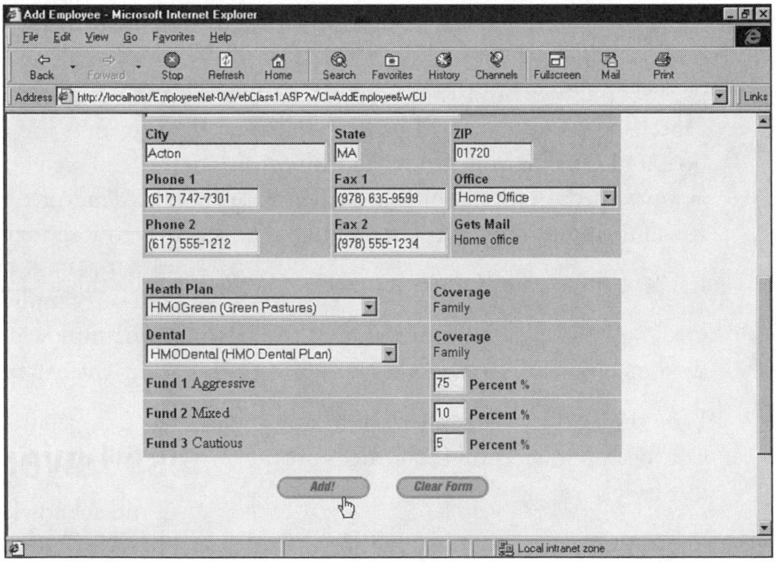

When this form is submitted, it is submitted back to itself. This means that the Respond method will be called, as shown in Listing 10.2, reproduced here for further analysis.

Listing 10.2—Revisited

```
0:   Private Sub AddEmployee_Respond()
1:       Dim theEmp                      As New employee
2:
3:       If Request.Form.Count < 1 Then
4:           Set HealthPlanRS = theEmp.GetAllHealthPlans
5:           Set officesRS = theEmp.GetOffices()
6:           Set FundRS = theEmp.GetFunds
7:           AddEmployee.WriteTemplate
8:       Else
9:           Dim item
10:          Dim i                       As Integer
11:          Dim args()                  As String
12:          ReDim args(1, Request.Form.Count - 1)
13:
14:          For Each item In Request.Form
15:              args(0, i) = item
16:              args(1, i) = Request.Form(item)
17:              i = i + 1
18:          Next
19:
20:          Session.Contents("EmployeeID") = _
21:          theEmp.AddEmployee(args)
22:
23:          If Session.Contents("EmployeeID") > 0 Then
24:              Set NextItem = ResultOutput
25:          Else
26:              AddEmployee.WriteTemplate
27:          End If
28:
29:      End If
30:
31:  End Sub
```

This time, the form having been submitted, the If statement fails, and we enter the Else clause beginning on line 9. We will now build our familiar array based on the elements in the form and pass that array to the AddEmployee method of the Employee business object.

DNA—Business and Data Access Layers

Before we analyze the AddEmployee method, let me acknowledge that I intermixed the business layer and the data access layer in this code and in much of the code we've seen so far.

In a larger, more complicated program, the business object would know about the semantics of the business rules but would know little or nothing about the database schema. Thus, business objects would interact with data access layer objects, passing disconnected recordsets or user-defined types from one to the other.

10

EXCURSION

Visual Basic

A user-defined type, or UDT, is a small structure defined in a VB program. It can be populated in one method and passed by reference (not making a copy) to another method in a different module.

The data access layer object would interact with the database, typically calling stored procedures. Because of the simplicity of the business object in this example, and because I want to simplify the interaction among objects to maintain focus on the creation and manipulation of WebClasses, I combined the data access layer and the business layer into a single object: Employee.

For smaller projects, I would argue that this is a reasonable choice. In fact, for many projects the three layers look like Figure 10.6.

Figure 10.6

n-Tier architecture.

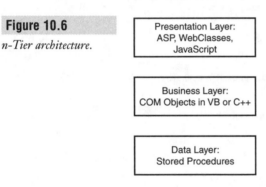

In this simplification of three-tier architecture, the business layer talks directly to stored procedures (and, oh my!, even uses SQL directly!). Even though this doesn't scale very well and requires that the business objects be rebuilt when the data schema are rebuilt, it is a more than reasonable price to pay in an otherwise simple application.

Only in more complex projects would I divide things along the lines shown in Figure 10.7.

In this more robust approach, the business object is decoupled from the database by a data access layer. The business object requests and receives recordsets. The recordsets the business object deals with are high-level abstractions of data, which may well be divided among various database tables at the database layer, but the business object is oblivious to this fact. The data access layer manages the mapping between business objects and data objects.

Figure 10.7

Further divided.

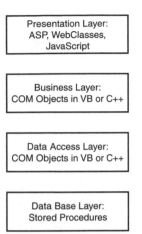

```
Presentation Layer:
ASP, WebClasses,
JavaScript
```

```
Business Layer:
COM Objects in VB or C++
```

```
Data Access Layer:
COM Objects in VB or C++
```

```
Data Base Layer:
Stored Procedures
```

As Listing 10.5 indicates, I asked the Employee object to encapsulate all the business logic *and* all the data access logic because, with all that, it remains a fairly simple object.

 Note This code is longer than it otherwise would be because I shortened many lines to fit in the format of this book.

Listing 10.5

```
0:  Public Function AddEmployee(args() As String) As _
1:      Integer
2:
3:      Dim myDict          As New Scripting.Dictionary
4:      myDict.CompareMode = DatabaseCompare
5:      Dim i               As Integer
6:
7:      For i = LBound(args, 2) To UBound(args, 2)
8:          Call myDict.Add(args(0, i), Replace(args(1, i), _
9:              "'", "''"))
10:     Next i
11:
12:     '********create a new address**********'
13:     Dim Addrcmd         As New Command
14:     Addrcmd.CommandText = "spAddAddress"
15:     Addrcmd.CommandType = adCmdStoredProc
16:     If Not myDict.Exists("Address1") Then _
17:         myDict("Address1") = ""
18:     If Not myDict.Exists("Address2") Then _
19:         myDict("Address2") = ""
```

continues

 10

Listing 10.5—continued

```
20:     If Not myDict.Exists("City") Then myDict("City") = _
21:         ""
22:     If Not myDict.Exists("State") Then myDict("State") _
23:         = ""
24:     If Not myDict.Exists("ZipCode") Then _
25:         myDict("ZipCode") = ""
26:     If Not myDict.Exists("Phone1") Then _
27:         myDict("Phone1") = ""
28:     If Not myDict.Exists("Phone2") Then _
29:         myDict("Phone2") = ""
30:     If Not myDict.Exists("Fax1") Then myDict("Fax1") = _
31:         ""
32:     If Not myDict.Exists("Fax2") Then myDict("Fax2") = _
33:         ""
34:     Addrcmd.Parameters.Append _
35:         Addrcmd.CreateParameter("@returnValue", _
36:         adInteger, adParamReturnValue)
37:     Addrcmd.Parameters.Append _
38:         Addrcmd.CreateParameter("@AddressLine1", _
39:         adVarChar, adParamInput, 50, _
40:         myDict("Address1"))
41:     Addrcmd.Parameters.Append _
42:         Addrcmd.CreateParameter("@AddressLine2", _
43:         adVarChar, adParamInput, 50, _
44:         myDict("Address2"))
45:     Addrcmd.Parameters.Append _
46:         Addrcmd.CreateParameter("@City", adVarChar, _
47:         adParamInput, 50, myDict("City"))
48:     Addrcmd.Parameters.Append _
49:         Addrcmd.CreateParameter("@State", adChar, _
50:         adParamInput, 2, myDict("State"))
51:     Addrcmd.Parameters.Append _
52:         Addrcmd.CreateParameter("@ZipCode", adVarChar, _
53:         adParamInput, 50, myDict("ZipCode"))
54:     Addrcmd.Parameters.Append _
55:         Addrcmd.CreateParameter("@Phone1", adChar, _
56:         adParamInput, 10, myDict("Phone1"))
57:     Addrcmd.Parameters.Append _
58:         Addrcmd.CreateParameter("@Phone2", adChar, _
59:         adParamInput, 10, myDict("Phone2"))
60:     Addrcmd.Parameters.Append _
61:         Addrcmd.CreateParameter("@Fax1", adChar, _
62:         adParamInput, 10, myDict("Fax1"))
63:     Addrcmd.Parameters.Append _
64:         Addrcmd.CreateParameter("@Fax2", adChar, _
65:         adParamInput, 10, myDict("Fax2"))
66:     Dim AddressID       As Integer
67:     Addrcmd.ActiveConnection = "EmployeeNet"
68:     Addrcmd.Execute
69:     AddressID = Addrcmd.Parameters("@ReturnValue")
70: '*********add new employee*********
```

```
71:      Dim cmd                As New Command
72:      cmd.CommandText = "spAddEmployee"
73:      cmd.CommandType = adCmdStoredProc
74:      If Not myDict.Exists("FirstName") Then AddEmployee _
75:          = 0
76:      If Not myDict.Exists("MiddleName") Then _
77:          myDict("MiddleName") = ""
78:      If Not myDict.Exists("LastName") Then _
79:          myDict("LastName") = ""
80:      If Not myDict.Exists("Title") Then myDict("Title") _
81:          = ""
82:      If Not myDict.Exists("Suffix") Then _
83:          myDict("Suffix") = ""
84:      If Not myDict.Exists("OfficeID") Then _
85:          myDict("OfficeID") = 11
86:      cmd.Parameters.Append _
87:          cmd.CreateParameter("@returnValue", adInteger, _
88:          adParamReturnValue)
89:      cmd.Parameters.Append _
90:          cmd.CreateParameter("@FirstName", adVarChar, _
91:          adParamInput, 50, myDict("FirstName"))
92:      cmd.Parameters.Append _
93:          cmd.CreateParameter("@MiddleName", adVarChar, _
94:          adParamInput, 50, myDict("MiddleName"))
95:      cmd.Parameters.Append _
96:          cmd.CreateParameter("@LastName", adVarChar, _
97:          adParamInput, 50, myDict("LastName"))
98:      cmd.Parameters.Append cmd.CreateParameter("@Title", _
99:          adVarChar, adParamInput, 50, myDict("Title"))
100:      cmd.Parameters.Append _
101:          cmd.CreateParameter("@Suffix", adVarChar, _
102:          adParamInput, 50, myDict("Suffix"))
103:      cmd.Parameters.Append _
104:          cmd.CreateParameter("@HomeAddress", adInteger, _
105:          adParamInput, 4, AddressID)
106:      cmd.Parameters.Append _
107:          cmd.CreateParameter("@OfficeID", adInteger, _
108:          adParamInput, 4, myDict("OfficeID"))
109:      cmd.Parameters.Append _
110:          cmd.CreateParameter("@MailAddress", adInteger, _
111:          adParamInput, 4, AddressID)
112:      cmd.ActiveConnection = "EmployeeNet"
113:      cmd.Execute
114:      Dim newEmpID           As Integer
115:      newEmpID = cmd.Parameters("@ReturnValue")
116:      '********health insurance
117:      Dim HealthCmd          As New Command
118:      HealthCmd.CommandText = "spAddHealthPackage"
119:      HealthCmd.CommandType = adCmdStoredProc
120:      If Not myDict.Exists("HealthPlan") Then _
121:          myDict("HealthPlan") = 1
122:      If Not myDict.Exists("DentalPlan") Then _
```

10

continues

Listing 10.5—continued

```
123:           myDict("DentalPlan") = 1
124:       HealthCmd.Parameters.Append _
125:           cmd.CreateParameter("@returnValue", adInteger, _
126:           adParamReturnValue)
127:       HealthCmd.Parameters.Append _
128:           cmd.CreateParameter("@EmployeeID", adInteger, _
129:           adParamInput, 4, newEmpID)
130:       HealthCmd.Parameters.Append _
131:           cmd.CreateParameter("@HealthPlanID", adInteger, _
132:           adParamInput, 4, myDict("HealthPlan"))
133:       HealthCmd.Parameters.Append _
134:           cmd.CreateParameter("@DentalPlanID", adInteger, _
135:           adParamInput, 4, myDict("DentalPlan"))
136:       HealthCmd.Parameters.Append _
137:           cmd.CreateParameter("@HealthCoverageType", _
138:           adInteger, adParamInput, 4, 1)
139:       HealthCmd.Parameters.Append _
140:           cmd.CreateParameter("@DentalCoverageType", _
141:           adInteger, adParamInput, 4, 1)
142:       HealthCmd.ActiveConnection = "EmployeeNet"
143:       HealthCmd.Execute
144:       '*******Portfolio information
145:       Dim PortCmd        As New Command
146:       PortCmd.CommandText = "spAddPortfolio"
147:       PortCmd.CommandType = adCmdStoredProc
148:       PortCmd.Parameters.Append _
149:           cmd.CreateParameter("@returnValue", adInteger, _
150:           adParamReturnValue)
151:       PortCmd.Parameters.Append _
152:           cmd.CreateParameter("@EmployeeID", adInteger, _
153:           adParamInput, 4, newEmpID)
154:       PortCmd.ActiveConnection = "EmployeeNet"
155:       PortCmd.Execute
156:       Dim portfolioID    As Integer
157:       portfolioID = PortCmd.Parameters("@ReturnValue")
158:       If Not myDict.Exists("Fund1Pct") Then _
159:           myDict("Fund1Pct") = 0
160:       If Not myDict.Exists("Fund2Pct") Then _
161:           myDict("Fund2Pct") = 0
162:       If Not myDict.Exists("Fund3Pct") Then _
163:           myDict("Fund3Pct") = 0
164:     ' Add test here for must add to 100%
165:       Dim AACmd          As New Command
166:       AACmd.CommandText = "spAddAssetAllocation"
167:       AACmd.CommandType = adCmdStoredProc
168:       AACmd.ActiveConnection = "EmployeeNet"
169:       AACmd.Parameters.Append _
170:           cmd.CreateParameter("@returnValue", adInteger, _
171:           adParamReturnValue)
172:       AACmd.Parameters.Append _
173:           cmd.CreateParameter("@PortfolioID", adInteger, _
```

```
174:              adParamInput, 4, portfolioID)
175:          AACmd.Parameters.Append _
176:              cmd.CreateParameter("@WhichFund", adInteger, _
177:              adParamInput, 4)
178:          AACmd.Parameters.Append _
179:              cmd.CreateParameter("@WhatPercent", adInteger, _
180:              adParamInput, 4)
181:
182:          If myDict("Fund1Pct") > 0 Then
183:              AACmd.Parameters("@WhichFund") = 1
184:              AACmd.Parameters("@WhatPercent") = _
185:                  myDict("Fund1Pct")
186:              AACmd.Execute
187:          End If
188:
189:          If myDict("Fund2Pct") > 0 Then
190:              AACmd.Parameters("@WhichFund") = 2
191:              AACmd.Parameters("@WhatPercent") = _
192:                  myDict("Fund2Pct")
193:              AACmd.Execute
194:          End If
195:
196:          If myDict("Fund3Pct") > 0 Then
197:              AACmd.Parameters("@WhichFund") = 3
198:              AACmd.Parameters("@WhatPercent") = _
199:                  myDict("Fund3Pct")
200:              AACmd.Execute
201:          End If
202:
203:          AddEmployee = newEmpID
204:
205:  End Function
```

The job of this bit of code is to take the information for a new employee, already extracted from the form into an array, and feed it to a series of stored procedures: spAddAddress, spAddEmployee, spAddHealthPackage, spAddPortfolio, and spAddAssetAllocation.

I made a few controversial, even debatable, design decisions. For example, I might well have decided to combine all five of these stored procedures into a single stored procedure.

The argument in favor would be that this division of labor is dictated by Declarative Referential Integrity; we must add the address before we can add the employee, and we must add the employee before we add the HealthPackage. Only the database ought to know about these constraints; therefore, there should be a single stored procedure that dictates this logic. This is a powerful argument.

The counterargument, which I find more compelling, is that by breaking these steps out into individual stored procedures, they are easier to create, understand, and maintain.

Here's how it works. On lines 7–10, the contents of the array are (again) copied into a dictionary. We saw this logic in previous chapters.

On line 13 a new command object, Addrcmd, is declared, and its CommandText parameter is set to spAddAddress on line 14. This indicates that when this command is executed, the stored procedure spAddAddress will be called. The type of this command is set on line 15.

Lines 16–33 ensure that all the needed values in the dictionary have a default value if they do not already exist. That is, if no value was passed in as part of the array of values extracted from the form, then we assign a default value here.

Lines 34–36 initialize the first parameter to the stored procedure, indicating that it will hold the return value from the stored procedure. In this case, as you'll see, the stored procedure returns the identity value it creates for the new record.

Lines 37–65 initialize each of the parameters that will be passed to the stored procedure.

On line 68 the stored procedure is executed, and on line 69 the return value is extracted from the @ReturnValue parameter created on line 35.

The stored procedure that is called is shown in Listing 10.6.

Listing 10.6

```
0:   create proc spAddAddress
1:   @AddressLine1 varchar(50),
2:   @AddressLine2 varchar(50),
3:   @City varchar(50),
4:   @State char(2),
5:   @ZipCode varchar(50),
6:   @Phone1 char(10),
7:   @Phone2 char(10),
8:   @Fax1 char(10),
9:   @Fax2 char(10)
10:  as
11:  insert into Address
12:  (
13:  AddressLine1,
14:  AddressLine2,
15:  City,
16:  State,
17:  ZipCode,
18:  Phone1,
19:  Phone2,
20:  Fax1,
21:  Fax2
22:  )
23:  values (
```

```
24:  @AddressLine1,
25:  @AddressLine2,
26:  @City,
27:  @State,
28:  @ZipCode,
29:  @Phone1,
30:  @Phone2,
31:  @Fax1,
32:  @Fax2
33:  )
34:  return @@identity
```

This stored procedure is very straightforward. It is divided into four sections.

Section 1 begins on line 0. The stored procedure is created and named. A list of parameters is provided from lines 1 through 9, where each is declared and given a name and a type.

Section 2 defines the stored procedure using the keywords as on line 10 and insert into on line 11 and providing the table (Address) on line 11 and then the list of fields on lines 12–22.

Section 3, lines 23–33, provides the values for each of these fields, feeding in the parameters declared earlier.

Section 4 is a single line, line 34, in which the identity column's value is returned. This value is extracted in the @ReturnValue parameter in the business object.

Calling the Other Stored Procedures

This pattern is repeated four times. From lines 70 to 115 of Listing 10.5 the parameters for the stored procedure spAddEmployee are created. That stored procedure is shown in Listing 10.7.

Listing 10.7

```
0:   CREATE proc spAddEmployee
1:   @firstName varchar(50),
2:   @MiddleName varchar(50),
3:   @LastName varchar(50),
4:   @Title varchar(50),
5:   @Suffix varchar(50),
6:   @HomeAddress int,
7:   @OfficeID int,
8:   @MailAddress int
9:   as
10:  insert into employee
11:  (
12:  firstname,
13:  middleName,
```

continues

10

Listing 10.7—continued

```
14:    lastName,
15:    Title,
16:    Suffix,
17:    HomeAddress,
18:    OfficeID,
19:    MailAddress )
20:    values (
21:    @firstName,
22:    @MiddleName,
23:    @LastName,
24:    @Title,
25:    @Suffix,
26:    @HomeAddress,
27:    @OfficeID,
28:    @MailAddress
29:    )
30:    return @@identity
```

Similarly, the parameters for spHealthPackage are created on lines 116–143, for Portfolio on lines 145–157, and for AssetAllocation on lines 158–200. Finally, the employeeID, which was created when the employee was added, is returned on line 203.

Transaction Support and Error Code

A critical flaw in the code as shown is that there is no transactional support. If we were to encounter an error in adding the portfolio, there would be no easy way to report that error, much less to roll back (undo) the creation of the employee, already added to the database.

It was a design decision of this book not to show error reporting and transactions, in an effort to keep this code reasonably simple and manageable, but in a commercial system such issues would become critical.

Buying Error Support

Visual Basic does provide some error support, but creating your own error tracking is tedious and time-consuming. Commercial products that will instrument your code and provide full logging and error management are available and may be a viable alternative if you are developing a commercial product. In any case, these issues are, once again, beyond the scope of this book.

Order Is Important

The order in which data are added to the database is critical. Because we defined Referential Integrity Constraints among these tables, it is not legal to create an

Employee record without already having an Address record to assign to that employee. Similarly, we can't create an AssetAllocation record unless there already is a Portfolio record to relate it to, and we can't create a Portfolio record if there is no Employee record to own the Portfolio record.

The Structure of the Database

It isn't always easy to understand the structure of the database and which constraints exist and how they relate the various tables. SQL Server does provide a diagramming tool, which is an excellent starting point. Figure 10.8 shows the diagram generated by SQL Server for the EmployeeNet tables.

Figure 10.8

SQL diagram.

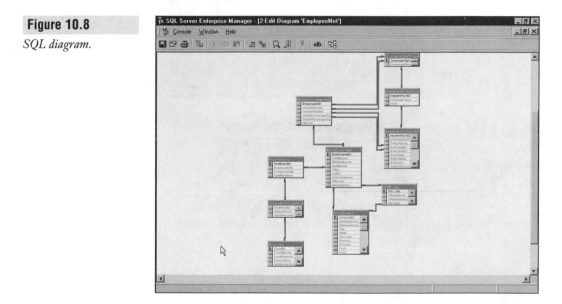

It is difficult to read this diagram when it is small enough to see the entire diagram, so let's focus on just one section, as shown in Figure 10.9.

Here we can see that there are primary key constraint relationships among these various classes. However, from this diagram, it is difficult to get a handle on what these constraints are.

We can highlight and explore each relationship in turn by right-clicking on a relationship and opening the Relationship Properties window, as shown in Figure 10.10.

These diagrams provide a good bit of information, but what I really want is the ability to add comments to the relationships and to each of the fields in the database.

10

Figure 10.9

Diagram close-up.

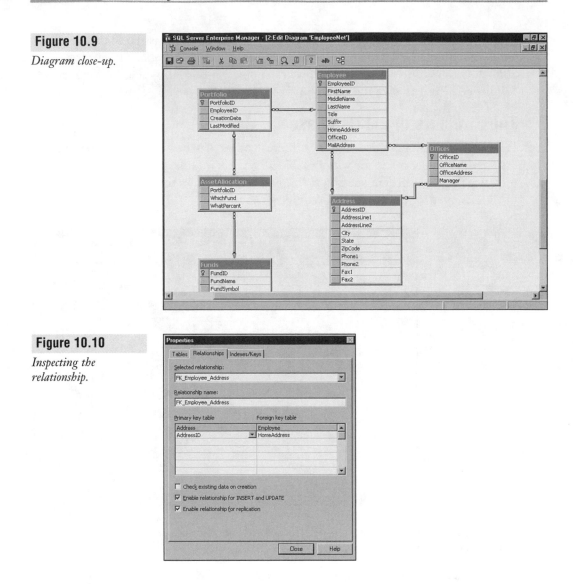

Figure 10.10

Inspecting the relationship.

Next Steps

Fortunately, a friend and co-worker, Mike Kraley (mike@kraley.com) has created a wonderful utility named SQueaL, which provides *exactly* this capability. Even more fortunate, he has agreed to allow me to include SQueaL in this book.

Chapter 11 describes this utility in detail, both because it will help us to understand the underlying database better and because it illustrates some advanced features of WebClasses.

Chapter 11

Data Utilities

In this chapter, we review a pair of simple, quick-and-dirty utilities for managing the data in EmployeeNet.

The first, SQueaL, is a free utility written by Mike Kraley to comment SQL Server databases. I find it terribly frustrating (and surprising!) that SQL Server does not provide this ability. Reading through a complex database without comments can be a confusing and difficult experience. SQueaL provides the necessary documentation—at the database, field, and relationship levels—so that you can explain what it is you are doing and why.

Note

Please note that SQueaL is designed for use by programmers and so provides no error checking at all. SQueaL is one of the most useful utilities I've ever seen; my hope is that Mike will develop a commercial release with even more features. If so, he'll announce it on my Web site (http://www.libertyassociates.com).

SQueaL is included on the CD. Please note that it is *not* public domain; it is Copyright © 1999 by Mike Kraley. (For details, see http://www.fsf.org/copyleft/gpl.html. Note, however, that neither Mike nor I will be providing ongoing support for the version included in this book.) Please see the "About Box" within SQueaL's Help for complete details, including this notice: "SQueaL comes with ABSOLUTELY NO WARRANTY." This is not an offering that can only be made by prospectus. Your mileage may vary. Offer is not good where prohibited. Contents are hot.

Using SQueaL

The purpose of SQueaL is to provide insight into the structure of a database. SQueaL allows you to add comments on every field of every table, on the table itself, and on its indexes and relationships with other tables.

Getting Started

When you first start SQueaL, it will prompt you for an SQL Server, as shown in Figure 11.1.

Figure 11.1

Prompting for a database.

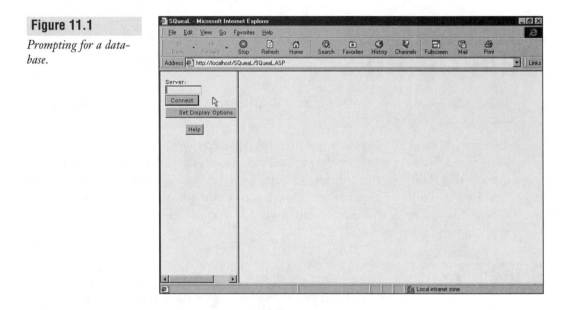

When you fill in the server and press Connect, it offers a drop-down of all the databases on that server, as shown in Figure 11.2.

After you make your choice, each of the tables is listed in the left-hand frame. Clicking on any table shows its structure in the right-hand frame, as shown in Figure 11.3.

You can click on an existing comment to edit it, or you can click on a field without a comment to add one, as shown in Figure 11.4.

Notice that, in addition to comments for the table name itself and each of the fields in the table, the indexes are represented (and can be commented) and the relationships can be commented.

Figure 11.2

Choosing the table.

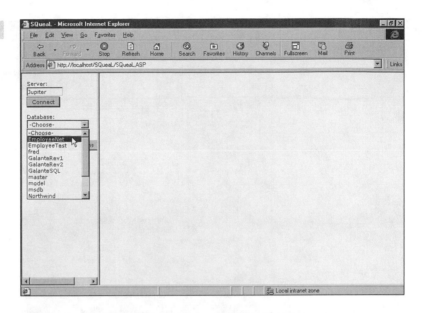

Figure 11.3

A table structure with comments.

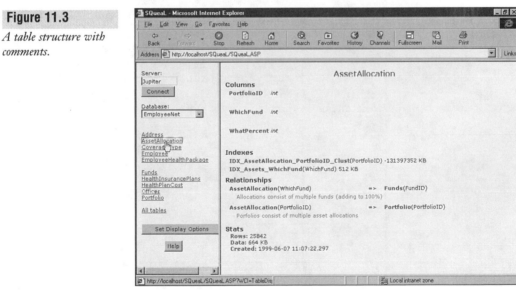

You can also generate a report on all the tables (suitable for printing) by clicking All Tables, as shown in Figure 11.5.

Other features include the ability to display a help file and to set the display options (as shown in Figure 11.6). Finally, SQueaL uses cookies to keep track of your preferences as well as the database to which you want to connect.

11

Figure 11.4

Adding a comment.

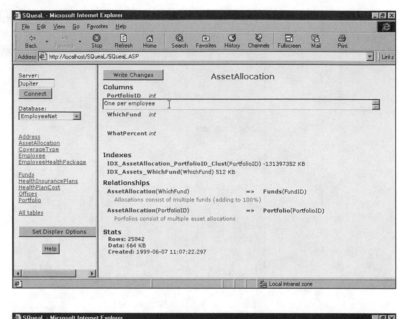

Figure 11.5

All the tables.

SQueaL Internals

SQueaL starts, appropriately enough, by setting NextItem to SQueaL—the frameset in which the results will be displayed. Listing 11.1 shows the source HTML for this page.

Figure 11.6

Setting options.

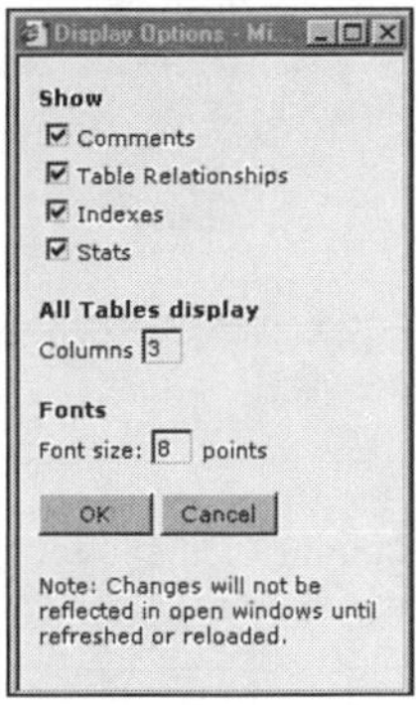

Listing 11.1

```
0:   <!DOCTYPE HTML PUBLIC "-//W3C//DTD
1:   HTML 4.0 Transitional//EN">
2:   <HTML><HEAD><TITLE>SQueaL</TITLE>
3:   <META content="MSHTML 5.00.2314.1000" name=GENERATOR>
4:   <META content="text/html; charset=iso-8859-1"
5:   http-equiv=Content-Type>
6:   </HEAD>
7:   <FRAMESET cols=20%,* frameBorder=1 frameSpacing=1>
8:       <FRAME name=tableList src="
9:       <wc@TableListName></wc@TableListName>">
10:       <FRAME name=contents src="about:blank">
11:   </FRAMESET>
12:   </HTML>
```

This is a straightforward frameset except that the left frame, named tableList, has its src set in the wc@TableListName tag.

The Respond method calls WriteTemplate, which emits this HTML, calling ProcessTag to process the TableListName tag, as shown in Listing 11.2.

Listing 11.2

```
0:   Private Sub SQueaL_ProcessTag( _
1:   ByVal TagName As String, _
2:   TagContents As String, _
3:   SendTags As Boolean)
4:       Select Case TagName
5:           Case "wc@TableListName"
6:               TagContents = URLFor(TableList)
7:       End Select
8:   End Sub
```

The net effect of this code is to substitute the appropriate URL for the TableList page; thus TableList Respond is called, as shown in Listing 11.3.

11

Listing 11.3

```
0:   Private Sub TableList_Respond()
1:       Dim fs As Variant
2:
3:       ServerName = Request("server")
4:       dbName = Request("db")
5:
6:       If ServerName = "" Then
7:           'get saved values from cookie
8:           ServerName = Request.Cookies("SQueaL")("server")
9:           dbName = Request.Cookies("SQueaL")("db")
10:      End If
11:      fs = Request.Cookies("SQueaL")("fontSize")
12:
13:      If ServerName <> "" Then
14:          dbServer.Connect ServerName, "sa", ""
15:      End If
16:
17:      'if we don't have a cookie, then set defaults
18:      If fs = "" Then
19:          Response.Cookies("SQueaL")("ShowComments") = "on"
20:          Response.Cookies("SQueaL")("ShowDRI") = "on"
21:          Response.Cookies("SQueaL")("ShowIndexes") = "on"
22:          Response.Cookies("SQueaL")("ShowStats") = "on"
23:          Response.Cookies("SQueaL")("fontSize") = 8
24:          Response.Cookies("SQueaL")("AllTRows") = 2
25:          Response.Cookies("SQueaL")("AllTCols") = 3
26:          fontSize = 8
27:      Else
28:          fontSize = fs
29:      End If
30:
31:      Response.Cookies("SQueaL")("server") = ServerName
32:      Response.Cookies("SQueaL")("db") = dbName
33:      Response.Cookies("SQueaL").Expires = _
34:      DateAdd("yyyy", 1, Date)
35:
36:      TableList.WriteTemplate
37:  End Sub
```

On lines 3 and 4, we ask the Request object for the server object and then the db value. The variables serverName and dbName, along with the others used in this code, are created as module-level variables and thus are available to all the methods in this file.

If the name we get back for db is empty, then we will ask the Request object for a cookie.

A *cookie* is a small bit of text that is saved on the client machine in a file. In this case, we've created a collection of such cookies named SQueaL. Within that collection, each individual cookie may be requested by name. The cookies themselves are retrieved from the cookies collection of the Request object. They are placed back on the client machine through the cookies collection of the Response object. Line 8 illustrates how you extract a single value from these collections:

```
8:          ServerName = Request.Cookies("SQueaL")("server")
```

On lines 17–29, we set defaults if there is no cookie. Notice that this assigns values to cookies that may not yet exist; it is this act of assigning to them that creates them. On lines 31–32, we update the server and database cookies (or create them if they don't exist) and finally set the SQueaL cookie to expire in one year. An expiration date tells the client to throw the cookie away after it has expired. This prevents old cookies from rotting on your hard disk, making crumbs, which are difficult to clean and which bring mice. (Have you noticed that there is a mouse near just about every computer these days? It's those darn cookie crumbs!)

We then write the TableList file, whose HTML is shown in Listing 11.4.

Listing 11.4

```
0:   <HTML>
1:   <HEAD>
2:   <META NAME="GENERATOR" Content="Microsoft Developer Studio">
3:   <META HTTP-EQUIV="Content-Type" content="text/html;
4:   charset=iso-8859-1">
5:   <TITLE>Table List</TITLE>
6:   <STYLE>
7:   .controls {font-family:Verdana;font-size:
8:   <wc@fontSize></wc@fontSize>pt}
9:   BODY {font-family:Verdana;font-size:<wc@fontSize>
10:  </wc@fontSize>pt}
11:  </STYLE>
12:  </HEAD>
13:
14:  <BODY>
15:  <form id=form1 method=post>
16:  Server:
17:  <br><input name=server size=10 class=controls
18:  value="<wc@ServerName></wc@ServerName>">
19:  <input type=submit value=Connect name=newServer
20:  class=controls><br><wc@noServer>
21:
22:  <br>Database:
23:  <br><select name=db class=controls onchange="form1.submit();">
24:  <wc@DBList></wc@DBList>
25:
26:  </select>
27:  <br><wc@TableList></wc@TableList>
28:
```

continues

11

Listing 11.4—continued

```
29:   </form></wc@noServer>
30:
31:   <center><input type=button class=controls
32:   value="Set Display Options" style="margin-top:3px"
33:       onclick="window.open('<wc@urlDispOpt></wc@urlDispOpt>',
34:       null,
35:         'height=330px,width=200px,status=no,toolbar=no,menubar=no,
36:         location=no');">
37:   <br><input type=button class=controls value="Help"
38:       onclick="window.open('<wc@urlHelp></wc@urlHelp>', null,
39:         'height=500px,width=400px,status=no,toolbar=no,menubar=no,
40:         location=no,scrollbars=yes');">
41:   </center>
42:   </BODY>
43:   </HTML>
```

A few advanced techniques are at play here. First, on line 6, we begin a style section. This defines how any HTML that is declared to use this style will be displayed.

EXCURSION

HTML

Cascading style sheets sound scarier than they are. The devil is in the details, but the overall idea is not that difficult.

Let's take a quick look at another page: Table Display. The opening lines look like this:

```
<STYLE>
{font-family:Verdana;font-size:<wc@fontSize></wc@fontSize>pt}
TD {font-family:Verdana;font-size:<wc@fontSize></wc@fontSize>pt}
TH {font-family:Verdana;font-size:<wc@fontSize></wc@fontSize>pt}
.controls {font-family:Verdana;font-size:<wc@fontSize></wc@fontSize>pt}
.dbName {font-size:<wc@fontSize>2</wc@fontSize>pt;font-weight:bold;}
.tableName {font-size:<wc@fontSize>4</wc@fontSize>pt;font-weight:bold;
➥text-align:center;color:blue;<wc@cursorHand></wc@cursorHand>}
.coname {font-size:<wc@fontSize></wc@fontSize>pt;font-weight:bold;
➥padding-left:5;color:blue;<wc@cursorHand></wc@cursorHand>}
.cotype {font-size:<wc@fontSize></wc@fontSize>pt;font-style:italic}
.comment {font-size:<wc@fontSize></wc@fontSize>pt;padding-left:20;
➥padding-bottom:5;color:green;<wc@cursorHand></wc@cursorHand><wc@commentVisible>
➥</wc@commentVisible>}
.section {font-size:<wc@fontSize>2</wc@fontSize>pt;font-weight:bold;
➥padding-top:5;color:black;}
.itemName {font-size:<wc@fontSize></wc@fontSize>pt;font-weight:bold;color:blue;}
.itemHead {padding-left:5}
</STYLE>
```

This code says that the font family for the entire page will be Verdana, with a size set to whatever we substitute for the `fontSize` tag. It then says that this will be overridden for anything within a TD tag (which will potentially change the font size) and also overridden for anything with a TH tag (again, which may override the size).

Next, this code creates some named classes, including .controls, .dbname, and .tableName. Each is defined with its own modifications of the style.

Later in the code, these specific style overrides can be applied using the class keyword. For example, in Listing 11.4 on line 17, the input object is assigned the style controls by use of the phrase: `class=controls`. This tells HTML to apply the .controls style to that object.

The style ends on line 11. In the body of the page, we create an input field with the value set to the tag wc@ServerName. This allows us to fill in this value when we know it (from the cookie). On line 20, this input statement ends with `class=controls`, which indicates that the style controls (defined earlier) ought to be applied.

Conditional Tags

Line 20 ends with a tag <wc@noServer>, which is not closed until line 29!

We haven't seen this technique before. Here's how it works: If the tag is *not* processed, then the tags are removed, but everything between the tags is left intact. If the tags are processed, then everything between the tags is replaced.

Mike will examine the state of the system. If he does not know the server, then he will not want this code to be processed, so he will remove it. If he does know the server, then he will ignore this tag (providing no substitution) and the HTML (including other embedded wc tags!) will be processed by ProcessTags.

To review, if we don't know the server then we want to remove all the HTML and tags on lines 21–29. We thus replace noServer with an empty string, as shown on line 8 of Listing 11.5. If, on the other hand, we do know the name of the server, then we simply ignore the noServer tag, which leaves lines 21–29 intact. They are then processed like any other HTML.

Note also that there are tags on lines 24 and 27. These tags live *within* the noServer tags. Normally, the WebClass engine makes just one pass through the code, and so these tags would be ignored. You can override this, however, by clicking on the individual WebItem in the list of HTML Template WebItems and then setting the ReScanReplacements property to true as shown in the lower-right corner of Figure 11.7.

Returning to Listing 11.4, Mike set up the link that will open the Options window on lines 31–36. On lines 37–40, he set up the help screen with his nifty copyright notice.

11

Figure 11.7

*ReScanReplacements
property.*

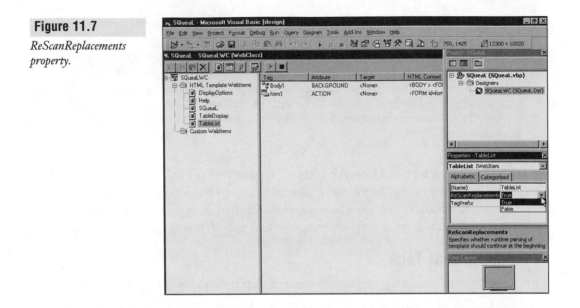

The bulk of the work of this form is done in the processing of the `TableList` tags, as shown in Listing 11.5.

Listing 11.5

```
0:  Private Sub TableList_ProcessTag( _
1:  ByVal TagName As String, TagContents As String, _
2:  SendTags As Boolean)
3:
4:      Dim db As Database, ta As Table
5:      Select Case TagName
6:        Case "wc@noServer"
7:        'omit most stuff if no server name yet
8:          If ServerName = "" Then TagContents = ""
9:        Case "wc@ServerName"
10:          TagContents = ServerName
11:       Case "wc@urlHelp"
12:          TagContents = URLFor(Help)
13:       Case "wc@urlDispOpt"
14:          TagContents = URLFor(DisplayOptions)
15:       Case "wc@fontSize"
16:          TagContents = fontSize
17:       Case "wc@DBList"
18:         'a select/option list of all databases on this server
19:         If dbName = "" Then
20:           'encourage user to choose one,
21:           'if none already selected
22:           TagContents = _
```

```
23:                 "<option SELECTED>-Choose-</option>" & vbCrLf
24:             End If
25:             For Each db In dbServer.Databases
26:                TagContents = TagContents & _
27:                "<option" & IIf(db.name = dbName, " SELECTED >", ">") _
28:                 & db.name & "</option>" & vbCrLf
29:             Next
30:           Case "wc@TableList"
31:              'if we have a database chosen, then present a list of
32:              'links to each of the tables
33:             If dbName <> "" And dbName <> "-Choose-" Then
34:                Set db = dbServer.Databases(dbName)
35:                For Each ta In db.Tables
36:                    'don't bother with system tables - or our own
37:                    If Not ta.SystemObject And ta.name <> _
38:                    "sysTableComments" Then
39:                      TagContents = TagContents & _
40:                      "<BR><A href=""" & URLFor(TableDisplay) _
41:                       & "&ta=" & ta.name & "&db=" & dbName _
42:                        & "&server=" & ServerName _
43:                        & """ target=contents>" _
44:                        & ta.name & "</A>" & vbCrLf
45:                    End If
46:                Next
47:                'add a link to display all tables
48:                TagContents = TagContents & _
49:                "<BR><BR><A href=""" & _
50:                URLFor(TableDisplay) & "&ta=*&db=" & dbName _
51:                 & "&server=" & ServerName & _
52:                 """ target=contents>All tables</A><BR><BR>"
53:             End If   'end if dbName
54:       End Select
55:    End Sub
```

This code begins by creating a database object and a table object. On line 8, `TagContents` is set to empty for the `noServer` tag if `ServerName` is unknown. As discussed earlier, this effectively blanks out some of the other tags.

Otherwise, the `ServerName` is filled in, links to the help screen and display options pages are created, and the font size is set.

On lines 18–29, all the database list box is populated. Lines 30–54 fill the list of tables. On line 36, we begin a loop in which each table is examined and then added; a link is created to the display page for each table.

Displaying the Table

When the link for a given table is followed, the TableDisplay_Respond method is invoked, as shown in Listing 11.6.

11

Listing 11.6

```
0:   Private Sub TableDisplay_Respond()
1:       Dim a() As String, i As Long
2:
3:       ServerName = Request("server")
4:       dbName = Request("db")
5:       taName = Request("ta")
6:
7:       ' we need both SQL DMO and ADO connections to the database
8:       dbServer.Connect ServerName, "sa", ""
9:       Set theDB = dbServer.Databases(dbName)
10:
11:      Set DBConn = New ADODB.Connection
12:      DBConn.Open "Provider=SQLOLEDB.1;Server=" & ServerName _
13:      & ";DB=" & dbName & ";UID=sa;PWD=;"
14:      DBConn.DefaultDatabase = dbName
15:
16:      ' make sure we have a comments table in this db
17:      DBConn.Execute _
18:      ("if not exists (select * from sysobjects _
19:      where name='sysTableComments') " _
20:       & "create table sysTableComments _
21:       (TableId int not null, colId int not null, _
22:       CommentText varchar(8000))")
23:
24:      GetAllOptions
25:
26:      'set some variables to help turn comments off
27:      If options("ShowComments") = "on" Then
28:          cursorHand = "cursor:hand;"
29:          commentVisible = "display:normal;"
30:      Else
31:          cursorHand = ""
32:          commentVisible = "display:none;"
33:      End If
34:
35:      'no comment editing allowed in all tables view
36:      If taName = "*" Then cursorHand = ""
37:
38:      If taName <> "*" Then
39:          'showing a particular table - set globals
40:          Set theTable = theDB.Tables(taName)
41:          tableId = theTable.ID
42:
43:          ' write out any previous changes
44:          If Request("Edit") <> "" Then
45:              a = Split(Request("Edits"), "¦")
46:              For i = LBound(a) To UBound(a) - 1 Step 2
47:                  DBConn.Execute ("delete from sysTableComments _
48:                  where TableId = " & tableId & " and ColId = " _
49:                  & a(i))
```

```
50:                         DBConn.Execute ("insert into sysTableComments _
51:                         (TableId, ColId, commentText) VALUES(" & _
52:                         tableId & ", " & a(i) & ", '" _
53:                         & Replace(a(i + 1), "'", "''") & "')")
54:              Next
55:          End If
56:      End If
57:
58:      TableDisplay.WriteTemplate
59:      Set DBConn = Nothing
60:  End Sub
```

On line 6, a connection is made to the server for DMO, which is the internal object model for SQL Server itself. DMO is used to manipulate and extract information about the tables and indexes. However, DMO is well beyond the scope of this book and of marginal interest to Web developers unless they are building utilities for SQL Server. We will skip over the details here.

On line 24, Mike calls a subroutine he wrote to extract the options saved as a cookie on the user's machine. GetAllOptions is shown in Listing 11.7.

Listing 11.7

```
0:  'routines for DisplayOptions window
1:  Sub GetAllOptions()
2:      GetOptions "ShowComments", "on"
3:      GetOptions "ShowDRI", "on"
4:      GetOptions "ShowIndexes", "on"
5:      GetOptions "ShowStats", "on"
6:      GetOptions "AllTCols", 3
7:      GetOptions "AllTRows", 2
8:      GetOptions "FontSize", 8
9:      fontSize = options("FontSize")
10: End Sub
```

This subroutine in turn calls GetOptions, shown in Listing 11.8.

Listing 11.8

```
0:  Sub GetOptions(name As String, default As String)
1:      Dim r As String
2:      r = Request.Cookies("SQueaL")(name)
3:      If r = "" Then r = default
4:      options.Add name, r
5:  End Sub
```

GetOptions in turn takes the name of the option and a default value. The name is used as an index into the SQueaL cookie collection. If no cookie is returned, then the default value is returned. In any case, the option's value is added to the options dictionary, which was declared earlier.

11

Returning to Listing 11.6, Mike then sets up his cursors and the tableID he will display. On line 58, he calls WriteTemplate, which displays the TableDisplay HTML file.

I'll stop my analysis here because the rest of this program is focused on the DMO aspects of the project, which are not of concern to us.

SQueaL Summary

Even though there are more details involved in making SQueaL work, they involve DHTML manipulation of the text of the page and the internals of talking with the database, all of which are beyond the scope of this book. The complete source code is provided on the CD if you have a morbid curiosity about how it works its magic.

The Data Generator

To provide data for this book, and to help me debug the application, I whipped together a very fast data generator program. This is not a robust or commercial-quality undertaking, but it does illustrate a useful technique.

Often, when working with new databases, you cannot easily test your code unless you have records to work with. After I created the AddEmployee module, it was fairly easy to use that same logic to create dummy data with which I could fill the database.

To accomplish this, I created a *very* simple standalone application called PopulateEmployees. It has a single form, as shown in Figure 11.8.

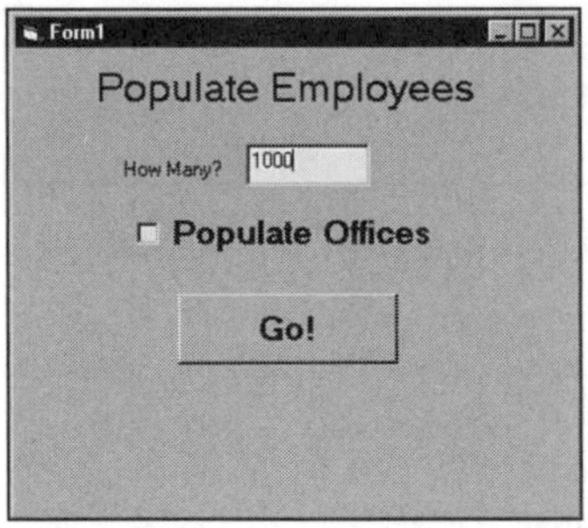

Figure 11.8

Populate employees.

You may use this form either to create new offices (by checking the check box) or new employees. When you press the Go button, the employees are added, and a text box announces completion when it finishes. It's fairly simple.

Note

This code was whipped together in fewer than two hours; it is hardly an example of well-designed or even robust programming, but it gets the job done. On the other hand, it's a pretty good example of the kinds of hacks that professional programmers throw together to accomplish a limited task on the way to delivering a commercial product, and so I've included a brief analysis of it here.

The trick is in creating the records. The work is done in the GoButton_Click() method, shown in Listing 11.9.

Listing 11.9

```
0:   Private Sub GoButton_Click()
1:
2:       Dim OneOfFour        As Integer
3:       Dim binaryChoice     As Integer
4:       Dim Title            As String
5:       Dim address          As Integer
6:       Dim zipCode          As String
7:       Dim phoneNumber      As String
8:       Dim IsOff            As Boolean
9:
10:      ' Add to office?
11:      If cbIsOff.Value = 0 Then
12:          IsOff = False
13:      Else
14:          IsOff = True
15:      End If
16:
17:      ' open recordset for first name
18:      Dim FNrs             As Recordset
19:      Set FNrs = New ADODB.Recordset
20:      Call FNrs.Open("select Name from FirstNames", _
21:          "PopulateEmployee")
22:
23:
24:      'open recordset for last name
25:      Dim LNrs             As Recordset
26:      Set LNrs = New ADODB.Recordset
27:      Call LNrs.Open("select Name from LastName", _
28:          "PopulateEmployee")
29:
30:      ' open recordset for city name
31:      Dim CNrs             As Recordset
```

continues

11

Listing 11.9—continued

```
32:        Set CNrs = New ADODB.Recordset
33:        Call CNrs.Open("select Name from CityNames", _
34:            "PopulateEmployee")
35:
36:        ' open recordset for state name
37:        Dim SNrs           As Recordset
38:        Set SNrs = New ADODB.Recordset
39:        Call SNrs.Open("select Name from StateNames", _
40:            "PopulateEmployee")
41:
42:        ' open recordset for street name
43:        Dim ANrs           As Recordset
44:        Set ANrs = New ADODB.Recordset
45:        Call ANrs.Open("select Name from StreetName", _
46:            "PopulateEmployee")
47:
48:        ' open recordset for employeeID as office manager
49:        Dim Mrs            As Recordset
50:        Set Mrs = New ADODB.Recordset
51:        Call Mrs.Open("select employeeID from employee", _
52:            "EmployeeNet")
53:
54:        'open recordset for office id to put new employee in
55:        Dim Offrs          As Recordset
56:        Set Offrs = New ADODB.Recordset
57:        Call Offrs.Open("select officeID from Offices", _
58:            "EmployeeNet")
59:
60:
61:        ' open recordset for health plan id
62:        Dim HIPrs          As Recordset
63:        Set HIPrs = New ADODB.Recordset
64:        Call _
65:            HIPrs.Open("select HealthPlanID from " _
66:            & "HealthInsurancePlans where TypeOfInsurance = 1", _
67:            "EmployeeNet")
68:
69:        'open recordset for dental plan id
70:        Dim HIDrs          As Recordset
71:        Set HIDrs = New ADODB.Recordset
72:        Call _
73:            HIDrs.Open("select HealthPlanID from " _
74:            & "HealthInsurancePlans where TypeOfInsurance = 2", _
75:            "EmployeeNet")
76:
77:        Dim firstName      As String
78:        Dim lastName       As String
79:        Dim cityName       As String
80:        Dim stateName      As String
81:        Dim streetName     As String
82:        Dim howMany        As Integer
```

```
83:
84:        howMany = txtHowMany
85:
86:        ' create connection to the DB
87:        Dim cn                As ADODB.Connection
88:        Set cn = New ADODB.Connection
89:        cn.Open ("EmployeeNet")
90:
91:        Dim myDict           As New Scripting.Dictionary
92:        myDict.CompareMode = DatabaseCompare
93:
94:        ' update the window
95:        Message.Caption = "Working..."
96:        Message.Refresh
97:
98:        ' for each employee you want to create...
99:        For ctr = 1 To howMany
100:            ' clear the dictionary each time through
101:            myDict.RemoveAll
102:
103:            ' create the first name
104:        If FNrs.EOF Then
105:                FNrs.MoveFirst
106:            End If
107:            firstName = FNrs!Name
108:            FNrs.MoveNext
109:            Call myDict.Add("FirstName", firstName)
110:
111:            ' create the last name
112:        If LNrs.EOF Then
113:                LNrs.MoveFirst
114:            End If
115:            lastName = LNrs!Name
116:            LNrs.MoveNext
117:            Call myDict.Add("LastName", lastName)
118:            binaryChoice = Int((2 * Rnd) + 1)
119:
120:            ' randomly chose mr or ms.
121:        If binaryChoice = 1 Then
122:                Title = "Ms."
123:        Else
124:                Title = "Mr."
125:            End If
126:
127:
128:            Call myDict.Add("Title", Title)
129:
130:            ' build a random street address
131:        If ANrs.EOF Then
132:                ANrs.MoveFirst
133:            End If
134:            streetName = ANrs!Name
```

continues

Listing 11.9—continued

```
135:          ANrs.MoveNext
136:          address = Int((999 * Rnd) + 1)
137:          binaryChoice = Int((2 * Rnd) + 1)
138:          If binaryChoice = 1 Then
139:              street = "St."
140:          Else
141:              street = "Ave."
142:          End If
143:
144:          Dim address1    As String
145:          address1 = address & " " & Trim(streetName) & _
146:              " " & Trim(street)
147:          Call myDict.Add("Address1", address1)
148:          If IsOff Then Call myDict.Add("offAddress1", _
149:              address1)
150:
151:
152:          ' build city and state
153:
154:          If CNrs.EOF Then
155:              CNrs.MoveFirst
156:          End If
157:          cityName = CNrs!Name
158:          CNrs.MoveNext
159:          Call myDict.Add("City", cityName)
160:          If IsOff Then Call myDict.Add("offCity", _
161:              cityName)
162:
163:          If SNrs.EOF Then
164:              SNrs.MoveFirst
165:          End If
166:          stateName = SNrs!Name
167:          SNrs.MoveNext
168:          Call myDict.Add("State", stateName)
169:
170:          If IsOff Then
171:              Call myDict.Add("offState", stateName)
172:              Dim officeName As String
173:              officeName = Trim(cityName) & address
174:              Call myDict.Add("OfficeName", officeName)
175:          End If
176:
177:          ' assemble a 5 digit random zip code
178:          zipCode = ""
179:
180:          For i = 1 To 5
181:              zipCode = zipCode + CStr(Int(10 * Rnd))
182:          Next i
183:
184:          Call myDict.Add("zipCode", zipCode)
185:          If IsOff Then Call myDict.Add("offZip", _
```

```
186:            zipCode)
187:
188:        ' assemble phone number
189:        phoneNumber = ""
190:
191:        For i = 1 To 10
192:            phoneNumber = phoneNumber + CStr(Int(10 * _
193:                Rnd))
194:        Next i
195:
196:        Call myDict.Add("Phone1", phoneNumber)
197:        If IsOff Then Call myDict.Add("offPhone1", _
198:            phoneNumber)
199:        phoneNumber = ""
200:
201:        For i = 1 To 10
202:            phoneNumber = phoneNumber + CStr(Int(10 * _
203:                Rnd))
204:        Next i
205:
206:        Call myDict.Add("Phone2", phoneNumber)
207:        If IsOff Then Call myDict.Add("offPhone2", _
208:            phoneNumber)
209:        phoneNumber = ""
210:
211:        For i = 1 To 10
212:            phoneNumber = phoneNumber + CStr(Int(10 * _
213:                Rnd))
214:        Next i
215:
216:        Call myDict.Add("Fax1", phoneNumber)
217:        If IsOff Then Call myDict.Add("offFax1", _
218:            phoneNumber)
219:        phoneNumber = ""
220:
221:        For i = 1 To 10
222:            phoneNumber = phoneNumber + CStr(Int(10 * _
223:                Rnd))
224:        Next i
225:
226:        Call myDict.Add("Fax2", phoneNumber)
227:        If IsOff Then Call myDict.Add("offFax2", _
228:            phoneNumber)
229:        HIPrs.MoveNext
230:
231:        ' get health insurance plan id
232:        If HIPrs.EOF Then
233:            HIPrs.MoveFirst
234:        End If
235:
236:        Call myDict.Add("HealthPlan", _
237:            HIPrs!HealthPlanID)
```

continues

Listing 11.9—continued

```
238:            HIDrs.MoveNext
239:
240:            ' get dental plan id
241:            If HIDrs.EOF Then
242:                HIDrs.MoveFirst
243:            End If
244:
245:            Call myDict.Add("DentalPlan", _
246:                HIDrs!HealthPlanID)
247:            If Not Mrs.EOF Then Mrs.MoveNext
248:
249:            ' get manager id
250:            If Mrs.EOF Then
251:                Mrs.MoveFirst
252:            End If
253:
254:            Call myDict.Add("Manager", Mrs!EmployeeID)
255:            If Not Offrs.EOF Then Offrs.MoveNext
256:
257:            If Offrs.EOF Then
258:                Offrs.MoveFirst
259:            End If
260:
261:            Call myDict.Add("OfficeID", Offrs!officeID)
262:
263:
264:            ' decide on one of four investment
265:            ' distributions
266:
267:            OneOfFour = Int((4 * Rnd) + 1)
268:
269:            Select Case OneOfFour
270:
271:            Case 1
272:                Call myDict.Add("Fund1Pct", 100)
273:                Call myDict.Add("Fund2Pct", 0)
274:                Call myDict.Add("Fund3Pct", 0)
275:
276:            Case 2
277:                Call myDict.Add("Fund1Pct", 50)
278:                Call myDict.Add("Fund2Pct", 25)
279:                Call myDict.Add("Fund3Pct", 25)
280:
281:            Case 3
282:                Call myDict.Add("Fund1Pct", 30)
283:                Call myDict.Add("Fund2Pct", 10)
284:                Call myDict.Add("Fund3Pct", 60)
285:
286:            Case 4
287:                Call myDict.Add("Fund1Pct", 40)
288:                Call myDict.Add("Fund2Pct", 30)
```

```
289:                Call myDict.Add("Fund3Pct", 30)
290:            End Select
291:
292:            Dim j           As Integer
293:            Dim args()      As String
294:            ReDim args(1, myDict.Count - 1)
295:            j = 0
296:
297:            For Each Key In myDict
298:                args(0, j) = Key
299:                args(1, j) = Trim(myDict(Key))
300:                j = j + 1
301:            Next Key
302:
303:            Dim theEmp       As New employee
304:
305:            If IsOff Then
306:                theEmp.AddOffice args
307:            Else
308:                theEmp.AddEmployee args
309:            End If
310:
311:        Next ctr
312:
313:        Message.Caption = "Done."
314:
315:   End Sub
```

Listing 11.9 begins by creating variables to hold the values we will add to the employee or office record. Lines 10–14 check the cbIsOff object's value to see if we are adding to an employee record or an office. (cbIsOff is the check box that indicates that we are adding to an office. It stands for Check Box Is Office.)

Lines 17–75 open a series of recordsets, each of which looks into a table in the PopulateEmployee database.

The PopulateEmployee database is a small database I threw together just for this purpose. It has a number of tables that contain names I can draw from to create the first and last names and street names I need. It is included on the CD.

These tables each have a pair of fields: an ID and a text string. For example, the firstName table has a firstNameID field and a Name field. Each record in the Name field has a different first name (for example, Jesse, Stacey, John, Peter).

Note

My technical editor, Donald Xie, points out that if this were not a quick utility, but rather a "real" commercial application, this approach of opening and closing lots of recordsets would be unacceptably inefficient. The answer is to create a single ADO connection and use it for all the recordsets.

Similarly, the LastName table has LastNameID and Last Names (for example, Jones, Smith, Liberty), and the CityNames table has a CityID and City Names (for example, Warsaw, Rockville, Woburn).

Lines 77–84 declare variables to hold the values I'll add to the new employee record. Lines 87–89 create a connection to the EmployeeNet database so that I can insert records.

Starting on line 104, a record is extracted from each of the databases, filling in the first and last name of the new employee.

Beginning on line 130, I assemble an address. I do this by pulling a street name from the database and prepending a random number between 1 and 999. I then end with either *Street* or *Avenue*, chosen at random.

Lines 180–182 assemble a random 5-digit Zip code.

Random 10-digit phone numbers are generated for each of the phone fields from line 191 to line 229. Lines 231–247 make the health insurance decision.

Line 267 picks a random number between 1 and 4 and uses that number on lines 269–290 to pick an income investment distribution.

The key lines in this entire listing are lines 306 and 308, which make the actual addition to the database by calling the exact same code that is called when really adding an employee through the user interface.

In short, even though the presentation layer is the Web in the real application but is entirely simulated in this application, the business layer is unchanged. This is the essential power of DNA: The n-tier approach allows us to reuse the AddEmployee method of the employee object without regard to how the data are generated.

Next Steps

We have covered a great deal of material in reviewing our simple employee Web project. In the next and final chapter, we quickly look at a few advanced topics to round out the discussion.

Chapter 12

Advanced Topics

This chapter wraps up our discussion of the EmployeeNet Web site by filling in some of the details about client-side data validation. It then goes on to look at some of the issues we haven't considered in this project.

Client-Side Validation

In Chapter 10, we looked at how the data are gathered from the user in a form and how records are added to the database using that data. The employee business object was responsible for ensuring that the data entered into the database were valid.

Before the business object receives the data, however, the presentation layer has an opportunity to validate the data at the client. This makes for better performance because the data do not need to be returned to the server, checked, and then sent again to the user for correction.

In this chapter, we examine more closely the JavaScript used to validate the information entered by the user before it is submitted to the server.

EXCURSION

JavaScript

If you are a C++ or Java programmer, JavaScript is quick and easy. If you are a VB programmer, or not a programmer at all, then JavaScript makes for a gentle introduction into the syntax and general approach of Java.

Don't be fooled, however. JavaScript is not Java. It is not type-safe, it is not fully object-oriented, and it bears only a passing resemblance to its eponym.

You will find references in the appendix for books on JavaScript.

JavaScript

In Chapter 10, we looked at the HTML for the AddEmployee page. Let's look at an excerpt of that page again, as shown in Listing 12.1.

Listing 12.1

```
0:   <HTML>
1:   <HEAD>
2:
3:   <SCRIPT LANGUAGE="JavaScript" SRC="AddEmpCheck.js"></SCRIPT>
4:   <script language="JavaScript">
5:
6:   function SetTheFocus(where)
7:   {
8:       // do we have this element at all?
9:       if ( document.forms[0].elements[where] )
10:      {
11:          // is an array
12:          if ( document.forms[0].elements[where].length )
13:              document.forms[0].elements[where][0].focus();
14:          else                      // not an array
15:              document.forms[0].elements[where].focus();
16:      }
17:
18:  }
19:
20:  function CheckVals()
21:  {
22:      return ( validateAddEmployee(document.frmAddEmp) &&
23:      fixupFields(document.frmAddEmp) )
24:
25:  }
26:  </script>
27:
28:
68:    <form method="post" action="" onSubmit="return CheckVals()"
69:      name="frmAddEmp" >
70:     <table width="500" border="0" cellspacing="1"
71:         cellpadding="3">
72:      <tr valign="top" bgcolor="#cccccc">
73:       <td colspan="4"><b><font face="Arial, Helvetica,
74:           sans-serif" size="2">Title:</font>
75:         </b><WC@TITLE></WC@TITLE>   </td>
76:      </tr>
77:      <tr valign="top" bgcolor="#cccccc">
78:       <td width="30%"><font face="Arial, Helvetica,
79:           sans-serif" size="2"><b>First
80:         Name</b><br><WC@FIRSTNAME></WC@FIRSTNAME>
```

The logic of this page that is of concern to us now begins on line 68, which in this listing immediately follows line 28 (I left out 40 lines of code that are not relevant to this discussion).

On line 68, we create the form and set the onSubmit event to return the value from CheckVals().

CheckVals() is JavaScript, which is shown on lines 20–25. All CheckVals() does is call ValidateAddEmployee, passing in the document and the form, and then calls fixUpFields, again passing in the document and form. Finally, it ANDs their return values and returns the result. That is, if (and only if) they *both* return true, CheckVals will return true. If CheckVals returns true, then the values are okay, and we can submit this form.

EXCURSION

JavaScript

When you AND two values (by using the logical AND operator: &&), you are saying, if A and B are both true, then the expression is true; otherwise, it returns false.

So where do we find ValidateAddEmployee() and fixUpFields()? After all, neither is in the <SCRIPT> portion of this file, where you might expect them.

Let's look at line 3. There is a script tag here that says its source (SRC) is in the file AddEmpCheck.js. This effectively "includes" that file into the current file, as if you had typed the contents of AddEmpCheck.js right into AddEmployee.htm.

Listing 12.2 shows the contents of this included file, AddEmpCheck.js.

Listing 12.2

```
0:   // Constant Declarations
1:
2:   var digits = "0123456789";
3:   var phoneNumberDelimiters = "()- ";
4:   var validUSPhoneChars = digits + phoneNumberDelimiters;
5:   var validZIPCodeChars = digits + ZIPCodeDelimiters
6:   var whitespace = " \t\n\r";
7:   var ZIPCodeDelimiters = "-"
8:   var digitsInUSPhoneNumber = 10;
9:   var digitsInZIPCode1 = 5
10:  var digitsInZIPCode2 = 9
11:
12:  var strCity = "the City"
13:  var strCompanyName = "the Company Name"
14:  var strCountry = "the Country"
15:  var strAddress1 = "the Street Address"
```

continues

12

Listing 12.2—continued

```
16:   var strAddress2 = "Additional Address Information"
17:   var strBlur = " "
18:   var strEntryPrompt = "Please enter "
19:   var strFax = "the Fax Number"
20:   var strFirstName = "a First Name"
21:   var strInvalidPhone = "This field must be a 10 digit phone ";
22:   strInvalidPhone += "number (like 415 555 1212). "
23:   var strInvalidZIPCode = "This field must be a 5 or 9 digit ";
24:   strInvalidZIPCode += "ZIP Code (like 94043). "
25:   var strLastName = "a Last Name"
26:   var strMiddleName = "a Middle Name"
27:   var strPhone = "the Phone Number"
28:   var strState = "a 2-digit State Abbreviation"
29:   var strSuffix = "an (optional) Suffix (Jr.)"
30:   var strTitle = "an (optional) Title (Mr./ Ms.)"
31:   var strZip = "the Zip Code"
32:
33:   function validateAddEmployee(form)
34:   {
35:       return (
36:       checkString(form.elements["LastName"],strLastName) &&
37:       checkString(form.elements["FirstName"],strFirstName) &&
38:       checkString(form.elements["Address1"],strAddress1) &&
39:       checkString(form.elements["City"],strCity) &&
40:       checkZIPCode(form.elements["ZipCode"]) &&
41:       checkUSPhone(form.elements["Phone1"],false) &&
42:       checkUSPhone(form.elements["Fax1"],true) &&
43:       checkUSPhone(form.elements["Phone2"],true) &&
44:       checkUSPhone(form.elements["Fax2"],true)
45:       )
46:   }
47:
48:   function fixupFields(form)
49:   {   return (
50:       prepPhone(form.elements["Phone1"]) &&
51:       prepPhone(form.elements["Fax1"]) &&
52:       prepPhone(form.elements["Phone2"]) &&
53:       prepPhone(form.elements["Fax2"])
54:
55:       )
56:   }
57:
58:   function prepPhone(theField)
59:   {
60:       var normalPhone =
61:           stripChars(theField.value, phoneNumberDelimiters);
62:       theField.value = normalPhone;
63:       return true;
64:   }
65:
66:   function stripChars (s, coll)
```

```
67:  {
68:      var i;
69:      var returnString = "";
70:      for (i = 0; i < s.length; i++)
71:      {
72:          var c = s.charAt(i);
73:          if (coll.indexOf(c) == -1) returnString += c;
74:      }
75:
76:      return returnString;
77:  }
78:
79:  function checkString (theField, s)
80:  {
81:      if (isWhitespace(theField.value))
82:          return Empty(theField, s);
83:      else return true;
84:  }
85:
86:  function checkZIPCode (theField)
87:  {
88:     var normalzip =
89:       stripChars(theField.value, ZIPCodeDelimiters)
90:        if (! (isInteger(normalzip ) &&
91:           (normalzip.length == digitsInZIPCode1) ||
92:         (normalzip.length == digitsInZIPCode2)) )
93:           return Invalid (theField, strInvalidZIPCode);
94:      else
95:      {
96:          theField.value = normalzip;
97:          return true;
98:      }
99:  }
100:
101:  function checkUSPhone (theField, emptyOK)
102:  {
103:      var normalPhone =
104:          stripChars(theField.value, phoneNumberDelimiters)
105:
106:      if ( normalPhone.length == 0 && emptyOK)
107:          return true;
108:      if (!isUSPhoneNumber(normalPhone))
109:      {
110:          return Invalid (theField, strInvalidPhone);
111:      }
112:      else
113:      {
114:          theField.value = reformatUSPhone(normalPhone)
115:          return true;
116:      }
117:  }
118:
```

continues

12

Listing 12.2—continued

```
119:  function isEmpty(s)
120:  {
121:      return ((s == null) || (s.length == 0))
122:  }
123:
124:  // Returns true if empty or white space only
125:  function isWhitespace (s)
126:  {
127:      var i;
128:
129:      if (isEmpty(s)) return true;
130:      for (i = 0; i < s.length; i++)
131:      {
132:          var c = s.charAt(i);
133:          if (whitespace.indexOf(c) == -1) return false;
134:      }
135:
136:      return true;
137:  }
138:
139:
140:  function reformat (s)
141:  {
142:      var arg;
143:      var sPos = 0;
144:      var resultString = "";
145:
146:      for (var i = 1; i < reformat.arguments.length; i++)
147:      {
148:          arg = reformat.arguments[i];
149:          if (i % 2 == 1) resultString += arg;
150:          else
151:          {
152:              resultString += s.substring(sPos, sPos + arg);
153:              sPos += arg;
154:          }
155:      }
156:      return resultString;
157:  }
158:
159:
160:
161:  function isUSPhoneNumber (s)
162:  {
163:      return (isInteger(s) &&
164:          s.length == digitsInUSPhoneNumber )
165:  }
166:
167:  // Display prompt string s in status bar.
168:
```

```
169:   function prompt (s)
170:   {
171:       window.status = s
172:   }
173:
174:
175:
176:   // Display data entry prompt string s in status bar.
177:
178:   function promptEntry (s)
179:   {
180:       window.status = strEntryPrompt + s
181:   }
182:
183:   function blankEntry ()
184:   {
185:       window.status = ""
186:   }
187:
188:   function Empty(theField, s)
189:   {
190:       theField.focus()
191:       alert("You did not enter a value into the "
192:       + s + " field. This is a required field. "
193:       + "Please enter it now.")
194:       return false
195:   }
196:
197:   function Invalid (theField, s)
198:   {
199:       theField.focus()
200:       alert(s)
201:       return false
202:   }
203:
204:   function reformatUSPhone (USPhone)
205:   {
206:       return (reformat (USPhone, "(", 3, ") ", 3, "-", 4))
207:   }
208:
209:   function isInteger (s)
210:   {
211:       var i;
212:       for (i = 0; i < s.length; i++)
213:       {
214:           var c = s.charAt(i);
215:           if (c < "0" ¦¦ c > "9") return false;
216:       }
217:       return true;
218:   }
```

12

Netscape offers an exhaustive validation script on their Web site (http://developer.netscape.com/docs/examples/javascript/formval/overview.html). The material in Listing 12.2 was loosely based on this code from Netscape. I am grateful to them for making this material available.

We start by declaring the constants that we use throughout the rest of the script. Lines 2–10 define the valid characters and delimiters for valid zip codes and phone numbers, as well as how many digits ought to be in each.

Lines 12–31 set up a number of prompts that we use to send warning or error messages to the user if the fields are not valid.

Lines 33–46 make up the driving program in this script: validateAddEmployee. This method is passed a form, and it ticks through elements in this form, checking each for validity. Notice that this method knows the structure and meaning of the AddEmployee form. This is not a flexible way to write this script, but it is far simpler than making it more general. Lines 36–39 check four entry fields to ensure they are not empty, line 40 checks the zip code to make sure it is in valid form, and lines 41–44 check the four phone numbers. Notice that line 41 passes false as the second parameter, whereas the other three pass true. We'll see why in just a moment.

The checkString method is fairly simple and is shown on lines 79–84. The field is passed in along with a prompt string (s). On line 81, we check to see if the field is empty using the isWhitespace method. This calls into line 125 where the string is passed in. If it is empty or if every character is white space, then the method returns true.

Returning to line 81, if isWhitespace returns false, we return true on line 83; that is, the string "checks out" and is fine (it isn't empty). If we get true back from isWhitespace, however, then we return the value we get from passing the same field and string to Empty(), which is shown on line 188. This method alerts users that they must enter a value into the field, and then it returns false.

On the one hand, there is no good reason to return false from Empty and then return that value from CheckString. However, we could just as easily have Empty return void, and return false after calling Empty. The way I've done it allows for the option of making this method more general. In the future, we might decide that Empty might return true or false, depending on some condition or on some user action, and we could incorporate this change back into the calling method.

The net effect of CheckString is to issue an error message if the field is nothing but white space. This brings us to line 40:

```
40:        checkZIPCode(form.elements["ZipCode"]) &&
```

which calls checkZIPCode, shown on lines 86–99:

```
86:  function checkZIPCode (theField)
87:  {
88:     var normalzip =
89:      stripChars(theField.value, ZIPCodeDelimiters)
90:        if (! (isInteger(normalzip ) &&
91:          (normalzip.length == digitsInZIPCode1) ||
92:         (normalzip.length == digitsInZIPCode2)) )
93:           return Invalid (theField, strInvalidZIPCode);
94:      else
95:      {
96:          theField.value = normalzip;
97:          return true;
98:      }
99:  }
```

There are three steps to this function. First we remove all valid zip-code delimiter characters (defined on line 7 to be nothing but the dash). We do this by calling the stripCharacters routine, which returns the string with all dashes removed. We then pass the result to isInteger, which checks that the entire string is nothing but an integer. If this is true, we also check that the length of this string is equal to the values defined either in digitsInZIPCode1 (5) or in digitsInZIPCode2 (9). If any of this fails, we call Invalid, and pass in the zip code; otherwise, we store the "normalized" value back into the field.

The result of storing the normalized value back into the field is that, when the user switches fields, all the dashes are removed. This may or may not be what we want. If it is not what we want, we can comment out line 96.

Calling Invalid jumps us to line 197. All this function does is to set the focus on the field in question and to raise an alert box explaining the problem.

We return to line 41, where we call checkUSPhone passing in false as the second parameter. CheckUSPhone is shown starting on line 101.

We start by stripping all the phone number delimiters out of the phone and set the local variable, normalPhone, to the resulting string. If this resulting string has a length of zero *and* if the second parameter, emptyOK, evaluates to true, then the phone number is valid and we're done.

This is how we indicate that the first phone number is mandatory but subsequent phone numbers are not. We simply pass false as the second parameter for all required phone numbers and true for all optional ones.

12

On line 108, we pass the stripped-down string to isUSPhoneNumber. If the value that comes back is not valid, then we put up an error dialog box. If the value that returns is valid, we reformat the phone number the way we want it.

Before looking at how we reformat it, let's look at what isUSPhoneNumber does, as shown on line 161. This simple function just ensures that the phone number is nothing but digits and is of the right length.

Now let's look at how we reformat the phone number if it is valid. We make the call on line 114, and the reformatUSPhone function begins on line 204. This function calls reformat, passing in the USPhone string along with a series of parameters. Reformat itself starts on line 140.

On line 146, we set up a For loop to tick through each of the parameters. What, exactly, is this doing? It gets a bit complicated. The string, s, that is passed in looks like this:

```
USPhone, "(", 3, ") ", 3, "-", 4)
```

USPhone is a stripped-down phone number, such as "6177477301". Substituting this, we get

```
"6177477301", "(", 3, ") ", 3, "-", 4)
```

On lines 142–144, we set up some local variables, including establishing sPos to 0.

The For loop on line 146 ticks through the arguments. Given the string we passed in, with seven parameters, this line becomes

```
146:      for (var i = 1; i < 7; i++)
```

Line 148 picks out each argument in turn. The first time through i is 1, so we set arg to "(". On line 149, we test to see if i % 2 = 1 (which it does), so we add this argument to the result string. The result string is now "(".

The variable i is now incremented to 2, and arg is set to the second argument, 3. The test on line 149 fails this time (2%2 = 0), and the Else clause is invoked. The result string is concatenated with the substring of s (the entire parameter passed in) starting at 0 and ending at s+arg. Thus, 617 is added, and resultString now has (617. sPos is now incremented to 3.

The variable i is now incremented to 3, and arg is set to the next parameter, ") ". The modulus is checked, and resultString is now "(617) ".

Once again the variable i is incremented, this time to 4. Again 3 numbers are added, making resultString (617) 747.

With the next round the dash is added, followed by the end of the string. When we are done, resultString has (617) 747-7301. It springs into the proper format when the user leaves the phone field. Very cool.

This concludes our checking of each field. If all the fields are valid, then true is returned from ValidateAddEmployee. Let's look back at CheckVals in Listing 12.1.

```
20:   function CheckVals()
21:   {
22:       return ( validateAddEmployee(document.frmAddEmp) &&
23:       fixupFields(document.frmAddEmp) )
24:
25:   }
```

If ValidateAddEmployee returns true, then the second part of the If statement on lines 22–23 is invoked, and we return back into this file to call fixUpFields, again passing in the form. FixUpFields is shown on lines 48–56 of Listing 12.2:

```
48:   function fixupFields(form)
49:   {   return (
50:       prepPhone(form.elements["Phone1"]) &&
51:       prepPhone(form.elements["Fax1"]) &&
52:       prepPhone(form.elements["Phone2"]) &&
53:       prepPhone(form.elements["Fax2"])
54:
55:       )
56:   }
```

This calls into prepPhone, passing in each phone field. This time the goal is not to validate the number or to turn it into a nice presentation but instead to prepare it for insertion into the database. Our database definition calls for a 10-digit character string, and that is what we render with prepPhone, shown on lines 58–64:

```
58:   function prepPhone(theField)
59:   {
60:       var normalPhone =
61:           stripChars(theField.value, phoneNumberDelimiters);
62:       theField.value = normalPhone;
63:       return true;
64:   }
```

The delimiters are again stripped, and the resulting values are pasted back into the field. The user's experience is that the formatting disappears just as the form is submitted.

12

Error Handling

This book has intentionally avoided all discussion of error handling. This allowed me to write the code so that it is far simpler and easier to explain and understand.

Error handling in Visual Basic is somewhat more limited than it is in some other languages. In C++, for example, we differentiate between *bugs* on the one hand and *exceptions* on the other. Bugs are problems in your code, which should not make it into the final release.

In C++, you find bugs by peppering your code with ASSERT macros, which help you find the logical inconsistencies in your program but which disappear (poof!) when you compile the program for release to your customers.

Exceptions are *not* bugs. They are undesirable, emergency conditions that are predictable and unavoidable. For example, sooner or later the user will try to write something to the disk, and there will be no diskspace. Or the program will try to create an object, but the user will be out of memory. These are exceptional circumstances to which you must respond, but they are not bugs.

VB does not support this distinction: It has only errors. How you respond to these errors is up to you. You may be able to help the user recover without terminating the program (for example, by closing other applications or making room on the disk), or you may need to shut down and report the error. In either case, the decision is under your control using the standard error mechanisms.

Listing 12.3 reprises the ProcessTag method from ResultOutput, which we examined in Listing 8.9. This time, however, I added rudimentary error handling. (To save room here, I left out some of the processTag cases.)

Listing 12.3

```
0:   Private Sub ResultOutput_ProcessTag(ByVal TagName As String, _
1:      TagContents As String, SendTags As Boolean)
2:
3:      On Error GoTo errorHandler
4:      Dim rsAssets                As Recordset
5:
6:      Select Case TagName
7:
8:          Case "WC@EmployeeID"
9:              TagContents = CStr(DetailsRS.Fields("EmployeeID"))
10:
11:          Case "WC@Name"
12:              TagContents = CStr(DetailsRS.Fields("FirstName")) _
13:                  & CStr(" " & _
14:                  DetailsRS.Fields("MiddleName") & " ") _
15:                  & CStr(DetailsRS.Fields("LastName"))
```

```
16:
17:     '*************************************
18:     ' other cases left out to save space
19:     '*************************************
20:
21:          Case "WC@Continue"
22:               TagContents = TagContents & _
23:                    "<a href=""" & URLFor(Login) & _
24:                    """ Target=_top>Continue</A><br>"
25:          End Select
26:          Exit Sub
27:
28:     errorHandler:
29:          Session("ErrorMessage") = Err.Description
30:          Session("ErrorNumber") = Err.Number
31:          Response.Redirect URLFor(ErrorPage)
32:     End Sub
```

Notice that I left out a few case statements on lines 17–19 to consolidate the listing.

Line 3 tells VB what to do in the event of an error—it is to jump to the tag errorHandler, shown on line 28. If an error arises at any time in the course of this method, control will pass down to line 28.

If, on the other hand, there are no errors, then the Exit Sub command on line 26 will execute, and we'll never get to the error handler.

The error handler itself does nothing more than fill two session variables with the error message and then, on line 31, redirect the client's browser to our Error page, where the error itself is displayed.

How might an error be generated? Listing 12.4 modifies Listing 8.4 to add error handling.

Listing 12.4

```
0:  Public Function GetByID(myID As Integer) As Recordset
1:
2:       On Error GoTo errorHandler
3:
4:       Dim rs                     As New Recordset
5:       Dim sqlStmnt               As String
6:       Dim objConn                As New Connection
7:       objConn.Provider = "msdatashape"
8:       objConn.Open _
9:            "DataProvider = sqloledb; data source = " _
10:           & "EmployeeNet; initial catalog = " _
11:           & "EmployeeNet"
12:
13:           sqlStmnt = "Shape{{Call dbo.spEmployeeGetByID" _
```

12

continues

Listing 12.4—continued

```
14:              & "(" & CStr(myID) & ")}} as Employee " _
15:              & "APPEND({Select AssetAllocation.PortfolioID, " _
16:              & "AssetAllocation.WhatPercent, Funds.FundName, " _
17:              & "Funds.FundSymbol from AssetAllocation inner " _
18:              & "join funds on AssetAllocation.WhichFund = " _
19:              & "Funds.FundID} as AssetAllocation " _
20:              & "RELATE 'portfolioID' to 'portfolioID') " _
21:              & "as AssetAllocation"
22:
23:  ' uncomment to generate error
24:  '     sqlStmnt = "adfs"
25:
26:      rs.CursorType = adOpenStatic
27:      rs.CursorLocation = adUseClient
28:      rs.LockType = adLockBatchOptimistic
29:      Call rs.Open(sqlStmnt, objConn)
30:      rs.ActiveConnection = Nothing
31:      Set GetByID = rs
32:      Exit Function
33:
34:  errorHandler:
35:      Dim lf             As New LogFile
36:      Dim outputString    As String
37:      outputString = Err.Description & _
38:      "( " & CStr(Err.Number) & ")"
39:
40:      Call lf.WriteToLog(outputString, True)
41:
42:
43:  End Function
```

Once again, we see the same pattern. On line 2, VB is instructed to pass control to the handler at the bottom of the function should an error arise. On lines 23 and 24, we modify the SQL statement to ensure that SQL will return an error. This will cause processing to jump from line 29 to line 34. On lines 36–40, we write the error to our errorlog, and then, because we haven't cleared the error, it will propagate up to the calling function and be handled by the presentation layer.

Let's trace through what happens. When the user completes a search and clicks on a particular employee to see the details, GetByID is called. When the bogus SQL statement is passed to SQL Server on line 29 of Listing 12.4, an error is generated. This invokes the error handler on line 34, and the error log is updated.

Control then returns to the calling function, ResultOutput_ProcessTag, which will catch the error and invoke its own errorHandler, as shown on line 28 of Listing 12.3. This redirects the user to the ErrorPage's Respond method, which calls ErrorPage.WriteTemplate.

The first time I wrote this, I had errorPage use the session variables to display the error number and text, but then I realized that the end user had little use for this information. I then rewrote the page to display a simpler error message, as shown in Figure 12.1.

Figure 12.1

Handling the error.

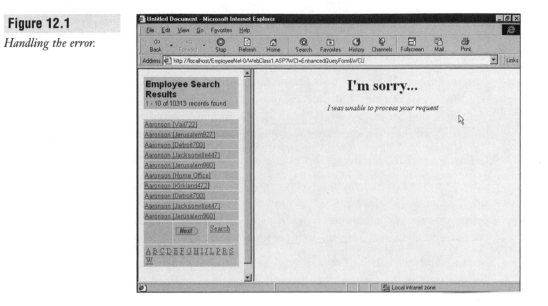

How much detail you provide is entirely up to you. A quick check of the error log, however, reveals that the information was captured properly:

```
1:24:46 PM: [Microsoft][ODBC SQL Server Driver][SQL Server]Could not find stored
➥procedure 'adfs'.( -2147217900)
```

We *could* show this error to the end users, but I'm not quite sure what they would do with the information.

Commercial Error-Handling Routines

Before we leave this topic, let me mention that there are many products on the market that will inject error-checking code into your program without your writing a line. NuMega's FailSafe product, for example, will add line numbers as well as "instrument" your code. When an error arises, you can instruct FailSafe to put up a dialog box, write to a log, or even send you email telling you what program, project, module, method, and code line had the problem in addition to what the problem was and when it arose.

Using products like this with WebClasses can be a bit tricky, of course, because you want to be careful about popping up dialog boxes on the server machine (where no

12

one will be around to see them!). Used with some care, however, these can save you hundreds of hours of work.

Scale

One of the issues we've not considered in great detail is scale. When programmers talk about scaling an application, they mean enabling large amounts of data and/or many simultaneous users.

The techniques discussed in this book are appropriate for the *overwhelming* majority of commercial projects, but they are not for every one. For the small percentage of Web sites that are hosted on Web server "farms" and visited by thousands or tens of thousands of simultaneous users, some modification will be required.

Before we continue, however, let me make a few quick points in my own defense.

First, you need to understand everything discussed in this book *before* you can consider the issues of massively scaled applications. Nothing covered here is wrong or a waste of time; you simply must modify what you have learned here when you subject your site to the kinds of numbers now under discussion.

Second, and at the risk of repeating myself, the overwhelming majority of projects are not so large that issues of scale enter into your decisions beyond what we've already covered.

So why is there so much hoopla about large-scale "enterprise solutions"? There are a few reasons.

First, historically, Microsoft has been weaker than, for example, UNIX on some of these issues, and so Microsoft has targeted this market as an area of expansion. Therefore, they are writing and talking about large-scale enterprise solutions and creating a great deal of interest in the topic.

Second, online commerce is a rapidly growing area of the Internet, and some of the scale issues we'll discuss in this chapter come into play in large online stores.

Third, it sells books. After you've bought your first books on HTML, WebClasses, and ASP, what can we sell you? One obvious choice is to help you solve your large-scale issues. This is as it should be; the books are there because the interest is there. But don't confuse cause and effect. Just because the books are there doesn't mean you have to be interested.

So the short answer is this: If you *are* building a massive application, then this can't be your last book. The appendix lists a number of excellent resources that you'll want to consult next. I'm confident that the background from *this* book will make those books easier to understand.

Issues with Large-Scale Applications

With that introduction, what *are* the issues? They fall into a few general categories:

- Performance
- State management
- Thread management
- Transaction management

In response to these concerns, a number of new technologies have emerged, the most notable among them being Microsoft's MTS and COM+. This section attempts to put all this into context.

Performance

For the vast majority of sites, the time it takes to pump your data through that tiny little telephone wire will swamp small differences in server-side performance. Thus, for the great majority of developers, it doesn't matter if your SQL statement takes 40 milliseconds or 200 milliseconds.

Still, for very large sites, small differences on the server can make an enormous difference in your ability to handle tens of thousands of requests.

To improve the performance of your application, you might consider two or three significant steps:

1. Improve your searching performance.
2. Improve your business object performance.
3. Improve your hardware.

We talked about improving searching performance in Chapter 9. Upgrading your hardware is often the least expensive and most overlooked solution to performance problems.

One way to improve the performance of your business objects may be to rewrite some of them in C++. Even though VB is *fantastic* for rapid development, and the performance is more than acceptable for most applications, when you do need that last millisecond of performance, C++ is perfect.

The ActiveX Template Library enables you to create COM controls that can be swapped in cleanly for the VB business objects that you've already created.

Unless you *know* that you are going to be building one of the 50 most popular Web sites in the world, however, I recommend starting with VB and then evaluating the performance after you are up and running. The likelihood of the project finishing is greatly improved if the development process is simplified.

12

Using State Variables

The EmployeeNet application makes generous use of session variables. I've been careful to put simple text strings into the session variables, rather than user-defined objects, Web classes, or controls, as Microsoft suggests. Nonetheless, the use of session variables makes it harder to create a Web farm because the session variables peg each session to a particular server. They also make it harder to *load balance* a popular site.

 Load balance—It is a goal of good engineering to balance the workload among machines so that no single machine is doing the bulk of the work.

If you are building one of the 1% or so of sites on which this will be an issue, you may need to move your session variables out to the database. There are complex trade-offs in these decisions, however, so again I urge you to build your site in a straightforward way and then optimize when it becomes necessary.

MTS and COM+

When I originally proposed this book, I thought I would write a lot about Microsoft Transaction Server technology. The more I learned about MTS, however, the more skeptical I became. Even though MTS is a great solution to specific problems in large-scale applications, it simply represents an unneeded complexity for the vast majority of development efforts.

With the advent of COM+, which incorporates the MTS technology right into the COM specification, MTS as an entity may pass into obscurity. COM+ promises to make the use of transactions somewhat simpler, but so far this is relatively uncharted territory.

What Is MTS?

In their book *Professional MTS and MSMQ with VB and ASP* (see the appendix), Alex Homer and David Sussman suggest that MTS should really have been named *Microsoft Component Server*, and I agree. Although MTS does help you with transaction management, it also helps with memory management and the creation and reallocation of COM components.

In short, MTS helps you manage your memory and other system resources more effectively than you can manage them yourself. This comes at the cost of added complexity, so again this tool should be used when the need presents.

MTS has *Transaction* as its middle name. A transaction is a way to bundle a series of actions and ensure that if any of the actions fail, all the others will be undone. For example, imagine that you are writing a banking application. One component is responsible for transferring funds from a customer's checking to savings.

Imagine that you issue the Database command to reduce the checking account balance, and it goes through with no trouble. When you go to add the money to the savings account, it turns out that the account is unavailable. If you stop there, the money will have "disappeared."

A transaction allows you to signify that should the second step fail (depositing the money), then the first step (withdrawing the money) ought to roll back (that is, it should be undone).

You certainly can do this by hand, but a transaction makes the logic simpler and less error-prone. There is much more to transaction processing, of course, and MTS helps you with all these details.

Even though MTS fits cleanly with the work we've covered in this book, it is a separate topic, and I would argue a more advanced topic of interest to only a small percentage of those of us who are writing Web applications. The appendix lists a number of books that can help you get started with this technology.

XML

In the last decade, we've seen a number of "hot" new technologies come along: Windows programming, object-oriented programming, HTML, the Web, Java, ASP, WebClasses, COM, and ActiveX. One might argue, however, that XML is the technology that will have the greatest effect on how we use computers in the *coming* decade.

XML is a specification for how to create markup languages. HTML is a markup language, but as XML is adopted, HTML will come to be seen as one of *many* markup languages.

HTML tells you how to display text. This excerpt from Listing 12.1 illustrates:

```
77:        <tr valign="top" bgcolor="#cccccc">
78:         <td width="30%"><font face="Arial, Helvetica,
79:            sans-serif" size="2"><b>First
80:         Name</b><br><WC@FIRSTNAME></WC@FIRSTNAME>
```

There are a number of HTML tags in these few lines: for rows and cells in a table and for formatting fields. The HTML tags tell you *nothing*, however, about the meaning of the data they enclose.

```
<b>First Name</b>
```

12

tells you that the string `"First Name"` ought to be in bold, but it doesn't tell you anything about what this first name *is*. XML does.

XML–compliant markup languages define data-aware tags so that you can signify that this First Name is the first name of a client or the first name of a book in a series.

> **Note** My editor asked, "What do you mean by 'XML-compliant markup languages'? I thought XML *was* a markup language!" Here's the answer. XML is *not* a markup language: It is a meta-language. XML tells you how to create a markup language, just as SGML does. HTML is an instance of an SGML-compliant markup language. XML will create a cornucopia of compliant markup languages (no doubt many of which will just be called XML!!).

The use of a semantically rich markup language allows you to store, forward, transact, interact, and otherwise manipulate this information in conjunction with others. XML will revolutionize the exchange of information across the Internet, and we're only just beginning to understand its potential.

Needless to say, XML is a book in itself, and we intend to offer that book, *XML from Scratch*, in the next few months. You can learn more about this forthcoming title on my Web site, http://www.libertyassociates.com, where you will also find an errata sheet, FAQ, and other supporting material for *this* book.

Next Steps

At the conclusion of our travel together, we find that we're not at the end of a trail but rather on the threshold of a new journey. There is more to learn and explore from here, and all this book can really do is to provide an annotated map of the terrain.

I urge you to read through the appendix to find further reading, to join in discussions on my book support group (http://www.delphi.com/libertybooks), and to join general newsgroups on WebClasses, ASP, VB, SQL, JavaScript, and so forth.

Thank you again.
Jesse Liberty
Summer 1999

Appendix

Reading List

As I said when we began, and again when we finished, my purpose in writing this book was to consolidate information about a wide range of topics including Visual Basic and IIS applications, WebClasses, object-oriented analysis and design, ASP, ADO, JavaScript, SQL, and SQL Server. My goal was to equip you with the necessary tools so that you could begin building robust commercial-quality Web applications.

No single book can present everything there is to know about all these topics. Therefore, I have included a reading list of books on these topics that I hope you will find useful.

Visual Basic and WebClasses

There are a number of good books on Visual Basic, most notably *Visual Basic 6 from Scratch* by Donald and Oancea (Que, 1999, ISBN 0-78972119-8) and *Beginning Visual Basic 6* by Peter Wright (Wrox Press, 1998, ISBN 1861001053). People I know who are VB experts have a lot of respect for *HardCore Visual Basic* by Bruce McKinney (Microsoft Press, 1997, ISBN 1-57231-422-2). I know of no book, other than the one in your hands, that is specifically about WebClasses, although they are covered briefly in *Visual Basic 6 Business Objects* by Rockford Lhotka (Wrox Press, 1998, ISBN 1-861001-07-X).

ASP

The single best book I've read on ASP is *Professional ASP* by Alex Fedorov et al. (Wrox Press, 1998, ISBN 1861001266). *ASP from Scratch* is forthcoming, and I'm looking forward to reading it.

JavaScript

By far the best book I've read on JavaScript is *JavaScript, the Definitive Guide* by David Flanagan (O'Reilly & Associates, 1998, ISBN 1565923928). This is a magnificent book, and it is no surprise it has been a runaway best-seller.

ADO

I kept the *ADO 2.1 Programmer's Reference* (Wrox Press, 1999, ISBN 1861002688) by Dave Sussman by my side while I wrote this book. I recommend it highly.

Transact SQL and SQL Server

The best book I've seen on SQL is *Transact SQL Programming* by Kevin Kline (O'Reilly & Associates, 1999, ISBN 1565924010). This terrific book takes you through all you need to know about SQL but were afraid to ask.

Inside Microsoft SQL Server 7.0 by Soukop and Delaney (Microsoft Press, 1997, ISBN 1572313315) is less about teaching you how to use SQL Server and more about why it is built the way it is. This is truly a great book.

MTS, COM, COM+, and Enterprise Applications

One of the most ambitious works on large-scale Web application development may be *Enterprise Application Architecture* by Joseph Moniz (Wrox Press, 1999, ISBN 1861002580).

MTS MSMQ with VB and ASP by Alex Homer and David Sussman (Wrox Press, 1998, ISBN 186100460) and *Professional VB 6 MTS Programming* by Mathew Bortniker (Wrox Press, 1999, ISBN 1861002440) are wonderful, in-depth examinations of MTS.

ActiveX and ATL

ActiveX and ATL are difficult topics, and there are many good introductions. However, the books that stand out in my mind are the matched set of *Beginning ATL Programming* by Richard Grimes et al. (Wrox Press, 1998, ISBN 1861000111) and *Professional ATL COM Programming* by Richard Grimes (Wrox Press, 1998, ISBN 1861001401). These are *wonderful* books.

Web Design and User Interface Design

If you are going to read one book on UI design, take a look at *Guide to Web Publishing* by Philip Greenspun and Morgan Kauffman (ApProfessional, 1999, ISBN 1558605347). Even though it is not strictly a programming book, it is an incredibly creative book and well worth your attention.

The Inmates Are Running the Asylum by Alan Cooper (Sams Publishing, 1999, ISBN 0672316498) and *The Design of Everyday Things* by David Norman (Doubleday Books, 1990, ISBN 0385267746) ought to be required reading for every developer in the United States. These are wonderful books about everything wrong in how we design software (and many other things!), and they are a delight to read. Put these at the top of your reading list.

XML

There are a number of very good if preliminary books on XML, including *Professional XML Design and Implementation* by Paul Spenser (Wrox Press, 1999, ISBN 1861002289), *XML Applications* by Frank Boumphrey et al. (Wrox Press, 1998, 1861001525), and *Style Sheets for HTML & XML* by Frank Boumphrey (Wrox Press, 1998, 1861001657).

The forthcoming *XML from Scratch* will endeavor to do for XML what *WebClasses from Scratch* has done for WebClasses—put the development of XML applications into the context of a real-world project.

Distributed interNet Applications

Designing Component Based Applications by Mary Kirtland (Microsoft Press, 1999, ISBN 0735605238) is a wonderful introduction to the Microsoft DNA architecture. I've had the pleasure of talking with Mary briefly, and she is simply a brilliant engineer. Her book is exceptional, and I recommend it highly.

Designing Distributed Applications by Stephen Mohr (Wrox Press, 1999, ISBN 1861002270) is a great overview of the issues involved in designing for distributed applications.

Object-Oriented Analysis and Design and Patterns

The OOAD field is suddenly awash in good books, although many are a bit academic for my taste. Certainly the flagship books must be *The Unified Software Development*

Process (Addison-Wesley, 1999, ISBN 0201571692), *The Unified Modeling Language User Guide* (Addison-Wesley, 1998, ISBN 0201571684), and *The Unified Modeling Language Reference Manual* (Addison-Wesley, 1998, ISBN 020130998x)—all by the "Three Amigos": Grady Booch, Ivar Jacobson, and James Rumbaugh.

I have two books in this category: *Beginning Object-Oriented Analysis and Design* (Wrox Press, 1998, ISBN 1861001339) and *Clouds To Code* (Wrox Press, 1997, ISBN 1861000952). *Beginning OOAD* is a tutorial and covers the UML as well as analysis, design, and architectural mechanisms including persistence, concurrency, and distributed objects. *Clouds To Code* is a detailed case study, written as it happened, of the development of a real-world application.

After you've read a book or two on object-oriented programming, be sure to pick up *Object-Oriented Design Heuristics* by Arthur J. Riel (Addison-Wesley, 1996, ISBN 0-201-63385-X). This wonderful book explains the difference between great designs and mediocre ones. It is filled with world-class advice and guidance, and I recommend it highly.

Perhaps the hottest and most interesting trend in software development in the past decade is the advent of design patterns. These are an attempt to capture, name, and describe design solutions that can be reused in a variety of situations. The seminal work is *Design Patterns—Elements of Reusable Object-Oriented Software* by Gama et al. (Addison Wesley, 1995, ISBN 0-201-63361-2).

Magazines and Publications

There are a number of good specialty magazines on VB, JavaScript, database programming, and so forth. The two magazines that you *absolutely* want to consider subscribing to are *Microsoft Systems Journal* and *Microsoft Internet Developer*. Both of these magazines are filled with information about emerging Microsoft technology.

Index

SQueaL is distributed under the GNU General Public License.Be sure to read this license before using SQueaL.

GNU GENERAL PUBLIC LICENSE

Version 2, June 1991
Copyright (C) 1989, 1991 Free Software Foundation, Inc.
675 Mass Ave, Cambridge, MA 02139, USA

Preamble

The licenses for most software are designed to take away your freedom to share and change it. By contrast, the GNU General Public License is intended to guarantee your freedom to share and change free software—to make sure the software is free for all its users. This General Public License applies to most of the Free Software Foundation's software and to any other program whose authors commit to using it. (Some other Free Software Foundation software is covered by the GNU Library General Public License instead.) You can apply it to your programs, too.

When we speak of free software, we are referring to freedom, not price. Our General Public Licenses are designed to make sure that you have the freedom to distribute copies of free software (and charge for this service if you wish), that you receive source code or can get it if you want it, that you can change the software or use pieces of it in new free programs; and that you know you can do these things.

To protect your rights, we need to make restrictions that forbid anyone to deny you these rights or to ask you to surrender the rights. These restrictions translate to certain responsibilities for you if you distribute copies of the software, or if you modify it.

For example, if you distribute copies of such a program, whether gratis or for a fee, you must give the recipients all the rights that you have. You must make sure that they, too, receive or can get the source code. And you must show them these terms so they know their rights.

We protect your rights with two steps: (1) copyright the software, and (2) offer you this license which gives you legal permission to copy, distribute and/or modify the software.

Also, for each author's protection and ours, we want to make certain that everyone understands that there is no warranty for this free software. If the software is modified by someone else and passed on, we want its recipients to know that what they have is not the original, so that any problems introduced by others will not reflect on the original authors' reputations.

Finally, any free program is threatened constantly by software patents. We wish to avoid the danger that redistributors of a free program will individually obtain patent licenses, in effect making the program proprietary. To prevent this, we have made it clear that any patent must be licensed for everyone's free use or not licensed at all.

The precise terms and conditions for copying, distribution and modification follow.

GNU GENERAL PUBLIC LICENSE

TERMS AND CONDITIONS FOR COPYING, DISTRIBUTION AND MODIFICATION

0. This License applies to any program or other work which contains a notice placed by the copyright holder saying it may be distributed under the terms of this General Public License. The "Program", below, refers to any such program or work, and a "work based on the Program" means either the Program or any derivative work under copyright law: that is to say, a work containing the Program or a portion of it, either verbatim or with modifications and/or translated into another language. (Hereinafter, translation is included without limitation in the term "modification".) Each licensee is addressed as "you".

Activities other than copying, distribution and modification are not covered by this License; they are outside its scope. The act of running the Program is not restricted, and the output from the Program is covered only if its contents constitute a work based on the Program (independent of having been made by running the Program). Whether that is true depends on what the Program does.

1. You may copy and distribute verbatim copies of the Program's source code as you receive it, in any medium, provided that you conspicuously and appropriately publish on each copy an appropriate copyright notice and disclaimer of warranty; keep intact all the notices that refer to this License and to the absence of any warranty; and give any other recipients of the Program a copy of this License along with the Program.

You may charge a fee for the physical act of transferring a copy, and you may at your option offer warranty protection in exchange for a fee.

2. You may modify your copy or copies of the Program or any portion of it, thus forming a work based on the Program, and copy and distribute such modifications or work under the terms of Section 1 above, provided that you also meet all of these conditions:

a) You must cause the modified files to carry prominent notices stating that you changed the files and the date of any change.

b) You must cause any work that you distribute or publish, that in whole or in part contains or is derived from the Program or any part thereof, to be licensed as a whole at no charge to all third parties under the terms of this License.

c) If the modified program normally reads commands interactively when run, you must cause it, when started running for such interactive use in the most ordinary way, to print or display an announcement including an appropriate copyright notice and a notice that there is no warranty (or else, saying that you provide a warranty) and that users may redistribute the program under these conditions, and telling the user how to view a copy of this License. (Exception: if the Program itself is interactive but does not normally print such an announcement, your work based on the Program is not required to print an announcement.)

These requirements apply to the modified work as a whole. If identifiable sections of that work are not derived from the Program, and can be reasonably considered independent and separate works in themselves, then this License, and its terms, do not apply to those sections when you distribute them as separate works. But when you distribute the same sections as part of a whole which is a work based on the Program, the distribution of the whole must be on the terms of this License, whose permissions for other licensees extend to the entire whole, and thus to each and every part regardless of who wrote it.

Thus, it is not the intent of this section to claim rights or contest your rights to work written entirely by you; rather, the intent is to exercise the right to control the distribution of derivative or collective works based on the Program. In addition, mere aggregation of another work not based on the Program with the Program (or with a work based on the Program) on a volume of a storage or distribution medium does not bring the other work under the scope of this License.

3. You may copy and distribute the Program (or a work based on it, under Section 2) in object code or executable form under the terms of Sections 1 and 2 above provided that you also do one of the following:

a) Accompany it with the complete corresponding machine-readable source code, which must be distributed under the terms of Sections 1 and 2 above on a medium customarily used for software interchange; or,

b) Accompany it with a written offer, valid for at least three years, to give any third party, for a charge no more than your cost of physically performing source distribution, a complete machine-readable copy of the corresponding source code, to be distributed under the terms of Sections 1 and 2 above on a medium customarily used for software interchange; or,

c) Accompany it with the information you received as to the offer to distribute corresponding source code. (This alternative is allowed only for noncommercial distribution and only if you received the program in object code or executable form with such an offer, in accord with Subsection b above.)

The source code for a work means the preferred form of the work for making modifications to it. For an executable work, complete source code means all the source code for all modules it contains, plus any associated interface definition files, plus the scripts used to control compilation and installation of the executable. However, as a special exception, the source code distributed need not include anything that is normally distributed (in either source or binary form) with the major components (compiler, kernel, and so on) of the operating system on which the executable runs, unless that component itself accompanies the executable.

If distribution of executable or object code is made by offering access to copy from a designated place, then offering equivalent access to copy the source code from the same place counts as distribution of the source code, even though third parties are not compelled to copy the source along with the object code.

4. You may not copy, modify, sublicense, or distribute the Program except as expressly provided under this License. Any attempt otherwise to copy, modify, sublicense or distribute the Program is void, and will automatically terminate your rights under this License. However, parties who have received copies, or rights, from you under this License will not have their licenses terminated so long as such parties remain in full compliance.

5. You are not required to accept this License, since you have not signed it. However, nothing else grants you permission to modify or distribute the Program or its derivative works. These actions are prohibited by law if you do not accept this License. Therefore, by modifying or distributing the Program (or any work based on the Program), you indicate your acceptance of this License to do so, and all its terms and conditions for copying, distributing or modifying the Program or works based on it.

6. Each time you redistribute the Program (or any work based on the Program), the recipient automatically receives a license from the original licensor to copy, distribute or modify the Program subject to these terms and conditions. You may not impose

any further restrictions on the recipients' exercise of the rights granted herein. You are not responsible for enforcing compliance by third parties to this License.

7. If, as a consequence of a court judgment or allegation of patent infringement or for any other reason (not limited to patent issues), conditions are imposed on you (whether by court order, agreement or otherwise) that contradict the conditions of this License, they do not excuse you from the conditions of this License. If you cannot distribute so as to satisfy simultaneously your obligations under this License and any other pertinent obligations, then as a consequence you may not distribute the Program at all. For example, if a patent license would not permit royalty-free redistribution of the Program by all those who receive copies directly or indirectly through you, then the only way you could satisfy both it and this License would be to refrain entirely from distribution of the Program.

If any portion of this section is held invalid or unenforceable under any particular circumstance, the balance of the section is intended to apply and the section as a whole is intended to apply in other circumstances.

It is not the purpose of this section to induce you to infringe any patents or other property right claims or to contest validity of any such claims; this section has the sole purpose of protecting the integrity of the free software distribution system, which is implemented by public license practices. Many people have made generous contributions to the wide range of software distributed through that system in reliance on consistent application of that system; it is up to the author/donor to decide if he or she is willing to distribute software through any other system and a licensee cannot impose that choice.

This section is intended to make thoroughly clear what is believed to be a consequence of the rest of this License.

8. If the distribution and/or use of the Program is restricted in certain countries either by patents or by copyrighted interfaces, the original copyright holder who places the Program under this License may add an explicit geographical distribution limitation excluding those countries, so that distribution is permitted only in or among countries not thus excluded. In such case, this License incorporates the limitation as if written in the body of this License.

9. The Free Software Foundation may publish revised and/or new versions of the General Public License from time to time. Such new versions will be similar in spirit to the present version, but may differ in detail to address new problems or concerns.

Each version is given a distinguishing version number. If the Program specifies a version number of this License which applies to it and "any later version", you have the option of following the terms and conditions either of that version or of any later version published by the Free Software Foundation. If the Program does not specify a version number of this License, you may choose any version ever published by the Free Software Foundation.

10. If you wish to incorporate parts of the Program into other free programs whose distribution conditions are different, write to the author to ask for permission. For software which is copyrighted by the Free Software Foundation, write to the Free Software Foundation; we sometimes make exceptions for this. Our decision will be guided by the two goals of preserving the free status of all derivatives of our free software and of promoting the sharing and reuse of software generally.

NO WARRANTY

11. BECAUSE THE PROGRAM IS LICENSED FREE OF CHARGE, THERE IS NO WARRANTY FOR THE PROGRAM, TO THE EXTENT PERMITTED BY APPLICABLE LAW. EXCEPT WHEN OTHERWISE STATED IN WRITING THE COPYRIGHT HOLDERS AND/OR OTHER PARTIES PROVIDE THE PROGRAM "AS IS" WITHOUT WARRANTY OF ANY KIND, EITHER EXPRESSED OR IMPLIED, INCLUDING, BUT NOT LIMITED TO, THE IMPLIED WARRANTIES OF MERCHANTABILITY AND FITNESS FOR A PARTICULAR PURPOSE. THE ENTIRE RISK AS TO THE QUALITY AND PERFORMANCE OF THE PROGRAM IS WITH YOU. SHOULD THE PROGRAM PROVE DEFECTIVE, YOU ASSUME THE COST OF ALL NECESSARY SERVICING, REPAIR OR CORRECTION.

12. IN NO EVENT UNLESS REQUIRED BY APPLICABLE LAW OR AGREED TO IN WRITING WILL ANY COPYRIGHT HOLDER, OR ANY OTHER PARTY WHO MAY MODIFY AND/OR REDISTRIBUTE THE PROGRAM AS PERMITTED ABOVE, BE LIABLE TO YOU FOR DAMAGES, INCLUDING ANY GENERAL, SPECIAL, INCIDENTAL OR CONSEQUENTIAL DAMAGES ARISING OUT OF THE USE OR INABILITY TO USE THE PROGRAM (INCLUDING BUT NOT LIMITED TO LOSS OF DATA OR DATA BEING RENDERED INACCURATE OR LOSSES SUSTAINED BY YOU OR THIRD PARTIES OR A FAILURE OF THE PROGRAM TO OPERATE WITH ANY OTHER PROGRAMS), EVEN IF SUCH HOLDER OR OTHER PARTY HAS BEEN ADVISED OF THE POSSIBILITY OF SUCH DAMAGES.

END OF TERMS AND CONDITIONS

Appendix: How to Apply These Terms to Your New Programs

If you develop a new program, and you want it to be of the greatest possible use to the public, the best way to achieve this is to make it free software which everyone can redistribute and change under these terms.

To do so, attach the following notices to the program. It is safest to attach them to the start of each source file to most effectively convey the exclusion of warranty; and each file should have at least the "copyright" line and a pointer to where the full notice is found.

<one line to give the program's name and a brief idea of what it does.>

  Copyright (C) 19yy <name of author>

This program is free software; you can redistribute it and/or modify it under the terms of the GNU General Public License as published by the Free Software Foundation; either version 2 of the License, or (at your option) any later version.

This program is distributed in the hope that it will be useful but WITHOUT ANY WARRANTY; without even the implied warranty of MERCHANTABILITY or FITNESS FOR A PARTICULAR PURPOSE. See the GNU General Public License for more details.

You should have received a copy of the GNU General Public License along with this program; if not, write to the Free Software Foundation, Inc., 675 Mass Ave, Cambridge, MA 02139, USA.

Also add information on how to contact you by electronic and paper mail. If the program is interactive, make it output a short notice like this when it starts in an interactive mode:

Gnomovision version 69, Copyright (C) 19yy name of author Gnomovision comes with ABSOLUTELY NO WARRANTY; for details type `show w'. This is free software, and you are welcome to redistribute it under certain conditions; type `show c' for details.

The hypothetical commands `show w' and `show c' should show the appropriate parts of the General Public License. Of course, the commands you use may be called something other than `show w' and `show c'; they could even be mouse-clicks or menu items—whatever suits your program.

You should also get your employer (if you work as a programmer) or your school, if any, to sign a "copyright disclaimer" for the program, if necessary. Here is a sample; alter the names:

Yoyodyne, Inc., hereby disclaims all copyright interest in the program `Gnomovision' (which makes passes at compilers) written by James Hacker.

<signature of Ty Coon>,
1 April 1989
Ty Coon,
President of Vice

This General Public License does not permit incorporating your program into proprietary programs. If your program is a subroutine library, you may consider it more useful to permit linking proprietary applications with the library. If this is what you want to do, use the GNU Library General Public License instead of this License.

CD-ROM Installation

Windows 95 Installation Instructions

1. Insert the CD-ROM disc into your CD-ROM drive.

2. From the Windows 95 desktop, double-click the My Computer Icon.

3. Double-clock on the icon representing your CD-ROM drive.

4. Double-click on the icon titled START.EXE to run the CD-ROM interface.

 Note
If Windows 95 is installed on your computer and you have the AutoPlay feature enabled, the START.EXE program starts automatically whenever you insert the disc into your CD-ROM drive.

Windows NT Installation Instructions

1. Insert the CD-ROM disc into your CD-ROM drive.

2. From File Manager or Program Manager, choose Run from the File menu..

3. Type *<drive>*\START.EXE and press Enter, where *<drive>* corresponds to the drive letter of your CD-ROM. For example, if your CD-ROM is drive D:, type D:START.EXE and press Enter. This will run the CD-ROM interface. .